Southern Biography Series
BERTRAM WYATT-BROWN, EDITOR

Kentucky Justice, Southern Honor, and American Manhood

Understanding the Life and Death of Richard Reid

James C. Klotter

Louisiana State University Press ✸ *Baton Rouge*

12 11 10 09 08 07 06 05 04 03   5 4 3 2 1

Designer: Amanda McDonald Scallan
Typeface: Sabon
Typesetter: Coghill Composition Co., Inc.
Printer and binder: Thomson-Shore, Inc.

Library of Congress Cataloging-in-Publication Data

Klotter, James C.
    Kentucky justice, southern honor, and American manhood : understanding the life and
death of Richard Reid / James C. Klotter.
        p. cm.—(Southern biography series)
    Includes bibliographical references and index.
    ISBN 0-8071-2857-0 (cloth : alk. paper)
        1. Reid, Richard, 1838–1884. 2. Judges—Kentucky—Biography. 3. Justice,
Administration of—Kentucky—History. I. Reid, Richard, 1838–1884. II. Title. III. Series.

KF368.R45 K58   2003
347.769′014′092—dc21
    [B]   2002043097

The paper in this book meets the guidelines for permanence and durability of the Committee on Production
Guidelines for Book Longevity of the Council on Library Resources. ♾

In memory of Hambleton Tapp

Contents

Illustrations

Acknowledgments

Authors usually have numerous people to thank, many academic debts to pay, and little space to do so. Faced with that situation as well, I can only hope that my brief words of acknowledgment convey at least some of the deep gratitude that I feel for the aid given. For without the help of those listed below, this would be a much poorer book.

Perhaps the place to start is where a project usually begins—in the archives. My thanks go: to Mary Margaret Lowe, Glen Taul, and the late Ora Lunceford at Georgetown College; to William J. Marshall of Special Collections, University of Kentucky, as well as those in other libraries there—Young, Law, and Medical; to James Prichard of the Kentucky Department for Libraries and Archives; to Lynn Hollingsworth, Mary Winter, and Nathan Prichard of the Kentucky Historical Society; to those in the Clerk's Office in both Bourbon and Montgomery Counties; to James Holmburg of the Filson Historical Society; and to various archivists at the University of North Carolina and at the Library of Congress. Support for research came from the Kentucky Historical Society and from Georgetown College, including the latter's Goode funds. Georgetown also provided support through the efforts of Ashlie Wrenne, Vanessa Carper, Dara Edgington, and Sarah O. Hardin.

To place Reid in the proper perspective requires an understanding of his home area. A great deal of aid was forthcoming, both in materials and information and in hospitality. In particular, Caswell Lane of Mount Sterling took much time to share his historical knowledge, as well as to comment on an early stage of the manuscript. Ann and Curt Steger provided not only research items but also access to the Reid house, where they live. Illustrations and other information came from Terry Murphy of Mount Sterling and Henry Prewitt of Paris, Kentucky. Leads to people and sources resulted from David and Lalie Dick of Bourbon County and the late Kate Prewitt. From Cincinnati, former Mount Sterling resident John Marshall Prewitt shared his expertise in the area as well.

More specific information, on matters as varied as law, psychology, medicine, and literature, came from John C. Klotter of Louisville, Richard Lozano and Karen Lozano, both of Birmingham, Robert S. Weise of Eastern Kentucky University, and, from Georgetown College, Susan Bell, Barbara Burch, Robert Snyder, and most members of the History Department.

But perhaps the greatest scholarly debt owed goes to those who look over various drafts of a book, commenting on weaknesses, probing the author's thesis, offering ideas for new sources, locating everything from embarrassing typos to questionable conclusions. They should challenge a writer to think and rethink each page, each viewpoint, each idea. In the end, not all suggested will be accepted, but the process itself is the important thing. My readers have done much to make this work better, and each brought different strengths to the project. For that, and for taking time from their own work to help, I give my great thanks to Lindsey Apple of Georgetown College, Thomas H. Appleton Jr. of Eastern Kentucky University, Terry Birdwhistell of the University of Kentucky, John David Smith of North Carolina State University, Christopher Waldrep of San Francisco State University, Margaret Ripley Wolfe of East Tennessee State University, and Bertram Wyatt-Brown of the University of Florida.

Finally, and foremost, the love, friendship, and support of my wife, Freda, remains the most important gift anyone has made to this work. As always, to her go my greatest thanks.

Introduction

He was the soul of honor.
— The Rev. H. R. Trickett, May 1884

Why study Richard Reid? Answering that query involves the question of why historians write books at all. First of all, and simply said, the historian is a detective—as Robin Winks has noted—a person searching out clues to answer questions from the past, seeking solutions to unresolved mysteries, looking for explanations from a world long gone to help understand a world all around us. Here were mysteries to be solved.

Yet historical study goes beyond that. As Winthrop Jordan emphasized in his brilliant *White over Black,* understanding history produces two almost opposite advantages for those who comprehend: "It makes us aware of how different people have been in other ages and accordingly enlarges our awareness of the possibilities of human experience, and at the same time it impresses upon us those tendencies in human beings which have *not* changed and which accordingly are unlikely to at least in the immediate future." Reid's life speaks to those universal understandings of the human condition.[1]

But more than that, Reid played center stage in a tragedy that garnered front-page attention and editorial notice from a wide range of national and regional journalists and commentators. His life, and subsequent manner of death, would raise important issues about the nature of Kentucky justice, southern honor, and American manhood. While he may not have been a major figure, Reid, in his attempt to escape the coils of melancholy and the surrounding culture of primal honor, and in the way he lived and died, showed vividly the tensions between an older southern way and the newer, secular, commercial forces.

Reid's life thus personified so many issues not only central to his era, but important to us as well. To understand many nineteenth-century concepts, the starting place remains at the local—or even personal—level. Resulting details, placed in context, take what might seem just a single study of one man's life and death, and move it to another plane, where larger understandings of the state, regional, and national mindset stand revealed. What happened to Richard Reid in 1884 not only shows the prevailing views of a broader society at that one moment in time, but also provides a benchmark to evaluate how that era weighed and honored different values, values we continue to debate.

Finally, the study of Reid's life explores, in some ways, an even broader question—that of the individual versus that person's surrounding culture and society. In this case, can one man be a part of a place—live *in* the culture—but not yet be *of* that culture? How much can an individual effect change by defying long-continuing codes of conduct, rules, and expectations? In short, can a dissenter change the existing values, can an individual cause societal remodification of the culture, can one person make a difference?

If these philosophical debates operate at several levels, so too does this book contain several approaches to those issues. The first third of the work may seem to be rather conventional biography, as it sets the stage for much that follows. The middle third begins to look at backgrounds and then actions that define Reid's life. Finally, the last third seeks to solve mysteries and to place it all in context. For his is not a story that ends with his death; if it is, then his life is even more a tragedy than it was. Instead, his example focuses on issues and answers with us yet.

To do justice to Richard Reid's life, and to understand fully his death, meant that the normal paths historians follow to solve a historical maze would not suffice in this case—psychology and sociology, gender studies, honor and the Lost Cause, manhood matters, legal works, examinations of violence, medical concerns, and more—all had to be part of the story. That meant that in addition to the usual historical suspects, sources had to include diverse journals ranging from the *Harvard Law Review* to the *Journal of Forensic Sciences* to the *American Sociological Review* and the *Journal of Clinical Psychiatry*. Physicians, lawyers, and psychologists, as well as historians, aided with excellent insights, and my acknowledgments only reveal part of my debt to them all. Whether I learned much from them, readers will have to decide.

At the same time, the poet Shelley wrote, "Forget the dead, the past? Oh, yet there are ghosts that may take revenge for it." If I have not done justice to Reid, a man deserving of justice at last, or if I have not properly used the sources and advice of many, then ghosts—or book reviewers—may well exact their revenge. But through it all, the pasts of Richard Reid's history must continue to be explored, and new mysteries perpetually studied. For only then can we better understand that which has shaped us, and molds us still.[2]

Kentucky Justice, Southern Honor,
and American Manhood

Prologue

It all began innocently enough. On 16 April 1884, in Mount Sterling, Kentucky, attorney John Jay Cornelison asked barrister and Superior Court judge Richard Reid to come to his office to look at some legal papers. After taking care of other matters, Judge Reid arrived around two P.M. in his fellow church member's place of business. Cornelison asked him to sit down and handed him some items regarding a case. As the seated Reid examined the material, Cornelison asked if he had written it. When Reid answered, "No," Cornelison suddenly yelled out, "Liar! That opinion is a great outrage to me and you are responsible for it!"[1]

Before Reid could say much in response, the strong and robust Cornelison started hitting him over the head and shoulder with a large hickory cane. Dazed, Reid stumbled from his chair and tried to get away from the blows. His assailant drew out a hidden cowhide whip and began lashing him, over and over, as Reid fled into the street. The number of blows may have been two dozen; it may have been a hundred. Reid only knew that he had to get away from them and from the man who would not stop. He ran more than a block, down a crowded street, with Cornelison continuing to strike him. Finally, Reid went into a store and asked for someone to make it end. After three or four more blows, a person finally stepped in, and the whip at last went silent. Cornelison triumphantly said, "I only gave him a good cowhiding, which he deserved." Reid—bruised, bloodied, and almost in a stupor—could say nothing.[2]

It was over. But, in fact, the story had just begun, and the past inexorably shaped that future.

Chapter 1

A Man of Books

People looked at the adult Richard Reid and described a man whose life appeared almost perfect, filled with success after success. A brilliant scholar, exceptional attorney, and model religious figure, he had a happy home life and much respect. But tragedies, both hidden and known, lay behind that façade, and his personal history would play an immense role in destroying that seemingly perfect life.

Happy moments had filled much of his childhood. When Richard Reid was born on the family farm in Montgomery County, Kentucky, on 3 October 1838, his place of birth lay in the outer parts of the central Bluegrass, but also looked over its shoulder at the not-far-distant Appalachians. The fertile, slightly rolling land delighted the eye, provided good farming, and offered a young boy room to roam. Reid's surroundings were comfortable, his situation prosperous. Very early, he could also place himself in time and know his roots, for the family Bible not only recorded his coming into the world, but also traced the progenitors back to a great-great-great-great-grandfather in County Antrim, Ireland. The names showed that the Reids, like others from that island, had migrated to the New World in the early 1700s and then, in another generation, made the move to the promise of the New West of Kentucky.[1]

At nearly the same time, Irish immigrant James Davis concluded his Revolutionary War service and came to what would be the first state west of the mountains. By then, most of the Indian threat had ended, and settlers could turn to building a new commonwealth out of a rough frontier. While not everyone found the land and wealth they sought in this "Garden of the

West," the Davises did. In 1797, son Josiah Davis was born in Kentucky, and he would go on to become a Whig legislator. When he and Patsy Chandler Smith married in 1820 and moved to Montgomery County, they came in contact with the Reids. On 4 January 1838, their sixteen-year-old daughter Elizabeth married twenty-seven-year-old Henry Prather Reid. Children soon followed: nine months to the day after the wedding came Richard, named for Henry's father, and then in 1840 Josiah Davis Reid, named for Elizabeth's. Those who knew Reid's mother remembered her as a tall, erect person of "splendid physique," with black hair and dark eyes, a woman of "wonderful vivacity."[2]

Devoted to family, she went to care for some relations who had "the fever." She too contracted the disease and died on 21 October 1841, at the age of twenty. Richard Reid, three years and eighteen days old, and his brother, Davis Reid, not yet two, had lost their mother.[3]

As was often the case with a single father, the boys went to live with their nearby grandparents. While they stayed there only a year, they would forge a strong bond and long remain close to them as a result. It proved a time of learning and listening. Grandmother Mary Reid could tell of how she once had been walking down the road when General Andrew Jackson had invited her into his coach, and how they talked till he delivered her to her destination. Such stories made the people of history real to Reid and a personal part of his past. On the Davis side, Reid could hear his grandfather tell of his legislative days, years as a colonel in the state militia, and sense of service to the people. Humorous and hospitable, Colonel Davis opened use of his fine library, strong in Burns and Shakespeare, not only to friends but to the family that included his grandchildren. Meanwhile Grandmother Patsy Davis took the opportunity to teach Richard to memorize the Scriptures as well.[4]

Change came once more to Richard Reid's life, on Christmas, 1842. That day his Aunt Mary Davis, his dead mother's seventeen-year-old sister, married Reid's thirty-two-year-old father. The two boys moved back to that household and soon found themselves surrounded by siblings, who came rapidly at two-year intervals. By 1850, the now-twenty-five-year-old Mary Davis Reid had stepsons Richard, age fourteen, and Davis, ten, plus her own children Flora, age six, William, five, Patsy, three, and one-year-old Mary, all to raise. She would bring two more children into the world before her childbearing ended in 1861.[5]

Richard Reid remembered his father as patriarchal, stern, remote, and even repressive toward the family. The blue-eyed, auburn-haired Henry Reid remained a strong, steady farmer, one who purchased in three separate transactions some 173 acres for over $5,300, in the year of his remarriage. He likely left most of the childrearing to his wife. The father and his oldest son would not be close.[6]

Part of the reason for that resulted from early misfortune, one which, in essence, would shape Reid's entire life-course. When only fifteen months old, Richard had been seized by a servant in such a way as to cause what was described as "a serious injury." Constantly in pain, unable to engage in most physical activities, he withdrew from the usual world of childhood, into one of books and the mind. At a time when, as one author notes, "traits such as size, strength, speed, and endurance earned a boy respect among his peers," Reid remained outside all that. To a father involved with the physical work of the farm, or to the boy's active friends, Reid could not measure up to their standards. He might recount the birth dates of his ancestors before he was three, yet he could not impress many of those he respected because they valued other attributes more.[7]

One who knew Reid in those years recalled that he became attached to those who returned his love, "with an intensity amounting almost to worship." Yet he grew sensitive, reserved, and occasionally reclusive, for he told no one outside the family of his problems. His world, increasingly, became himself.[8]

Whether because of all that, or in addition to it, Reid also slept poorly and became a sleepwalker. His family would find him wandering the halls or even outdoors and could awaken him only with difficulty. At other times, he could not sleep at all and lay in the solitude and loneliness of a quiet, dark house. Reid grew nervous and sometimes melancholy; those problems he would take with him into adulthood. Yet children often adjust to difficult situations and fashion reasonably happy lives as a result. Despite the injury and the changes it caused, despite the death of his mother and emotional distance of his father, despite the sleepwalking and sleeplessness, a resilient Richard Reid drew strength from his loving grandparents, his books, his sense of place, and his internally constructed world. He would not just survive; he would excel.[9]

The first step in that process centered on schooling. At the time of his birth, Kentucky had just initiated a system of state-funded public schools, and only after Reid left that system did it become strong in the antebellum era.

Generally, it featured few schools, ill-prepared teachers, and one-room log buildings, when extant. At age six, he entered one of those places of instruction, taught by a "Northern man," and had thereafter a series of teachers, good and bad, over the next eight years. Then, at age fourteen, in August 1852, Reid became a student at the Highland Literary Institute, a boarding and day school in Mount Sterling. Its principal, Episcopal minister Daniel S. C. M. Potter, had made it an excellent institution, one where Reid developed an even greater love of learning. Virtually every day (since he seldom missed a class), he packed his lunch, then got on his horse, and made the roundtrip of some seven miles from his home to the school and back. He often stayed after classes ended, for additional work.[10]

Both the Reverend Mr. Potter and Reid's fellow pupils remembered him as an exceptional student. Potter, a strict disciplinarian, found Reid conscientious almost to "an exceeding extreme" and gave him no punishments or demerits. A classmate his age, Edward O. Guerrant, would later be a Confederate soldier, physician, well-known minister, and author. He called Reid "the best student and the best scholar I ever knew . . . a man of books." Yet Guerrant recognized that he and Reid were different: "Modest as a girl," the "delicate" and "sensitive" Reid did not play sports as the others did. He preferred seclusion and therefore never became particularly popular with most of his classmates (who, like Guerrant, did not know of Reid's physical problems). Yet Guerrant liked and, most of all, respected Reid.[11]

Probably through Potter's influence, in 1852 Reid also professed religion and was baptized. Thereafter, the church formed an important part of his being. It gave him some solace and comfort amid his pain, both physical and mental. His success in school provided an additional measure of confidence. When he graduated, Reid had begun to emerge, bit by bit, from his carefully constructed, isolated life. College would continue that process.[12]

New institutions of higher learning in Kentucky, the South, and the nation had sprung up on a regular basis in the nineteenth century. Some survived; many did not. Still others flourished when a particularly good teacher or administrator led them, but soon failed when that individual left. In Kentucky, Transylvania University had been a major regional and national school for a time, but by the 1850s, when Reid entered college, it had become only a shell of its earlier self; its initial glory days had passed. Among the other colleges around, none dominated, but several showed signs of future strength. For practical reasons as well as academic ones, Reid chose a religiously oriented college less then forty miles from his home. There he would mature as a scholar and as a person.[13]

Georgetown College, like others of that era, had both a mixed history and uncertain prospects. Situated near Lexington, in Georgetown, Kentucky, it sprang from an academy started around 1787 by a Baptist minister–businessman–bourbon maker named Elijah Craig. Later, as Rittenhouse Academy, it had attracted good principals, including the Reverend Barton Stone, one of the founders of the Christian (Disciples of Christ) Church. He described the town as "notorious for irreligion and wickedness" and soon devoted his full time to converting those sinners. By the 1820s, the academy had closed, but when the college received its charter in 1829—as one of the oldest Baptist schools in America—it took over the old academy site. On 1 January 1830, Georgetown College opened its doors to thirteen students. Among the more notable members of its classes over the next dozen years was a ministerial student, Robert Sallee James, who married Zerelda Cole in 1841. Their move to Missouri soon thereafter meant that their sons, Frank and Jesse James, would be born there.[14]

But overall, the school had mostly struggled in the two decades before Reid arrived. In an inauspicious start for the college, the first president died before even stepping foot on the campus. Others stayed only briefly, or died in office. With little continuity of leadership, student enrollment fluctuated as well. In 1852, however, Duncan R. Campbell, a thirty-eight-year-old native of Scotland and a Baptist minister, became the seventh president in just over two decades, and the school's fortunes improved. Georgetown seemed a good choice for the young graduate of Highland Literary Institute.[15]

In September 1855, Richard Reid, age sixteen, paid the forty-dollars-a-year tuition and entered Georgetown College. Most students lived off-campus in private homes and paid around two dollars a week for room, board, and washing. When Reid went out to secure that housing, he saw the city that would be his home for several more years.[16]

Kentucky had been called the "dark and bloody ground," and Georgetown reflected that early history. Its first settlement was abandoned in 1777, following a battle that left its founder dead. Three years later, one of the members of the Johnson family, who so dominated the county later, reestablished a fort. A son, Richard M. Johnson, would gain his fame—and some said the vice presidency of the United States—by virtue of being declared the slayer of the Indian chief Tecumseh. Ironically, Johnson later started a school for Native Americans on his land.[17]

But then, contradictions abounded in Scott County, with its county seat of Georgetown. Johnson also lived openly with his mulatto mistress and raised their children as his own, while continuing to hold slaves. Elijah Craig, the Baptist minister, would be called by some the father of bourbon whiskey, which he certainly made. He too owned slaves—some thirty-two in 1800. In fact, by the eve of the Civil War some 41 percent of the population lived as slaves under the "peculiar institution." Yet overall, the county—like Kentucky—divided when war came. The rich farmland of hemp, wheat, corn, oats, and tobacco, worked by slaves, brought antebellum prosperity, but the existence of slavery meant future woes, and many deaths.[18]

Reid, whose family held slaves, and had for decades, made no public comments during his school years on that explosive issue. Instead, once he found a place to board in the town that would have 1,684 people by 1860, he went about the business of simply being a college student, trying to live up to his own expectations and the school's many rules.[19]

According to the college, inducements to sin lay all around the all-male student body. The Georgetown Female Seminary stood only a block or so from campus, but appeared worlds away both to the male college students and to the 140 tightly regulated and strictly chaperoned young seminary women. More attainable, apparently, were other temptations. Rules stated that students could not leave their rooms after seven o'clock at night except to attend church or special events. Daily devotions were required as well. "Frolics" of a "noisy, disorderly or immortal [sic?] nature" could not occur, nor could students frequent a barroom or "tippling house" or fight a duel. While two students had been expelled years before for yelling "Down with the Yankees" to two New England faculty members, in Reid's era discipline went to those "drinking and shooting turkeys," misbehaving at chapel, and stealing chickens and strawberries from townspeople.[20]

Reid apparently broke none of the many college rules. A classmate recalled that Reid never missed a lecture and did not drink, play cards, smoke, or even swear. Few students of any era would earn that memory. In 1855, the year he entered Georgetown College, he stood as one of 134 college students, 80 percent of them from Kentucky. Of the rest, virtually all came from southern states. His class was a particularly strong one. Fellow students included James E. Cantrill, later lieutenant governor of Kentucky; J. Q. A. Ward, a future Superior Court judge; John L. Peak, afterwards minister to Switzerland; future businessman John M. Atherton; and numerous young men who would go on to be clergy.[21]

The five college professors taught sophomores Latin and Greek, geometry, trigonometry, and "Grecian Antiquities," with an emphasis on Cicero, Homer, Horace, and Plato in all their studies. Juniors studied Greek and Roman literature, chemistry, natural philosophy, botany, logic, literary criticism, and "mechanics." Finally, as seniors, Reid and the others took classes in English literature, geology, zoology, astronomy, Christianity and religion, political economy, the U.S. Constitution, the history of philosophy, and Hebrew.[22]

Reid earned a 7.99 in his college career, out of a possible 8.00, the highest grades ever attained in the college's twenty-five-year history to that point. Not surprisingly, one of his fellow scholars remembered him as the "most brilliant student among us," particularly in Latin and Greek. His roommate termed Reid "the best student I ever knew—methodical, conscientious, untiring."[23]

But while Reid excelled in learning in classes, his real development came outside the academic halls, in both writing and speaking. He and five others started the short-lived *Georgetown College Magazine* in 1857. In one of the first issues, writing as "R.R." (Reid was the only R.R. on campus), he told of "The Martyr to Science," who turns from man's selfish nature to promote instead "the good of the world." Reid, who loved poetry, filled the piece with verse, references to Roman leaders, and much flowery prose. Stronger efforts came elsewhere, however.[24]

Since social fraternities and sororities did not yet dot most college campuses, and few student organizations existed, literary societies provided students camaraderie, unity, and even a sense of intellectual excitement outside the classroom. At Georgetown College, two such groups vied for the best students and the most attention. Tau Theta Kappa and the Ciceronian Society each had their own libraries—totaling two thousand volumes, compared to the college's six thousand overall—their own diplomas, and even (later) their own separate entrances to debating halls. Members wore their satin sashes to the weekly secret debates, cheered or jeered the speakers, and reveled in the knowledge that they could legally leave their rooms after 7:00 P.M. to attend.[25]

Reid joined the Ciceronian Society, which reported his talks and activities regularly in the college's *Ciceronian Magazine,* started his first year on campus. In its second issue, "R.R." wrote on "Music," and stressed how people through the ages enjoyed that pursuit: "To the lover of music, everything wears a cheerful aspect." For a seventeen-year-old, it showed solid prose, but on a safe subject. Five months later, in a more serious piece, entitled "Unity of Purpose in Life," Reid pondered why "eminent men" excelled and achieved. His answer? "Because unity of purpose characterizes every thought and action. They seem to be urged on by an irresistible devotion to attain one great object, to accomplish one great end." In a sense speaking about himself, he said that aspirants for earthly glory must focus their attentions, for "without unity of purpose in life you will . . . pass from the stage of human action unwept, unhonored, and unsung." Reid had the ability and desire to be successful, to win his battles outside the physical realm. He believed he needed only the will now to do that.[26]

Already gaining a reputation for his scholarship and writing ability, Reid gave the featured address to the junior class annual exhibition in February 1857, and the *Ciceronian* printed that as well, with Reid's full name this time. In "The Old Age of the Scholar," an eighteen-year-old Reid stressed, in essence, why teachers never get old, why scholars do not fear the passing of time. In many ways, the talk reflected Reid's own maturity:

> Such is the old age of every scholar. Upon him the imbecilities of advanced life are not visited. . . . Old age, to the world a desolate waste—a Sahara boundless and drear, he knows not, hence does not dread. . . . Nature may refuse to perform her functions, the blood loses its youthful warmth and active flow . . . but his form is erect; his eye burning and undimmed; his mental horizon unclouded. . . . If it be asked why the scholar never becomes old, be this our answer. *He has not time.* . . . In youth, in manhood, in hoary ages [*sic*], he toils. He sees a new revelation written every night in the heavens. . . . He brings up the treasured wisdom of the past to bear on present emergencies. He dives into the chambers of his being. . . .
>
> His motto is, "onward, onward forever." He belongs to no set or party. The world is his country. . . . Planting his foot upon the grave of buried vanity, he presses on to the unfailing fountains of wisdom. This . . . keeps the scholar young.[27]

Reid then contrasted the scholar with the person "grown old in ignorance and folly." That individual, he argued, had none of the "elastic buoyancy" of youth, no fire or passion: "His mind is like a deserted temple." Look instead at the scholar, Reid suggested. In old age, Homer "struck the epic lyre," Sophocles "sang . . . his sweetest song," Franklin saw the power of lightning. "Do you long for happiness? The old age of the scholar alone is blessed. . . . For him philosophers think, poets sing. For him thoughts are uttered, books are written. . . . He is rich in thought." And when death comes, it brings no terror. While the warrior dies with "the guilty stain of murder" on his soul, and the statesman with the "frightful phantoms" of neglected issues on his, the scholar instead knows that he has done his duty and that "heaven shall be my home." If occasionally naïve and somewhat selective in argument, the talk, nevertheless, represented a remarkable summary from a young man. Reid obviously looked forward, as a man of letters and learning, to a long and fruitful life.[28]

That same mature, reflective Reid emerged in a series of letters he exchanged with his old principal, the Reverend Daniel Potter. Telling his mentor that he had made perfect grades, he confided that such "only adds fuel to the flame for honorable distinction, which has already been kindled within me." Then, repeating the themes he had spoken three weeks earlier to the junior class, he privately stressed that "I wish so to live that the small, still voice of an approving conscience may whisper to me in the winter of life. I wish to die with the blessed assurance that I have not lived in vain." But what should he do, once school had ended? He admitted his desire had been to be a minister, but now feared he was not competent, in his mind, to do that. Several months later, Reid once more took up similar themes with the Reverend Mr. Potter. "I have a work to do, a mission to perform," he affirmed, and he had determined to do something to ameliorate the condition of the world. In short, "I am resolved to render myself useful, to live and die with the peaceful consciousness of having attempted to do my duty." Duty, honor, conscience, mission—these guided Richard Reid as the end of his college career neared.[29]

During that time, the student's relationship with his classmates had remained mixed. Virtually everyone acknowledged his strengths—his wit, his mind, his fluent conversations, his amiable spirit, his modesty, his moral spirit. Yet the specific language used by some of his fellow students, as they later remembered those years, suggested that they did not fully accept him still. Businessman Atherton recalled that Reid did not engage in "manly sports" and concluded: "He was not a coward, but he was timid." Roommate William Welch indicated that Reid "had an almost feminine aversion to all forms of coarse dissipation," while classmate Peak remembered Reid as physically fragile, a man who "shrank from all kinds of rude contests with the timidity of a girl." Brilliantly successful as a scholar, essayist, and orator, popular as a student, Reid still could not fully penetrate the inner circles of masculine respect. He remained an outsider.[30]

On 24 June 1858, the twenty-three members of the senior class graduated, with nineteen-year-old Richard Reid receiving "first honors." Apparently long commencement exercises have a storied history, for his included two prayers, eleven musical interludes, and seventeen talks by others—including one in Latin, and addresses on Bunker Hill, Homer and Milton, and trial by jury, among the many. Reid spoke early on "The Destiny of the Anglo-Saxon," then again—as the nineteenth talk—in his valedictory. Finally came the awarding of diplomas, and Richard Reid now faced leaving his secure college world.[31]

But not yet. On the same day trustees awarded Reid the bachelor of arts degree, they named him principal of the Preparatory Department of the college, at a salary of $600. (The president received $2,000 that year.) Over the next two years, he would be officially listed as "Tutor in the Classical Academy," a title that disguised his varied duties. Chiefly, he taught the two dozen or so students not yet ready for the college curriculum, including four from China. At the same time, Reid aided the professor at the college in the fields of Latin and Greek. Gradually, however, he decided that another profession better suited "my peculiar bent of mind."[32]

"I came to the conclusion I would follow the law," Reid told Potter. During the time he taught, he found those duties took only four or so hours a day, so he asked Judge Alvin Duvall if he could study law under him. It was a good choice. Duvall had attended both Georgetown College and Transylvania University, had served in the legislature, then had been circuit judge. When he accepted Reid as a student and allowed him to board with his family—he had thirteen children—Duvall was a member of the state's highest tribunal, the Court of Appeals, and later would be named chief justice. Described as "unpretending, polite, dignified, and polished," he and Reid worked well together. In May 1860, the young legal student won his license to practice law.[33]

Still not satisfied that he knew enough about the "practical workings of the law," Reid arranged to study further under the direction of Thomas Payne Porter, then the acting lieutenant governor of Kentucky. That decision necessitated a move to Porter's practice in Versailles, some twenty miles away, in Woodford County. There Reid found a man, not yet fifty, who had been selected to preside over the state senate, and from that post had become the next in line to the governorship, since the elected lieutenant governor had died. Now, Porter headed the state senate just as the commonwealth—and the nation—faced the prospect of civil war.[34]

In 1861, Kentucky wanted both union and slavery. On the walls of the Washington Monument, the state had earlier inscribed the words, "Under the auspices of Heaven, and the precepts of Washington, Kentucky will be the last to give up the Union," and the ghost-words of Henry Clay's calls for unity echoed still to the people. Yet others pleaded the earlier arguments of the Kentucky Resolutions of 1798, calling for the rights of states, and warned of the dangers to slavery from the Kentucky-born Abraham Lincoln and his "Abolition Party." When another native of the Bluegrass State, Jefferson Davis, became president of the new Confederacy, that cemented the symbolism of a divided Kentucky. In a prescient essay written five years earlier in the *Ciceronian Magazine,* a student had suggested that "when the Union is dissolved, it will be by the withdrawal of the South; and in no event will that take place until the North elect a President. . . . The great question then will be, how will Virginia and Kentucky go?" Now that question required an answer. At that college in April, student divisions grew so strong that trustees suspended classes until the fall semester. Symbolically, Scott County itself furnished both a Union governor of Kentucky and a Confederate one; Mary Todd Lincoln found that most of her family had taken up arms against the cause her husband led; U.S. Senator John J. Crittenden saw one of his sons become a Union general, another a Confederate one; 1860 presidential candidate John C. Breckinridge went south, while his Unionist uncle's family sent two sons to the gray, two to the blue. Novelist John Fox Jr. later wrote, "As the nation was rent apart, so was the commonwealth; as the state so was the county; as the county, the neighborhood; as the neighborhood, the family; as the family, so brother and brother, father and son."[35]

The Reid family faced these same conflicts. Kentucky officially declared itself neutral in May 1861, and there existed three entities—the United States of America, the Confederate States of America, and Kentucky. But as Union forces won political victories, the South recognized that the state's future did not seem to favor formal secession, and a Confederate invasion brought an end to the commonwealth's neutrality. Kentucky went with a Union that had not yet made the end of slavery a stated war aim. When that changed as the conflict wore on, the state's sympathies altered as well. But for the commonwealth in 1861, it had already become the Brothers' War.[36]

Richard Reid's brother Davis and his father both supported the Union. With the same intensity, Richard sided with the South, as did his legal mentors Duvall and Porter. Although he had always abhorred bloodshed, Reid supported the cause so much that he secretly went to a physician and asked if his physical condition would allow him to enlist. It did not. Neither of the brothers entered the army, and they remained friends. But Lieutenant Governor Porter's actions forced him to leave the state for a time, and his— and new partner Reid's—practice suffered greatly as a result. With the courts meeting erratically, the entire legal profession lay in shambles. By February 1863, Reid wrote that he had virtually abandoned the law "until a better time" and had, once more, retreated to "obscure seclusion with my books." However, that did not tell the entire story. Richard Reid was in love.[37]

Chapter 2

A Perfect Life

Richard Reid felt comfortable in the company of women. In fact, he noted early, "I have always been so unfortunate as to fall in love with every beauty that showed me favor." Yet apparently the attention of those young women had never gone beyond kindness or courtesy to him. Or perhaps he simply could not lower the barriers he had so long established, and let emotion compete with reason, or permit physical feelings to win out over his long-cultivated reserve. His psychological shell had been built to protect himself from physical and mental distress, but he frankly admitted his growing susceptibility to "female charms." Confusing emotions pulled at the eager young man.[1]

For women, Reid offered many positive attributes. Physically he could impress—handsome, dignified, tall, slender, with long dark-brown hair, "brilliant" expressive blue eyes, and a flowing beard. Balancing all that was the fact that he constantly drooped his shoulders, wore ill-fitting clothes, and had pale skin, because he engaged in few outdoor activities.[2]

At the same time, intellectually Reid impressed almost everyone with his retentive memory and analytical mind. Well-read, he could easily quote poetry and the classics. His writing showed his thoughtfulness and ability to express ideas clearly. Moreover, his religious beliefs and internal makeup caused him, as one classmate said, to be "utterly devoid of ill-will toward any one." Others found a man of irreproachable character, a person of almost no personal vices—he did chew tobacco—"a practicing as well as professing Christian," "the most gentle, loving and amiable man I ever knew." Yet some of the "manly" qualities the age valued would not be found in

Richard Reid. He avoided fights and physical activity, and seemed sensitive and shy. Certain that such weaknesses outweighed his strengths, Reid confessed by the end of his college days that "I have not the slightest idea of marrying."[3]

Then Richard Reid met Sarah T. Jameson. Her father John Jameson had grown up in Reid's home county of Montgomery, had moved to Missouri before Reid was born, and there had tasted political success after success. A Fulton attorney, he had been a Democratic legislator, eventually serving as Speaker of the Missouri House, then had won election to Congress for three terms. Jameson had not sought reelection and went from politics to the pulpit as a Christian Church minister. His 1857 death brought daughter Sarah to move to Versailles, Kentucky, where her older sister operated a school. There in 1861, "Sallie"—as she was known—met young lawyer Reid, just as the Civil War opened.[4]

A family member praised the young Miss Jameson as a woman of "rich natural endowments, high culture, rare personal beauty," with a cheerful personality and sparkling wit. More unbiased observers echoed those descriptions, calling her a person of great beauty and "womanly grace." Sallie recognized Reid's strengths, and their friendship grew into romance. Richard, in turn, found the love he had perhaps never expected would be his. They became engaged to be married and set the date for 25 November 1863.[5]

Reid traveled to Missouri three months before that date, to meet her family. He found his betrothed "unchanged—sweet, lovely, glorious as an angel." Her hospitable, friendly relatives had only one fault, he admitted: they sought to feed him to death. The man who liked children and usually had a group of them following him around the streets of Versailles even enjoyed playing with his fiancée's baby niece, although, he confessed in a letter, that took him away too long from Sallie, "and I must look after her." The sheer joy of his love echoes throughout almost every line he wrote and emphasizes the correctness of his conclusion: "I am as happy as a man ever gets to be."[6]

Excited over the future, Reid returned to Kentucky to continue his struggling wartime legal practice over the next months and to prepare for married life. Then he received a telegram, telling him that Sallie had fallen ill with the fever in Missouri. He immediately rushed to her. By the time he arrived, she was dead. Sarah T. Jameson was twenty-one, a year older than Reid's mother when she died. Richard could not even see Sallie a last time, for the family had already buried her, in what would have been her bridal dress. She had died two weeks before the wedding.[7]

Sallie, in the last hours of her illness, had said, "I should like very much to live. The world is a very bright and beautiful place to me just now." So too it had been for Reid. Now all seemed darkness and dread. He had opened a very hidden part of himself to her love, but had found death and hurt instead. Just how strong was his own will to live, after that, remains unknown. Worried over his mental state, her family had to force Reid from Sallie's grave, for he would not leave her. His nervousness and sleeplessness increased, for with sleep came dreams. Two other things also suggest the depth of his loss. Soon after he came back to Versailles from Missouri, he left the town—her town—and did not return for some eighteen years. The memories there continued to be too strong, after all that time. And over twenty years after his death, people who knew Reid told how, in their view, he "never got out from under the shadow of that great sorrow." Her grave left a dark wound on an already scarred psyche.[8]

Reid's religion helped him deal with the loss; he told a minister that before the tragedy, he had never known the true worth of his beliefs. The death of Sallie, "a being so beautiful, so pure and angelic in body, soul, and spirit," he did not fully understand yet, but he expected that in time he would meet her in Heaven. He found solace also in his work. In 1864, Reid returned to his hometown of Mount Sterling and formed a partnership with his brother, J. Davis Reid, to begin in January 1865.[9]

The firm of Reid and Reid prospered, doing all manner of work in the chaotic postwar period. Their advertisement in the local paper stressed expertise in "claims against the United States Government," but they operated as master commissioners, tried court cases large and small, wrote mortgages, wills, and other legal papers—in short, did most of the things attorneys did in small towns. Since Davis Reid served, for a short time, as the county attorney as well—a part-time job that still provided a secure income base—the older Reid took on more of the daily duties of the firm. Now called "Dick" Reid, he seemed to be trying to work in order to forget. Seldom did he arrive in the office later than 7 A.M., and he kept equally long hours in the evening. His weight dropped to only 130 pounds on his six-foot frame.[10]

Other tragedies decimated much of what remained of the family. Half-sister Flora had died earlier, then ten-year-old James followed her. Next,

Reid's father passed away and his land went to Davis and Richard Reid in 1869. Three years after that, twenty-seven-year-old William, a half-brother to whom Reid had grown very close, became ill with typhoid fever, and within three weeks he had died. Dick Reid wrote: "We can not understand the dealings of Providence, and the blow seems too hard to bear." A half-sister's life ended in 1880, when she was nineteen, adding more sorrows.[11]

But life went on. The legal work proved very profitable, yet took its toll. Reid called the law "a cruel, dull, hard, confining business," one that required too much of its practitioners, since he had not been able to leave town for the past three weeks. Davis Reid apparently agreed and in 1869 dissolved the partnership in order to farm his father's land, on the place where Richard Reid had been born. There Davis and his wife, Nettie Prewitt Reid, raised ten children, including one named for his brother. The two siblings remained close, and Dick Reid frequently visited his brother's house—his own birthplace—over the ensuing years. There, several miles from town, Davis Reid lived in what had originally been an 1820s house that had been altered to Greek Revival style, probably in the 1850s. The story-and-a-half building soon would be given Victorian architectural features as well. Not far over the rich, rolling land sat the boyhood home of ex–Confederate general John Bell Hood, who visited there after the war. Across the road from Davis Reid's home lay the rapidly expanding Reid family cemetery.[12]

While brother Davis took up a new career, Dick Reid continued to be faithful to the legal profession. It might be a fickle mistress and he might grumble to be rid of it at times, but in truth Reid loved the orderliness of the law and its dependence on rules and precedents. His life needed that security and safeness. Accordingly, in January 1870, Reid became the junior partner in Apperson and Reid, which developed into one of the best law firms in town—if not the best. Richard Apperson Jr. had been born into a family where his father had been a Whig legislator and delegate to Kentucky's constitutional convention in 1849. The son had fought in the Mexican War as a sixteen-year-old, had married a grandniece of his old commander, Zachary Taylor, and had been selected circuit judge, on a Union ticket, during the Civil War. Now the forty-year-old Apperson and the thirty-one-year-old Reid formed a powerful partnership, since both men excelled in the law. It would be broken only by Apperson's death eight years later, in 1878. During that time, Reid continued to prosper, and it became clear that he had determined to make Mount Sterling his permanent place of residence. That increasingly seemed a good choice, although it may not have appeared so when he had returned in 1864, amid the war.[13]

Mount Sterling had been officially established as a town the same year Kentucky became a state, in 1792. Originally called Little Mountain Town for a large Indian burial mound there, the place had been named the county seat of the newly created Montgomery County four years later. But it had grown slowly, and then the Civil War had left its mark on the town. Confederate raiders and Union soldiers alike had occupied Mount Sterling, and in a March 1863 encounter Rebels had burned several buildings—a woollen mill, church, and hotel among them—in order to drive out Federal forces hidden in the structures. Nine months later, another Confederate raid had resulted in the destruction of the relatively new courthouse and many of its records. Then came the disastrous June 1864 raid by the "Thunderbolt of the Confederacy," the dashing cavalryman John Hunt Morgan. By that time, much of Morgan's original command had been captured, or killed, or dispersed, and a more unrestrained force rode into a town usually friendly to the Southern soldier. After defeating a Union force, the Rebels robbed the bank of some $60,000 and then looted stores. Reid's old Academy classmate E. O. Guerrant rode with Morgan and admitted his anger at his fellow soldiers: "bank robbed, stores plundered, universal pillage of private property! Am perfectly disgusted with Morganism. . . . Am ashamed to be caught in such company." The whole affair had been a blot on Morgan's mostly solid record, and the defeat he suffered soon afterwards ended his last raid. Behind he left a devastated town.[14]

When Reid arrived, he found Mount Sterling still "battle-scarred," with burned-out buildings everywhere. The city's fallen walls and coats of dust made it look like "a piece of worn-out linen that had been hastily washed out and hung out to dry." Union soldiers occupied the area, and Reid, "forlorn and desolate," questioned whether he had made the right decision in returning home. While there he saw the conflict's end firsthand, for on 1 May 1865, the few remnants of Morgan's old command rode into town. They had come, as Guerrant wrote, "to bury hopes that had been cherished for years" and to surrender to Federal forces. By July, the local newspaper noted the many ex-soldiers passing through town, as they made their way back to homes left long before. The Brothers' War in Kentucky had concluded. Now troops on both sides, and all Kentuckians, had to build new lives out of human and physical wreckage left by war. In the state, up to 140,000 had fought; 30,000 or more never returned, and their graves represented some of the best of the young antebellum generation. Reid had stepped into that leadership void, and his hometown had begun to rise with him.[15]

A minister who visited Mount Sterling near war's end found it at that time "a quiet little village, of no commercial importance whatever." Its citizens, he argued, displayed little ambition, except to have a happy and refined home where they could dispense gracious hospitality. Yet that all changed rapidly, and Reid resided in the city just as it experienced its greatest growth. That made it an exciting and vibrant place to live, but also brought conflict. Throughout the era, for example, the people out in the country competed with the city not only for power, but also for an outlook. Novelist James Lane Allen in his presentation of the Bluegrass Region remarked that even towns in the area—such as Mount Sterling—"bear the pastoral stamp." At a time when Americans increasingly portrayed those who toiled the soil as "hicks" or "rubes," being a central Kentucky farmer "implies no social inferiority, no rusticity, no boorishness." Indeed, Allen compared Kentucky to England and stressed that in the Bluegrass there still existed a landed aristocracy, living in homes their ancestors built, receiving some deference because of that.[16]

A contemporary of Allen's, the Reverend George O. Barnes, agreed: "There is a brotherhood of pride and prosperity; over all an ancestral love of estate, an aristocratic democracy." Davis Reid typified that part of the county's makeup, living on the old home place, working as a gentleman farmer. In a sense, he and many like him represented more the Old South and its outlook than the new one. A competing mindset came from those in Mount Sterling. While they still often worshipped at the shrine of the Lost Cause, and kneeled before the agrarian ideal yet, a new god increasingly appealed, one tied to the New South and to an urban outlook. During the time, then, of Reid's hometown's great growth, the city did not rule unchallenged, for those with an ethos tied to the land continued to confront the commercial ideal. A powerful agrarianism and an equally strong—and growing—small-town urbanism and boosterism warred with each other, causing clashes.[17]

Racial tensions added to the instability of the town. Before the war, some 85 percent of the households in Mount Sterling held slaves. In Civil War Kentucky, a loyal state officially—though a divided one—the Emancipation Proclamation had not legally affected slavery. Only when the Thirteenth Amendment went into effect in December 1865, long after the war's close, did slavery cease. But during the conflict, Congress had declared that slaves who fought for the Union and, later, their dependents were free. Many Kentucky slaves earned their freedom by fighting for it; others received theirs only after most African Americans elsewhere had already been freed.[18]

Reid's later law partner, then–circuit judge Richard Apperson Jr., had declared unconstitutional the congressional act freeing the families of slaves who fought, a decision supported by the state's highest court. That ruling became moot with the ratification of the Thirteenth Amendment. But Apperson's words accurately reflected the sentiment of the majority of Kentuckians, who gave up slavery reluctantly. Widespread violence against the newly freed ex-slaves caused many blacks to depart the state entirely, or to leave the farms for the city, or to build small rural hamlets where they could band together for some protection.[19] In Mount Sterling, the black population by 1870 had grown to 42 percent of the total population. Yet white efforts to help those in their midst had been tardy at best. The first "colored" school came only in 1881—sixteen years after freedom—and even then with much opposition from a local press protesting the taxes to support those efforts. By 1880, outmigration had reduced Mount Sterling's black population to 31 percent, but that poor and segregated segment held only 2 percent of the wealth. Often simmering below the surface, the tensions of racial inequality added another element to an increasing volatile urban mix.[20]

Population growth furthered that instability. From a town of 1,090 in 1870, Mount Sterling doubled in size in a decade, to 2,087, and had more than tripled in two decades, to 3,629 in 1890, the seventeenth largest city in a still very rural state. During that time, the county's overall population had gone from 4,858 to 12,367, but the city's part of that had increased faster. All those numbers meant that numerous young people, attracted by the opportunities there, had entered the urban mix, bringing with them no previous ties with the area. They began to challenge the old elites, whether urban or rural, even as that "aristocracy" itself remained divided. Many factors pulled the people apart.[21]

Yet various things also united the city, among them its growing economy. The railroad keyed that expansion. In 1872, the Elizabethtown, Lexington, and Big Sandy Railroad completed the line that tied Mount Sterling to the rapidly increasing national rail network. But what made that so crucial for the town was the fact that for seven years Mount Sterling stood at the end of that line and became the closest railhead for a large portion of eastern

Kentucky. By 1881, it connected to Ashland, Kentucky, and from there on to the East Coast. Earlier the Montgomery County city had attracted some of that regional trade by virtue of being on one of the several roads coming from the hills. Now the "Gate City" became even more important to the Appalachian market, as farmers drove cattle to Mount Sterling, as timbermen returned through there, after riding their logs on the Kentucky River to sawmills, as highland grocers picked up supplies from Louisville or Cincinnati at the railroad station and then took them to distant stores. As Reid told a politician friend, "We are a focal point and our influence reaches to all the mountains."[22]

Court Day symbolized that expanding market economy. Once a month, the roads filled as all classes of people came to town to bargain, observe, gossip, eat, and meet. Horses, cattle, chickens, and other manner of livestock all mixed their noises with the cries of vendors offering goods for sale to produce "a perfect Babel" of noise. Auctioneers shouted, politicians pleaded, children laughed, babies cried, and merchants bickered. Strolling through the crowded streets, people bought apples and peanuts, purchased anything from patent medicines to mules, and, as one recalled, simply enjoyed "the sights and the sounds." A description of Mount Sterling Court Day concluded: "Dust everywhere, or mud, knee deep, depending on the weather; . . . spurts of tobacco juice; women holding up their ankle length skirts as they crossed the streets, the men enjoying the scene, and being free with their comments; . . . some people bringing lunch and staying all day; . . . chairs in the back of jolt wagons for the women to ride; dog stealing; drunks; crowded taverns . . . ; pure copper whiskey at 25 cents a gallon; trading; and fantastic stories of good and bad deals." With liquor flowing so freely, people argued over politics, religion, and seemingly anything. Fights—occasionally deadly—broke out virtually every Court Day. But if some limped home or woke with a hangover, and others cursed a dishonest deal or an unfair price, many came back again and again, for Court Day gave excitement to lives and income to many.[23]

Before the railroad's arrival, an 1870 state directory noted that Mount Sterling already had wagonmakers, saddlemakers, butchers, saloons, shoemakers, blacksmiths, hardware and dry goods stores, dentists, doctors, carpenters, a jeweler, a flour mill, a hotel, a bank, and many churches. But after the railroad arrived, as the town grew, commerce expanded almost overnight. A distillery, more carriage factories, additional brothels, another newspaper and hotel, a public library, a gas works, a plow handle factory, and a new courthouse all symbolized that success. Others took note. A *Louisville Courier-Journal* reporter in 1881 commented on the city's thriving businesses, impressive buildings, and increasing trade. Favorably persuaded by the "energy and activity" of the people, he called Mount Sterling "the young, giant city of our eastern counties." A few months later, another story in that widely circulated newspaper praised the city as a "very favorable point for all kinds of enterprises." Not all the new endeavors survived, and other railroad lines would go into the mountains as the years passed, taking trade away. But the 1870s and 1880s represented a golden era for Mount Sterling businesses.[24]

Among those benefiting from the growth were the town's attorneys. In frontier times, Kentucky's convoluted land titles brought one author to conclude that the state quickly became "a happy hunting ground for lawyers." Now, in Mount Sterling, a similar situation existed, and a whole cadre of talented attorneys competed for business. By 1870, some thirteen practitioners of the law had offices there, including Apperson and Reid. Of the thirty wealthiest people in the community, four had been admitted to the bar; the richest man in Mount Sterling was attorney and congressman Thomas Turner, with property valued at $125,000. The other respected men of the law included former legislator Belvard J. Peters, who sat on the state's highest court from 1860 to 1878, serving the last two years as chief justice; William H. Holt, later another chief justice of that court; and James H. Hazelrigg, who also served in that post at the turn of the century. In short, from the four decades after 1860, some member of the Mount Sterling bar served on Kentucky's highest tribunal all but ten years of the forty. Attorney A. T. Wood ran for governor in 1891 on the Republican ticket as well. Yet of that talent, Richard Reid gained respect as the best legal mind in the group. Prosperous and successful, he settled happily into life as an attorney and less happily into what he called "permanent bachelorhood."[25]

After his fiancée's death, Reid had continued to correspond with Sallie Jameson's sisters. Writing to one of them, he described himself on New Year's Day 1873 as "a forlorn, desolate, forsaken bachelor," one who had been alone so much, by choice, that he found society "irksome." Reid admitted that his health was better, and that he had gained weight, to over 180 pounds, but doubted his marital status would ever change. His words revealed nothing about the pain he still felt from his earlier loss and ignored the question of whether he would have the courage to risk such hurt again.

Yet Reid's life had not been one filled with affection, and he still sought that.[26]

Dick Reid had also continued to write another of Sallie's sisters, Elizabeth. Known as "Bettie," she had been born in Missouri in April 1840, and had graduated at age sixteen, first in her class, from Christian College in that state. She had then come to Kentucky to teach at Daughter's College in Harrodsburg. When eighteen, Bettie Jameson accepted the principal's post at nearby Woodford College, a boarding school in Versailles, and younger sister Sallie had joined her there. Described as "the social queen of central Kentucky," Bettie dazzled with her "rare physical beauty," personality, and intellectual confidence: "Beauty of form and face, of mind and heart, belonged to her." Very close to her sister, Bettie had planned for them to have a double wedding—Sallie and Richard Reid, she and Benjamin F. Rogers, a widower from a wealthy Bourbon County family. Her sister's death had ended those hopes, but twenty-three-year-old Bettie and the forty-eight-year-old Rogers did marry a month later, at the end of November 1863, and she moved to "Sunnyside" in his home area. They had a child on 4 December 1866 whom she named Richard Reid Rogers. Then, after seven years of marriage, her husband died suddenly. She was a widow at age thirty.[27]

Reid had offered words of encouragement, for he knew something of the pain she felt. As before, they continued to exchange letters, as he asked about his namesake. Then one day, he quietly left town, and to many people's surprise, the two married, at her brother's home in Missouri. The date of their wedding, 13 November 1873, was—almost exactly to the day—ten years after Reid had arrived in Fulton, to find Sallie dead. Bettie, thirty-three, and Dick Reid, thirty-five, returned to Mount Sterling to create a new life and new marriage.[28]

Before they wed, Dick Reid had asked Bettie to be patient with him and to remember how alone he had been for so long: "Be kind and gentle to my sad introspective experiences." But two weeks after the wedding, a happy Reid told his new brother-in-law, "I have not words to describe the great light that has dawned upon my life. All that I had hoped for, for years, has been fully realized." By the New Year, the couple studied Latin together, with Reid admitting that his wife made better progress than he had done. With marriage, Reid found the missing piece to his happiness.[29]

Reid's single life had left him sleeping at times in his office, or staying in boarding houses, or residing with his brother. Now he and Bettie had to find a permanent home. Wealthy through her widowhood, the new Mrs. Reid aided in that search as well. According to her first husband's will, should Bettie remarry, she would relinquish her part—over half—of an estate valued at over $70,000, and receive outright $10,000 instead. The remainder would go back to be further divided among his children. She thus gave up much for her love. From his income and hers, in March 1877, Dick bought 6 acres, and then a few months later his wife, in her name, purchased a more expensive 6¾ acres more. (Kentucky law at that time decreed that any property a woman brought into a marriage legally went to her husband. Wives could make no will without their spouse's consent, could not keep any wages they earned, and could not even be legal guardians to their children. Nevertheless, Dick treated Bettie as a coequal legally. When money came in from the sale of some other land, for example, the deed went to Reid "and his wife," not the husband alone.) On their new land, the Reids built one of the fine houses of the city. Located at the edge of town, the two-story frame building sat on the top of a small knoll and overlooked picturesque farmland and the growing city. The place featured two large bay windows, a library, and a porch across the front—where the family spent summer evenings talking—as well as a sizable second-floor ballroom for entertaining.[30]

The Reids needed a large home, for they had an expanding household. However, it did not grow larger due to any children they had. A historian of sexuality in the nineteenth century has concluded that "the marriage night was an institutionalized trauma for the pure of both sexes." Bettie Reid, of course, had been married before, so it would be less so for her. But all the available evidence suggests that her husband had never had sexual relations before marriage. If such was the case, his later joyful letters suggest that Bettie had initiated him with minimal trauma. Still, at a time when Victorian America considered fatherhood the epitome of manhood, and when Kentuckians held, on the average, the largest families in the nation, the Reids remained childless. Most scientific thought of the time stressed not male infertility, but rather the "barren wife" as the source of that situation. In general circles, people blamed childlessness on the woman and did not see that as a reflection on the male. However, Bettie Reid had already had a child, so she obviously had not been barren. That issue remained something of a cloud over the marriage.[31]

Richard Reid turned instead to raising Bettie's son, his namesake Reid Rogers, as his own. Seven years old at the time of his mother's remarriage, the young boy, in turn, responded to Dick Reid's love and considered him, in essence, his real father. When his mother said, "Son tell your Uncle

Dick . . . ," he interrupted her saying, "He is my papa, now, and I intend to love him and call him papa." The two had deep affection for each other, so much so that Dick Reid could not bear to discipline his son and often left the house to avoid hearing any cries of hurt from him. His family doted on him, buying the boy the first bicycle in town, taking him on long vacations, tutoring him at home. Reid Rogers, in turn, became a well-liked member of the community and traveled frequently to Lexington by train, where the handsome young man became part of a particularly talented group of young people: later Nobel Prize recipient Thomas Hunt Morgan; future best-selling novelist John Fox Jr.; and two Breckinridges—Desha, later editor of the *Lexington Herald,* and Sophonisba, later a national leader in the field of social work. When Reid Rogers left the family household to attend Princeton, it hit husband and wife hard.[32]

But the Reids had been surrounded by more children than just Reid Rogers. A year after they married, Sarah "Sallie" Jameson, Mrs. Reid's niece and the namesake of Dick Reid's dead fiancée, came to live in their household and would be referred to as their "adopted daughter." Her very name daily reminded Richard Reid of his loss, but she received his love as well. She, like Reid Rogers, started her education at home, then, like him, attended the school of the Reverend Mr. Potter—as had Dick Reid years before. Described by a local paper as "one of the brightest and best girls that ever came to Mt. Sterling," Sallie went to college in Missouri, but poor health eventually caused her to seek the warmth of southern California.[33]

Then two orphans asked if the Reids would provide them a home and education. They agreed, and Lily and May Horton came in as full members of the family as well. The 1880 census listed the household as containing husband and wife, plus stepson Reid Rogers, fourteen, niece Sallie Jameson, seventeen, "Lillie" Horton, nineteen, May Horton, seventeen—each described as "boarders"—John Jameson, a thirteen-year-old nephew then there, and two black servants, mother Rebecca Rawls and son Jacob. At other times, for briefer intervals, Reid's mother-in-law and three or four other relatives lived in the Reid house.[34]

But to Richard Reid, the most significant person in his family remained his wife. He needed her respect. He needed her adulation. He needed her love. While a large part of the childrearing fell to her simply because of his long absences riding the circuit as a lawyer, and while contemporaries gave her high praise in that society by stressing that she ran a "well-ordered house," Reid depended on her not for those household issues but because she was vital to his own emotional health and well-being. Now that he had happiness and love, he did not want to be away from it, unless necessary. Reid filled his letters to "Dear Blessed Darling" or "Dear Darl" with descriptions of how "dreadfully and hopelessly lonesome" he was without her. When Bettie returned to Missouri to visit relatives, when she went back to the place where his Sallie had died, Reid reverted to his past physical problems, as he told her: "I fell into a troubled slumber, and was seized, I don't know by how many adult, robust, double-decked nightmares; and had . . . perturbed and terrible dreams, in which many of the old phantoms of my childhood came back, grown larger by age." When awake, he prowled the rooms of his house, "listening for your voice and looking for your face." Bettie Reid would have been unusual in those circumstances had she not felt guilty in being gone, particularly when he cried out, "For love's sake, don't stay away long." With her return, calm came back to the Reid home.[35]

Another important stabilizing influence on his life continued to be his religion. As in antebellum times, most churches had many more female members than male ones; to some, the sentiment remained that it was somehow unmanly for men to participate. Yet to others, the new age stressed that duty and service required a gentleman to be part of that religious effort. In Reid's case, he represented the new emphasis, though his devotion came less from duty than from conviction. As an elder in the Christian Church, he also taught Sunday school and usually attended Wednesday night prayer meetings. One who heard him offer thanks in one of those gatherings long remembered how tender and elevating had been his words: "He seemed to be talking face to face with God." Reid also aided his wife in organizing a Kentucky Christian Woman's Missionary Society, and Bettie Reid became a state president. She later became president of the Kentucky chapter of the Christian Women's Board of Missions. But more than a helper to his wife, a churchgoer, a teacher, and an organizer, Dick Reid *lived* his religion. He followed its principles; he set an example for others. Even when he did not understand why suffering went on, he emphasized that humans saw only through that glass darkly: "In a little while we shall see face to face."[36]

Just as some members of his generation considered it unmanly to attend church, they—and others—also worried that the entire culture around them might be too "effeminate." Henry James had one of his characters voice that attitude: "The whole generation is womanized; the masculine tone is passing out of the world." To counter that, men increasingly turned to the all-male fraternal organizations to preserve and strengthen manhood. The late nineteenth century would be termed the "Golden Age of Fraternity," and more than one in four American men belonged to such groups. At a time of great, ongoing change in society, clubs stressed rituals and rules, provided a form of family free of females, and, as a student of them concluded, offered "solace and psychological guidance," fraternity and friendship. For Reid, he valued and needed his domesticity and home life very much, but the clubs allowed him to meet another need and become more of a part of the male world that had often only included him on its fringe. The non-physical aspects of the groups meant he could join in and be "one of the boys." Reid associated with the popular International Order of Odd Fellows, which had originally been established in Great Britain and had made its way to Mount Sterling with a lodge there in 1830. Dick Reid became a frequent participant in its activites.[37]

Yet in taking three stands that he did, in that same time, he negated some of that sense of male togetherness. For instance, even though his church did not represent one closely tied to the Social Gospel movement, Reid himself strongly supported solving social issues through concerted religious action. Churches for years had tried to restrict drinking, one of the cornerstones of male culture. Now individuals sought that same restriction through formal legislation. Reid supported temperance laws and in 1877 gave a public address extolling that course of action. "A total abstainer," he criticized the inebriate, "besotted with the fumes of intemperance, and besmeared with the filth of the gutter." Such men squandered their inheritance and destroyed their families, he declared. Pointing out that too many of Kentucky's great leaders had dissipated their energies and had yielded to "the Delilah of drunkenness," Reid demanded that no one compromise with that great evil. When the issue of local option came up for a vote in Mount Sterling, it went down to defeat.[38]

Even more controversial was a second issue. Because electoral politics remained a male-only subculture, a proving place for manhood, women's demand for suffrage struck at another part of that masculine world. Opposition came quickly—and often. In 1874, for example, a Lexington paper stressed that "married women, that is, real women, prefer to be ruled than ruling," as it spoke out against such equal rights. Four years later a former Kentucky governor and U.S. senator emphasized his opposition, saying that he never believed "that God intended women . . . to be ought but ministering angels in the great loveliness of our homes." Two years after that, a state senator, concerned over the words of "strong-minded women," firmly declared, "Give me a wife that can love, honor, and look up to me as her lord and shield, or give me separation and death."[39]

In contrast, Richard Reid advocated more rights for women, equal treatment, and greater fairness. At an 1883 meeting, Bettie Reid had been asked to address a church audience about organizing a Christian Women's Board of Missions' auxiliary. A debate ensued over whether she, as a woman, should speak from the pulpit. In answer to that, her husband walked her to the pulpit, handed her talk to her, and returned to listen. Angry men, and some women, disapproved of the actions of both. Reid would continue to travel with her across the state, helping organize other chapters. In fact, Dick and Bettie worked very much as a team, for he respected her judgment. That attitude influenced him as he gave his thoughts to students of a female academy in Mount Sterling. Reid told the class that change is constant and old customs must be modified: "And in all the old that is passing out, and the new that is coming in, is the old, old life of woman, and the new emancipation that is awaiting her. It is useless to cry out against this any longer." He concluded by predicting equality—in wages, privileges, property, and education—and a glorious future for women. Yet his vision matched that of few other men in his hometown, home state, or generation.[40]

But perhaps his strongest statements came through his actions on the issue of race. When African Americans in Mount Sterling dedicated a new Christian Church, Reid was the only white person present. Impressed by the proceedings, he, as an elder in his own church, invited one of the ministers to come there and "preach for the white people." Some time after that, an influential member of the black congregation came to Reid privately and explained that the building contractors for that new facility demanded immediate payment of $1,000, which the church did not have on hand. Reid quickly wrote a promissory note for that amount, got nine others to cosign it, secured a bank loan as a result, and paid off the contractors. But the most public action came on a Sunday in 1875. That same black minister had gone to Reid's church to hear a special sermon and had quietly found a seat in the rear, near the door. As the building filled, ushers asked the man to move into the gallery: "Just at that minute Judge Reid came in and invited me to his pew to sit with him." That African American minister called Richard Reid "my greatest friend, among men, on earth."[41]

Reid never publicly advocated racial equality in his speeches or strongly endorsed full women's rights in public forums. Perhaps his search for approval kept him from taking that final, radical step. Even at that, however, his stance on those issues, and on temperance, separated him even more from the male world of his fraternity and even his society. But Reid's actions showed that on controversial issues, he would take the stand he believed church and conscience dictated.

Despite involvement in those issues of such considerable debate, the Reids devoted much of their time to less polemical and more pleasurable pursuits. They hosted parties at home, earning praise for Bettie for "entertaining as only Mrs. Reid knows how to serve." After one particular tea party, a reporter stressed the hospitality "cultivated people" such as the Reids provided. Nor did they just stay at home. At a friend's costume party based on Dickens characters, Richard Reid went as Pickwick, his wife as Mrs. Bardell. Going outside the town, they vacationed and partied as well. At White Sulphur Springs resort in West Virginia in 1882, Reid loved the beautiful grounds, but found the food disappointing, the dances long, the dinners interminable, and the conversations dull. Kentucky, he opined, had more attractive women as well. A week later, at Old Point Comfort, Virginia, the Reids sampled the attractions of Chesapeake Bay, and a relaxed Dick told May Horton, "You would laugh to see me running over the beach with breeches not quite up to my knees, and floundering about in the water."[42]

Back in Kentucky, both husband and wife enjoyed the use of their library at home. Boasting one of the best private collections in the state, the Reids could there peruse *Atlantic, Harper's, Scribner's, The Century,* and other journals to which they regularly subscribed. There, too, Reid read British authors, such as Macaulay, Milton, Thackeray, Scott, and Dickens, and American ones, such as Irving, Twain, Motley, Howells, "and some of our female writers." That library also served as his resource when he prepared an address for the 4 July 1876 centennial celebration. Published a few years later as an almost-seventy-page book entitled *Historical Sketches of Montgomery County,* that talk showed good research into early history and solid descriptions of the soil, roads, and other features of the county. A last section included biographical sketches of early leaders (and had presumably not been read aloud). A proud wife sent a copy to the State Historical Society, noting that she hoped one day the county would be less "poverty stricken" and could produce a full account of its past. But Reid's work, like his reading, showed his range of interests and his many talents.[43]

Still, none of these pursuits seemed to give Reid the enjoyment he received from simply being at home with his wife. At that time, marriage represented one of the marks of manhood and often produced a relationship in which the patriarch dominated the union. But by the time the Reids married, a more companionate matrimony had emerged. That ideal stressed mutual interdependence, not male dominance, and emphasized a more romantic relationship where the two partners respected the individuality of each other. That did not mean that Victorian society expected gender lines to dissolve, for that world still had not shaken free of the ideas of separate spheres—the domestic for the woman, the public for the man. Yet those lines increasingly blurred and grew more fluid. One study of that change noted that the era's model became more the concept of the "ideal self," a part of a person revealed through marriage. In the Reids' case, theirs certainly represented the marriage more of equals, of companions who eventually depended on each other, of people who revealed parts of their hidden self only to their spouse.[44]

But in Dick Reid's situation, his nuptials may have meant even more. In Bettie, he could psychologically see the mother figure, like the one who had died when he was three, or the romantic one, like the person he had lost long ago, or the nurturer, who kept the nightmares away, or the lover, like no one he had been with before. In the end, each person in the marriage put the other on a pedestal. Bettie Reid, who knew her husband better than anyone, protected him, in a sense, from the harshness of the world outside the home, and reveled in his public success and private love. But given his life history, Richard Reid needed his wife much more than she needed him. Her support ironically gave him the confidence and the comfort necessary for him to move more into the public arena, a place where threats to that happiness awaited.

For the moment the happy couple led people to extol their "Eden-like home" and their "almost perfect married life."[45]

Chapter 3

A Superior Judge

Secure and happy in his home life, Richard Reid continued to prosper in his professional career as well. But the death of partner Apperson in 1878 meant change, and soon a new, junior attorney joined the firm. Henry Lane Stone had been born in neighboring Bath County, to a distinguished family. His father, a cousin of Confederate general John Bell Hood, had been a state legislator and militia general; Stone's mother was a sister of a later Republican governor and U.S. senator from Indiana. The family moved to the Hoosier State, and when the Civil War came, three sons joined the Union army. Henry Stone, however, rode with Confederate general John Hunt Morgan. Captured, he had escaped from a northern prison, contacted another brother—a Chicago physician—and had walked openly around that city before brazenly buying a train ticket back to Kentucky. Soon recaptured there, Stone had again broken free and ended the war escorting Jefferson Davis in his failed escape attempt. Stone returned to his native region, was elected Bath County attorney, served a term in the Kentucky House, and formed a partnership with former circuit judge Newton P. Reid, Dick Reid's uncle. Now, in 1878, the thirty-six-year-old Stone came to Mount Sterling to be in the new firm of Reid and Stone. It proved a powerful combination, bringing together the studious and philosophical Dick Reid and the more aggressive and practical Stone. Each supported the Democratic Party; each worked very hard; each eschewed liquor; each had ambition. And each expressed frustration with Kentucky's legal system.[1]

They were not alone. The system of laws in the state obviously sought to protect the innocent and punish the guilty. Yet, to many citizens, that happened all too infrequently. The grand juries that first started the process of bringing a person to trial, by considering indictments, did so imperfectly. One state attorney general called for a new group of such jurors in one case, saying the current grand jury consisted of "the criminals, their close kin, and their steadfast friends and admirers." But generally that part of the process did work. However, once indicted and arrested, some defendants could not meet the requirements for bail and might spend six months or more in jail before having their day in court. With wealthy defendants not subjected to that, justice seemed to favor the well funded. When trials did begin, courts drew juries from a pool of white male citizens, but if that original list was exhausted—as frequently happened—then sheriffs usually selected the next group from bystanders. In some cases, "professional jurors" stayed near the courthouse, hoping to be chosen, for they sought the $1.50 per day pay in a cash-poor society. In such situations, defendants with sufficient finances could often "hire" one juror, in order to ensure at least a deadlocked outcome.[2]

The defense had several advantages under that system which made it harder to secure convictions. First, if attorneys did not like the judge before them, it only required two supposedly disinterested "reputable persons" to swear the judge was not impartial, and he had to step down. An appointed, perhaps friendlier, special judge would be substituted. Then when time came for the selection of jurors, the prosecutor had only five peremptory challenges, the defense twenty. Juries more favorable to the defense resulted. Even the prosecutorial system had flaws. Elected by the people, prosecutors could be out of a job if their actions angered powerful voters in the community. In other cases, the existence of groups that were virtual private armies meant that criminal elements could threaten a prosecutor or his family—and often did. As a result, some attorneys for the state simply quit challenging those groups. Then, if a prosecutor did take the case to trial, he often found himself outclassed by the defense. The individual commonwealth's attorney, usually overworked, underfunded, and inexperienced, might face a well-financed, veteran defense team of specialized talents.[3]

If found guilty, the defendant appropriately could appeal the verdict from the circuit court to the state's highest tribunal, the Court of Appeals, with its four elected justices. In 1881, the *Kentucky Law Journal* concluded that the court had too many cases on its docket to do good work, while the next year a Kentuckian who would soon become president of the American Bar Association told a friend that the Court of Appeals had lost the confidence of the people: "The judges are . . . not learned or experienced enough for the high discharge of the duties." That may not have been a fair evaluation, but it remained a common one.[4]

After all that, if the appeal failed and a convicted criminal remained incarcerated, a last option existed, and that one elicited much controversy. Kentucky had no parole board before 1888, so the final decision on whether a felon should go to prison or remain there for the full sentence lay with the governor, who had—and used—the power to pardon. No formal process existed, so family, friends, and defense attorneys peppered governors with petitions calling for mercy. Often the prosecutor's account was not even heard. Numerous pardons resulted, with one governor signing at least 845 in his first eighteen months in office. The *New York Times* blamed the "reckless exercise of the pardoning power by the Governor" for much of the attitude toward crime in Kentucky. With overcrowded prisons and no parole, pardons could be a force for good, but at the same time could be—and were—given for political motives.[5]

For people living in communities like Mount Sterling, or in more isolated, crime-infested areas, being a juror and making an impartial decision became difficult. If a citizen had voted guilty, but then the jury did not convict—perhaps because of tampering—then the freed defendant or his friends might take revenge. Since no state police force existed, and since sheriffs operated more as tax collectors than law enforcers, little public protection existed. And should a guilty verdict result, friends and political allies of the governor more easily received the abundant pardons. Such pardons made retribution, once again, more likely. Fearful jurors became timid ones. The *Louisville Commercial* termed the whole jury system "rotten and corrupt," while a Frankfort paper said juries handled horse-thieves harder than murderers. All that did not mean that the system never worked, for it often did, and worked well. Good judges, careful attorneys, and impartial jurors did serve, and justice did result, in many cases. But the inequalities and problems in the system caused many in the commonwealth, and others outside the state, to have little respect for Kentucky justice.[6]

Despite such problems in the legal apparatus, Richard Reid successfully navigated those judicial waters. But other public interests also increasingly called to him. Seemingly every attorney in Kentucky entertained political hopes, and Reid now proved no exception. Victory would bring many rewards and much satisfaction. But the Siren-like state political scene could also lure the ambitious and the unready, and wreck their hopes on the rocks of stark reality, just as easily as the legal world could. Success did not automatically come to the most talented.

Initially, the way to political triumph appeared clear and simple: join the dominant Democratic Party. That pathway, however, concealed as much as it revealed, for recent history and changing conditions made the situation much more fluid and complex. First of all, Kentucky remained an important state in the region and nationally, and a large corps of candidates sought to represent it. In the first third of the states in population, the commonwealth in 1870 also ranked first in the South in manufacturing and in the value of its farms. This prosperity relative to the rest of the South provided an opportunity for Kentucky drummers, whose wares supplied the once-Rebel states and tied Kentucky even more to those who had worn the gray. Moreover, the commonwealth as an officially loyal state, by virtue of not going through a formal Reconstruction, could become the "unconquered" voice of the region. The newly established *Louisville Courier-Journal* under Henry Watterson spoke for the South nationally and for a time enjoyed the largest circulation there.[7]

But more than that, the commonwealth now philosophically identified with the South. The excesses of what was virtually a Union army of occupation during the war—with scandals, political repression, and executions—angered many; the racial issue solidified the shift from supporting the Union at war's start to opposing it by conflict's end. As one historian noted, Kentucky "waited until after the war was over to secede from the Union." The commonwealth's violence against the newly freed ex-slaves equaled that anywhere in the region and caused the Freedman's Bureau to operate in Kentucky, as it did in former Confederate states. And that issue and the state's increasing identification with the South brought the Democrats, a minority party in the commonwealth for most of its existence, to become dominant, as in the rest of the South. In fact, historian C. Vann Woodward concluded of Kentucky that "no state below the Ohio River presented a more solidly Confederate-Democratic front in the decade after Appomattox."[8]

It is no wonder, then, that for three decades after the Civil War, the Democratic Party won every governor's race, took all congressional seats save one, as a rule, usually held over two-thirds of the legislative seats, and controlled most county governments, except in mountain counties and in some urban areas with sizable black populations (since African Americans voted

Republican almost entirely). The pockets of dissent—supported largely by blacks' early and continued exercise of the vote—meant that the minority Republicans did have enough presence electorally that Democratic defections or weaknesses could yield an occasional victory for what was still termed the Radical Republicans, or the party of "nigger equality" (as a candidate for circuit judge said in 1868). Yet if the party of Lincoln could not be completely ignored, it generally did not have to be feared either. Democrats ruled.[9]

Successful Democratic politicians of Reid's era followed either one or all of several paths to victory. First and foremost were racial arguments. When Reid's old mentor, Judge Alvin Duvall, ran for clerk of the Court of Appeals in 1866, the race became a testing ground, and bitter disputes resulted, with some twenty election-day deaths. Duvall's almost two-to-one margin, and the arguments used to achieve it, caused a newspaper in the state capital to conclude that ex-Unionists had been overwhelmed, "the great engine used against them, having been, as usual, the negro." Three years later, the *Lexington Observer and Reporter* frankly admitted, "We want a white man's state, and we intend to have it." In 1871, a delegate to the Democratic state convention explained what he saw as the difference between the two parties: "If he was a nigger, he would be a Radical, and, as he was a white man, he was a Democrat." If all other political appeals failed, candidates could always fall back on racial demagoguery and usually win. But Reid would not do that.[10]

A second road to winning meant emphasizing Confederate service or wartime sympathy. Even though twice as many Kentuckians had fought for the North as the South, and even though the Union had won the war, in Kentucky after 1865 the changing sentiments in favor of the South meant that the vanquished ruled the victors. Ex-Confederates quickly gained most of the leadership posts in the reborn Democratic Party. A visitor to one convention wrote that it seemed as if "all the Confederate troops in Kentucky" had assembled there, while another onlooker at a legislative meeting termed it "scarcely more than the meeting of a Confederate regiment." When the Democrats in 1867 won all nine congressional seats and 121 of 138 legislative contests, a Republican paper exclaimed that what the Confederates had failed to do on the battlefield—win the state—they had done on the political field of war. The *Frankfort Commonwealth* concluded: "The 'Lost Cause' is found again in Kentucky." As a result, candidates seeking victory usually needed that Confederate tie. The next six governors all qualified. As one diarist noted, he had voted at the polls for five Democrats, "most all old Confederate soldiers." That same tendency extended to the elective judiciary. Democratic candidates tied to the old Confederacy ran in all seven Court of Appeals races between 1874 and 1882 and won all seven. One nineteenth-century observer concluded that "worthy and capable ex-Confederate soldiers (especially if maimed)" would "invariably" be elected. Operating almost as a lodge or fraternity or union, the voting bloc of those who had supported the South dominated the Democratic Party. While Reid had indeed sympathized with the Confederate cause, he had done so only quietly. If he entered politics, he would not necessarily lose the Rebel vote, but it would not automatically go to him either, particularly if a foe demonstrated better Confederate credentials.[11]

A third possible factor in political success, though a lesser force as the stage grew larger, was the role that family played. As a son of one of the Confederate governors of Kentucky explained, "The Kentucky people are great sticklers for kinship, and if they can trace any relation, it immediately forms a strong bond of interest and sympathy between them." That bond extended to voting for them and ensuring that the extended family did so as well. Particularly in small communities, that could be crucial, for the family provided a network of ready allies. A minister stated of Kentucky: "As nowhere else on this soil, they hold family connection as almost divine heritage." In that area, at least locally, Dick Reid could compete with others. He did not have the Clay or Breckinridge name that gave statewide advantages, but the Reids had a large connection and many family ties in Montgomery and surrounding counties.[12]

Yet another approach to electoral success—and the one Reid tried to follow most of all—focused on speaking about the issues. An ex-Confederate, with family connections and with no hesitancy to use racial appeals, might seldom need to say much about matters of controversy. If discussions occurred, office-seekers usually dealt with the matters of states' rights or broad concerns. Candidates could win without delving into dangerous, issue-oriented discussions. But over and over, the same questions arose, calling for answers, and often they could be used to gain public attention. Almost every major political figure of the last third of the nineteenth century in Kentucky called for an end to violence, advocated low taxes, emphasized the need for better education, supported prison and convict labor reform, and extolled the virtues of agriculture. Stressing one or the other of those, a candidate might, in the right atmosphere, gain additional support. The plight of farmers and the formation of such agrarian-oriented organizations as the Grange, for example, meant that those running for office had to speak to those concerns or risk losing their vote. Reid sought a discussion of issues, for he held strength there as in perhaps none of the other roads to victory—or so it appeared.[13]

The final factor in any election in Kentucky focused on factional divisions in the controlling Democratic Party. Though the Democracy ruled, it did so very carefully, for the party rested on a fragile coalition of varied interests. First of all, the Democrats really combined two parties. Before the war, the Whigs of Henry Clay had dominated state politics. With that party's death in the 1850s, its former members had wandered in the political wilderness for a decade, never really supporting the Democrats, but finding no real home elsewhere. But with the war's end and Kentucky's general turn southward in sympathy, about half of the former Whigs went to the Democratic Party. The rest, together with black voters and some mountain whites, formed the Republicans. But the ex-Whig presence ran strong in the Democrats, and several leaders came out of that more centrally oriented background. At the same time, the ruling party had to deal with extreme sectionalism in Kentucky, which could tear it apart as well. The earlier dominant central Bluegrass and the newer regions of the west, the urban forces of Louisville and northern Kentucky and the small agrarian ones across the state, the old hemp farms and the new burley tobacco ones—all vied for control. Additionally, powerful lobbies, such as the Louisville and Nashville (L&N) Railroad, tried to influence actions, while railroad-poor regions competed against that strong force. And finally, two different philosophies governed the party, at least for a time after the war. The so-called Bourbon faction resisted any black rights—in voting, courts, or wherever—and looked back more wistfully to the prewar days of agrarian Kentucky. Strongly supporting states' rights, low taxes, and limited government, those leaders found many allies. The second faction, called New Departure Democrats, spoke for a New South, one based on acceptance of change in the status of blacks, on increased industrialization, and on a more Whig-like concept of government's role in the economy. Over the years, each faction won its victories, but each viewpoint continued to be an important force in the party. Reid's Democrats, then, represented an unstable—and its enemies said, an unholy—alliance of ex-Whigs and longtime Democrats, of people from different sections with different beliefs and desires, of business and agrarian forces, of New Departure and Bourbon factions.[14]

Those same kinds of divisions existed in Mount Sterling and Montgomery County. Before the Civil War, that area had generally supported the Whigs, often by margins exceeding 60 percent. But as with Kentucky generally, Democrats dominated after the war, capturing 86 percent of the vote in the 1868 presidential race, before blacks could vote. The Republican ballots of African Americans, after 1870, made the political competition closer, but that was all. Similarly, urban versus agrarian interests, New Departure versus Bourbon ones, and other party divisions operated as well. Still, political success had to start at the local level, and there Richard Reid finally entered the quicksand of Kentucky politics.[15]

In 1869, friends had persuaded Reid to seek the nomination for state senator, and he campaigned for a month. But he yielded to "the irresistible and omnipotent influence of the Confederate army" and dropped out of the race. A similar effort later for Congress ended with the same results. After those attempts, Reid seemed satisfied to stay away from politics and public life. But at the same time, his wife, who owing to her sex could not win political office and whose many talents could find outlet in only limited public ways, had ambition for him. That, coupled with his own quieter but still strong aspirations, meant that the right office at the right moment could draw Richard Reid once more into the political arena.[16]

That opportunity came through tragedy. On 26 March 1879, John Milton Elliott, a justice on the state's highest court, was walking toward the Capital Hotel in Frankfort. Thomas Buford approached him, they spoke briefly, and, as the judge turned away, Buford cried out, "Die like a man!" and fired a gunshot blast into Elliott's back. Elliott died almost instantly. Buford claimed he had acted because the judge had written the unanimous Court of Appeals decision upholding a lower court's ruling that had caused Buford's sister to lose her Henry County farm. Honor required him to respond to that affront, said the murderer, and the shooting victim "was the most ignominious game that my gun ever killed." A man of fiery temper, Buford had earlier fought a duel over a woman, had blinded an attorney in an argument over a civil suit, and had once stopped a train at gunpoint to demand reimbursement for a supposed wrong done him by the railroad. From a prominent family, Buford had never been prosecuted for any of those actions. In 1881, after two trials, with capable attorneys arrayed on both sides, a jury acquitted Buford, on grounds of insanity. (A Kentucky paper concluded of that decision: "The time seems to have come for every man to rely upon his own steady arm. Law in Kentucky is a miserable mockery.") Officials then committed Buford to the Central Kentucky Lunatic Asylum, near Louisville. Within a few months, he escaped across the Ohio River into Indiana and remained there for several years.[17]

Reid had been on a train, going to the state capital for business before the Appellate Court, when he heard the news of the assassination. He and Elliott had been good friends, and he would serve as one of the pallbearers at the funeral. It was a personal loss, one that Reid apparently felt deeply. But almost immediately, people began urging Reid to run for the vacant seat. Reid asked Bettie's advice. She told him to do what he wished, but if he entered, he should "strive to win." He decided to run.[18]

It would not be an easy canvass. The Democratic convention to select the party's nominee lay only a month away, which meant a candidate had to travel a great deal in that time to talk with voters and delegates in the thirty-nine counties that then composed the large judicial district. Moreover, Reid faced strong opposition for the nomination, chiefly in the person of Thomas Frazier Hargis. Born four years after Reid, in Breathitt County, Hargis and his family had moved from there to Rowan County, where his father served as county attorney. During the Civil War, Hargis had been a Confederate officer, had been wounded on at least three occasions, had been captured, and had escaped several times as well. He represented the hero for the Lost Cause. With the end of the conflict, he moved to Nicholas County, became an attorney, and then won election as county judge at age twenty-seven. Two years later, voters selected Hargis as state senator, then, later, as circuit judge. But his best qualification for the now-vacant court seat may have been the fact that he and the martyred Elliott had once been law partners.[19]

Reid brought his own strengths to the race and worked very hard to gain the victory. In one ten-day period, for instance, he traveled over six hundred miles in the mountains, seeking votes. That bore electoral fruit, for when the convention opened in Owingsville on 24 April 1879, Reid had good support and even greater good will. Eleven men received votes on the first ballot, with Hargis leading with 57½, and Reid in third place with 43. By the twenty-fifth ballot, Dick Reid stood second, as more and more candidates had dropped out. After midnight and forty ballots, the convention, still deadlocked, adjourned. Described as "one of the most turbulent, hotly-contested conventions of a state not unfamiliar with harrowing contests," the meeting went a second day without a decision, though much "log-rolling" and deal making did occur. Finally, on the third day, delegates selected Hargis—barely. Out of over 300 votes, Reid had lost by only 13. He immediately gave the victor his support in a strong speech that won him more friends. A nearby paper praised both candidates and proclaimed the winner a good choice, "not withstanding rumors detrimental to his character."[20]

Such rumors soon involved the firm of Reid and Stone as well. The origin of the stories went back to 1874, when Hargis had won the Democratic nomination for circuit judge. A political supporter of one of the defeated candidates soon questioned the victor's qualifications, saying that he had not been an attorney the requisite eight years. Thomas Green, the bitter editor of the *Maysville Eagle,* soon followed that claim with the charge that Hargis had mutilated and altered the judicial records to conceal the date of his admittance to the bar. Following the printing of that story, a Republican, buoyed by the Democratic infighting, took the circuit judgeship. Four years later, Hargis won the seat, but now, in 1879, the old charges resurfaced once more through the pages of the *Eagle.* Despite that, Hargis carried the appellate post over Republican William H. Holt of Mount Sterling. An angry editor Green then brought suit against Hargis for libel, since the new judge had called Green a liar. One of the lead attorneys for Hargis in the ensuing and controversial three-day trial was Reid's partner, Henry Stone. After Stone delivered a lengthy concluding defense statement—printed and distributed across Kentucky—the jury quickly found Hargis not guilty of the libel charges. The new judge had already admired fellow Christian Church–member Reid's actions at the convention, and he praised Stone's current conduct of the defense. The firm now had a powerful friend in Judge Hargis.[21]

Such support became important in 1882, for Richard Reid once again sought to become a judge, although this time at a different level. By 1880, the state's highest court had fallen a year behind in hearing and deciding cases, and to try to remedy that, the legislature had created a new court, called the Superior Court. It received limited appellate jurisdiction and would hear cases involving $3,000 or less. The three popularly elected judges—paid $3,600 annually—would take about half of the Court of Appeals cases. Reid ran for one of those new seats. In supporting him, his hometown paper noted that his father had been one of the "most thrifty and influential farmers" in the county, praised his overall family ties, and termed him "the most scholarly lawyer of Eastern Kentucky." Others, already impressed by his earlier race against Hargis, agreed, and by the time the nominating convention grew near, Reid had enough delegates to win. Another paper concluded: "He is well-qualified by natural ability . . . to make a

No. 1 jurist." In June 1882, at a meeting at the Lexington Opera House, Reid won by acclamation the nomination for the eastern district of the Superior Court, covering forty-five counties. Republicans respected Reid's chances so much that they declined to run a candidate in opposition. While one paper grumbled that two of the three winning candidates for the new court had been Hargis's attorneys and that he was "bossing the Kentucky Democracy," that proved the exception. Reid won, with little ill will and no opposition. He was now a Superior Court judge.[22]

The post proved difficult and challenging. The first year the jurists decided 445 cases, heard other petitions, and established the procedural rules for a new court. During that time, Judge Reid gained a reputation for writing clear, soundly analyzed opinions. Lawyers lauded his work, and he and the other two judges received much praise. All of that caused him to consider another try for the Court of Appeals seat, for Thomas Hargis had announced that he did not intend to run for a second term. Stung by the criticism he had received, Hargis instead gave his support to Reid for the 1884 race.[23]

With a longer time to campaign than previously, Reid started early, going all over the wide-flung district. He heard cases and wrote decisions during the week, then traveled by train to distant areas on the weekend. When larger breaks occurred, he went by carriage or horseback to those places untouched by railroads or without adequate roads. All that—as well as the absences from his wife—took their toll on Reid. In October 1883, he told Bettie how he had not slept during the previous night and how nervous and depressed he was as a result. In December, he had "one of my spells" and stayed in bed all day, eating nothing. Yet overall, the canvass gave him hope amid the physical exertions. In Laurel County, for example, he discovered "every powerful family interest and connection in the county" united against him but felt confident that he still would not be defeated there, for he found few supported his two opponents for the nomination—Boyd County's Laban T. Moore, a former Whig, Know-Nothing congressman, and Union colonel who sought support from those groups, and Robert Riddell, an Estill County circuit judge. They each represented, respectfully, the northern and mountain parts of the district, but Reid's reach covered the more populous central region. Respected as a judge and a person, backed by powerful political allies, Reid had excellent prospects for victory. Yet lurking out there were potential dangers for any candidate, and those were issues dealing with Kentucky justice, southern honor, and American manhood.[24]

Chapter 4

A Christian Gentleman

To many, the term "Kentucky justice" seemed an oxymoron. Or it at least suggested that justice in the state came chiefly through individual retribution rather than through legal means. Violence begat violence, and each generation's offspring added to the image of a violent and lawless Kentucky. Reid sought to be on the high court, in part, to change that perception and bring better order, truer justice, and greater respect for the law to the commonwealth where he had lived all his life. But as a student of history, and as an observer of current affairs, he likely knew that the effort would not succeed quickly or easily. The state had fully earned its violent reputation.

Almost from its first recorded history, Kentucky had been associated with killing. When Daniel Boone and others trudged across the mountains to this "new found paradise," they encountered various Indian tribes hunting the land. Conflicts broke out immediately in the "dark and bloody ground." Spectacular acts of cruelty came from both camps; so did extreme acts of courage and heroism. For some of the early colonial explorers, a seeming indifference to death resulted. They slept amidst danger, without guards, and often ventured alone into territory where large numbers of the enemy awaited.

At the same time, the frontier society stressed courage and manhood, even on occasion to its detriment. In 1782, a hastily gathered force of settlers outside Lexington had followed some retreating Native Americans and caught them at Blue Licks. Hugh McGary had lost a stepson to the Indians earlier, and once when he saw a tribal member wearing that son's shirt, McGary had killed him, hacked up the corpse, and then threw the body parts to his dogs. Now, as Boone and others warned of an ambush and cautioned patience, McGary cried out, "All who are not damned cowards, follow me!" and charged after them. The army followed and was virtually massacred. Even though reason had dictated otherwise, the fear of being branded a coward drove men on the frontier to risk death rather than to be so labeled.[1]

Though he lost a son at the Blue Licks defeat, Boone survived, and two years later, his supposed "autobiography" appeared. From it, all sorts of pirated versions would appear, making Boone the embodiment in American mythology of the heroic frontiersman, fighting the Indians with his Kentucky rifle, clearing a path for the "civilized world." That identification of Kentucky with such conflict continued in the War of 1812, where an estimate suggests that over 60 percent of those Americans killed came from Kentucky. At the Battle of the Thames in 1813, a group of twenty state volunteers, called the "Forlorn Hope," charged hundreds of hidden Indians, in an almost suicidal effort to draw their fire, so the main army could locate the Native American force and attack before they could reload. Of the twenty, fifteen died immediately and four others were wounded; only one escaped without being hit. Richard M. Johnson, one of the "Forlorn Hope," though wounded, continued to fight, and later supposedly killed Tecumseh. He would receive numerous political victories owing to his part in the violence.[2]

Indeed, Reid had read how the commonwealth seemed to reward politicians who killed, or sought to kill, particularly if they fought in duels. In 1809, Humphrey Marshall, a former U.S. senator from Kentucky and brother-in-law to the chief justice of the United States, angered young Henry Clay, and the two soon faced each other at ten paces. After the third round of shots, Clay was wounded. Seventeen years later, he fought John Randolph in Virginia in another affair of honor. One historian wrote that Clay had "demonstrated a calm bravery under fire which in no wise detracted from his public popularity." Yet the example he gave showed that the man who sought to use compromises politically to avoid conflict and settle disputes when national or sectional honor was at stake would readily resort to arms when he considered his personal honor threatened. When faced with the two competing ideals of honor—the one seeking violent actions, the other seeing such violence as a threat to the social order—Clay made his choice clear. That same spirit showed in 1838 when he was involved in the fringes of another duel, between two congressmen—William J. Graves of

Kentucky and Jonathan Cilley of Maine. In that affair, Graves killed Cilley, bringing mostly northern censure, but little state criticism. A writer from Louisville told of the attitude there regarding the Kentuckian's action: "Had not Mr. Graves . . . fought that duel, the finger of scorn would have been pointed at him on his return to Kentucky; he could not have represented this district in Congress." There stood both a congressman of the common-wealth and Kentucky's greatest statesman as models for Reid's generation—men who took up the pistol, rather than the pen, to settle disputes of honor.[3]

Such actions gave the state a decided reputation in the antebellum period. An 1818 visitor told how citizens "have the character of being the best war-riors of the United States." Traveler James Hall, seventeen years later, called the state "the cradle of courage and the nurse of warriors," a chivalrous place whose very name "is continually associated with the idea of fighting." A woman who came to the area soon thereafter noted how inhabitants had long been praised for their valor. Nathaniel S. Shaler, who would become a famous Harvard geologist, grew up in Kentucky in Reid's time and recalled that the attitude prevalent in his youth was that combat stood as "the fittest occupation of a man." Champ Clark, later Speaker of the U.S. House of Representatives from Missouri, grew to maturity in Kentucky before and during the Civil War and termed those of his native state "born warriors." He apparently embraced that attitude, for Clark would be expelled from a state college for shooting at a classmate. The warrior mentality—and re-spect for it—prevailed as Reid grew to maturity and entered public life.[4]

But other kinds of violence also permeated Reid's society, almost on a daily basis. The predominantly rural population killed chickens and slaugh-tered hogs in bloody force; the men hunted and brought back various dead animals to the table. Even sport might involve violence, as did, for instance, cock-fighting. In that society, also, children and adults alike might see slaves whipped and beaten and hear their cries. Opposition to foreigners resulted in the "Bloody Monday" riots of 1855, which left over twenty dead. And one northerner remembered how when he came to the state in the 1830s, "street-fights and duels were normal facts of Kentucky life," all made worse by heavy drinking. Kentuckian Robert Penn Warren's words about another era in the state's history applied to Reid's time as well: "There was a world of violence that I grew up in. You accepted violence as a component of life. . . . You heard about violence and you saw terrible fights. . . . There was some threat of being trapped into this whether you wanted to or not." It became too easy to grow inured to killing, to accept it as inevitable, to tolerate the causes. Frontier violence, wars, racism, nativism, alcoholism, duels—all fueled the commonwealth's aptitude for violence. Yet despite all that, in many ways Kentucky had not differed greatly from the South in that regard before the Civil War. As one historian has noted, there was an "overwhelming acceptance of violence by almost everyone in the society." The prewar years only set the stage for the postwar actions that followed and made it easier for them to occur. By the time Reid sought office, Kentucky events had produced an even stronger image of the Bluegrass State as a place of violence.[5]

After studying the era in which Reid lived, historian Robert M. Ireland concluded: "While nineteenth century Kentucky produced fine horses, hemp, and whiskey, she excelled most in crime." That violence took several forms, both group-oriented and individual, much of it a continuation of trends from earlier times, but some of it, unfortunately, the result of new forces of violence. Old forms of killing did not die away easily, however, and examples of that continued even as Reid served as judge and campaigned. Those who defended murderous actions by appeal to the "unwritten law" still found sympathetic jurors. On 27 April 1883, for example, Congressman Phillip B. "Little Phil" Thompson shot and killed Walter Davis, a man Thompson—probably erroneously—believed had seduced his wife months before. Henry Watterson's *Courier-Journal* echoed other state papers: "The forfeit of the life of the wife-seducer to the vengeance of the husband is accepted as unwritten, but inexorable, law." The trial jury's actions endorsed that sentiment, for they quickly freed Thompson. That acquittal once more supported the idea that moral order and manly honor compelled such action, even if outside the law.[6]

Many of these elements likewise emerged in what became known as the "Ashland Tragedy." On the day before Christmas 1881, three men—George Ellis, William Neal, and Ellis Craft—broke into the Gibbons home, raped the two teenage girls, and then killed them as well as a handicapped boy there. They then burned the house to conceal the deed. One of the criminals, the twenty-four-year-old George Ellis, turned state's evidence, and his two cohorts were quickly found guilty and given the death penalty. They appealed and received a new trial. Meanwhile, a jury convicted Ellis, and a judge sentenced him to life in the penitentiary. On 3 June 1882, a mob seized Ellis and hanged him. But they sought more vengeance and did not want to wait for the legal system, which was moving slowly. As Neal and Craft were being transferred to a new location, under the guard of over two hundred militia, another, larger mob formed. Others gathered to watch. The militia force took Neal and Craft to a riverboat; a group of people from Ashland moved out into the water in another vessel. One shot, then another, rang out, and the soldiers responded, with an estimated thousand or more rounds. Bullets struck those on shore as well, and when firing ceased, at least four had died and over twenty more had been wounded. A subsequent trial for Craft resulted in his execution, with some three thousand people watching on 12 October 1883. The final trial of William Neal began in April 1884, during Reid's race for the Court of Appeals. The whole affair showed the mob mentality for vengeance, and the ensuing outrage of the militia's actions meant that such a response might be less likely in the future.[7]

In fact, such group-oriented violence seemed to be spreading in postwar Kentucky. While traveler Charles Dudley Warner's comment that in Kentucky "lawlessness has only existed since the war" ignored decades of history, it correctly emphasized how much violence had occurred after that conflict. Part of it came from racial strife. The Ku Klux Klan rode in Kentucky, and in a five-year period after the Civil War, it and less organized groups lynched over one hundred people, most—but not all—of them black. Self-styled "regulators" virtually controlled several counties, bringing one judge to cry out that "human life in Kentucky is not worth the snapping of a man's fingers. . . . Acres of grass grow on the graves of murdered men in my district." Such lawlessness produced extralegal response. In 1883, a national newspaper story told how "a band of outlaws" in western Kentucky had been executed, "without the formality of jury trial." The next year, just in the two months of April and May, in the midst of Reid's race, state stories told of the northern Kentucky lynching of a black man who had stolen $120. They gave details of how a mob seized a white man and a black youth from an eastern Kentucky jail in "Bloody Breathitt" and hanged them from the courthouse. At almost the same time, another crowd seized a black prisoner in Hardin County, in the central part of the state, and hanged him as well.[8]

But despite all the personal killings, the lynchings, and the mob rule, it was a new feature of postwar Kentucky violence that chiefly gave the commonwealth a reputation for lawlessness that elevated it over most other states. Massive Appalachian feuds went on for over four decades after the Civil War, and left hundreds dead before they ceased. Since most occurred only in Kentucky, feuds associated its mountain people—and, by extension, all the state—with a developing stereotype of "violent irrationality." The people involved did not see it that way. They fought each other for a variety of reasons and in different ways. Often a minor dispute would implicate whole extended families and spread that way; others focused more on economic or political rivalries; some centered on conflicts over modernization of the mountains and transfers of power; a few included political or wartime animosities. The ensuing fighting might produce mostly lawless elements fighting almost as if for a feudal lord, or it might include family against family. But whatever form it took, the feud generally focused on the concept of justice. Frequently, groups battled over the physical control of the courthouse in a county, for that, in a sense, symbolized what they sought. For if justice could not be secured through the local courts—where one family might dominate or where one outlook might prevail—then the atmosphere of the era and the misconduct of the people justified a different form of justice: "Our only retaliation to speak of is the muzzle of our guns; when all else fails us we at least have that left us."[9]

That spirit produced feud after feud, one following in almost numbing fashion after another, decade after decade. One in Carter County during the 1870s seemed almost a conflict between lawless groups and the militia, while one deeper in the mountains, in Breathitt, raged for over thirty years, with more than one hundred deaths. The 1880s saw the outbreak of the "Rowan County War," on the fringes of Appalachia, not far from Reid's Mount Sterling; it ended eventually with one faction surrounding a hotel, gunning down their enemies as they fled, in an almost Western-style shootout. In one three-year period, twenty had died and sixteen had been wounded, in a county of only eleven hundred people. That same decade saw the Howard-Turner feud in "Bloody Harlan" and the French-Eversole one in Hazard, Kentucky. Important community leaders steered both; numerous deaths characterized each. In the same time period, the developing Hatfield-McCoy feud, though far from the bloodiest or largest of the mountain "troubles," attracted even more attention because it crossed state lines and involved the U.S. Supreme Court. Dime novels spread the feud story as well. In the nation's eyes, these so-called family "vendettas" seemed almost a peculiarly Kentucky form of violence. The state's image worsened.[10]

Feuding had occurred within thirty miles of Reid's home. But all around him in Mount Sterling and Montgomery County, other aspects of lawlessness almost constantly made him aware of the destructive force of unlawful actions since the Civil War. "A.D.," an African American living in Mount

Sterling, wrote to a newspaper in 1869, saying, "Our neighbor Ku Kluxes have just quit killing our people in this section. . . . They shot my father down in April, 1866, for nothing but prejudice." A white man recalled of that same time: "Many Negroes in my acquaintance were assassinated in their own houses." But violence knew no particular race: in 1870, Munell Tyree, white, had fallen victim to "Judge Lynch." The year 1878 proved particularly deadly. In February, a fight left one man dead of knife wounds, another injured; three months later, another clash, in a saloon, ended in three gunshots and another death. Then in November, a "riot" took place. When the city marshal, his deputy, his cousin, and several others tried to break up a fierce argument involving four men, the shooting began, and after some twenty or more shots had been fired, an innocent bystander lay dead, and four of the participants suffered wounds. That episode had little effect on town violence, for a month later, on Christmas Eve, the owner of a Mount Sterling bar ordered a storekeeper from his saloon and received major stab wounds for his words. In 1882, the local paper told of "Ku-Kluxing" still going on in the area and reported that a local woman, mistreated by her husband, had left him. But soon six men seized her and warned her to return home or be beaten. In June of that same year, five men took a black prisoner from the jail in Mount Sterling and hanged him from a railroad trestle outside of town. The correspondent who filed the story concluded: "The general impression is that Judge Lynch did a very good job." Smaller communities and places with little internal unity often produce high homicide rates. Still a small town, though one in transition, Reid's Mount Sterling represented a potentially high-conflict society, one tense and ready to explode.[11]

Behind much of that violence, whether at the state, local, or regional level, lay either an exalted sense of honor or a misplaced one. As historian Bertram Wyatt-Brown notes, honor represents a set of external, ethical rules supported by a collective community consciousness, a group of principles of socially expected conduct that establish what actions should be taken under what conditions. Honor also requires an inner strength and represents the individual's internal evaluation. Not only does honor thus define the self-respect and worth of individuals in their own eyes, but it also shows the whole society's estimation as well. Acting according to the code of honor justifies and sanctifies the actions taken in its name—and had for thousands of years. But even though the Hebraic, Christian, Middle Eastern, and other cultures all feature aspects of that code, and even while Ptolemy in the second century wrote of honor as one of the properties of the soul, the concept increasingly seemed an anachronism in the United States, part of a value system that went against what Edward L. Ayers terms the American idea that all individuals have intrinsic worth. The exception seemed to be the South. Throughout the nineteenth century, southerners valued, praised, and tried to live the code of honor. As historian Elliott Gorn pointed out, "Piety, hard work, and steady habits had their adherents, but in this society aggressive self assertion and manly pride were the real marks of status." Their culture and many others in the Western world could even view such ideas as a symbol of modernism. In France, Germany, and Italy, dueling grew more popular, particularly among the military, and the elites of other societies, such as Mexico's, adopted that attitude and increasingly defended their personal prestige on the dueling grounds. All of these places—as in the South— stressed that honor could not be arbitrated; an individual either had it or did not. As Wyatt-Brown argues, honorable individuals most feared not death but public humiliation, as a betrayal of manhood and honor. Honor required courage; cowardice meant shame; insults could not be tolerated. Action must follow, for only blood could cleanse the stains of honor.[12]

That code had long operated in the South and in Kentucky. Before the Civil War, the Bluegrass State had seen that, not only in a series of duels, but in other deadly ways as well. On a dark night in November 1825, a young man named Jeroboam Beauchamp assassinated Solomon Sharp, former state attorney general. When apprehended later, he defended his actions by stating that Sharp had earlier dishonored and impregnated Ann Cook and then had refused to acknowledge the action. Beauchamp had later married her and had thus acted to avenge his new wife's honor. Convicted of murder, Beauchamp—with his wife—tried to commit suicide in his cell. She succeeded; he died on the gallows. They were buried together in one grave. Their story provided material for Edgar Allan Poe, William Gilmore Simms, and other writers for a century, in accounts based more on romance and honor than death. Nearly three decades later, in 1853, a different insult resulted in a similar outcome. A Louisville school principal punished the younger brother of Matt Ward and when ordered to apologize for the action and for calling the boy a liar, the principal refused. Ward pulled a pistol and killed the man for insulting the family honor. Defended by prominent attorneys, including John J. Crittenden, Ward went free. While many protested the decision, the powerful code of honor had prevailed.[13]

Often, the insulted person responded not with a pistol, but with a whip—usually made of cowhide because that was the kind used on slaves and thus represented the ultimate dishonor. In 1807, a Georgia political leader attacked a judge that way. A more famous example took place in 1851 in North Carolina. After attorney William W. Avery declared that his fellow legislator, Samuel Flemming, had engaged in fraudulent activities, the larger Flemming waited outside the courtroom and attacked Avery with a whip when he emerged. He later boasted of the action, calling Avery a coward. Three weeks later, the two met in court and Avery drew a pistol, fired it at point-blank range, and killed the man who had whipped him earlier. Avery's defense attorney claimed that any man who cowhided another man of honor had forfeited his right to live. The jury, after deliberating ten minutes, accepted that view, and Avery won acquittal. Two years later, in Kentucky, a man demanded that newspaper editor Richard H. Collins—later author of one of the major histories of the state—retract charges made in the paper. He threatened to cowhide Collins if he did not. When Collins later saw the man approach him with whip in hand, he promptly pulled a pistol and shot him. Such actions made clear the differences between a culture of dignity and a culture of honor, as expressed in a saying: "Call a man a liar in Mississippi, and he will knock you down; in Kentucky, he will shoot you; in Indiana he will say, 'You are another.' "[14]

Some of the elements of honor helped drive southerners to secession and Civil War in 1861. Angry, frustrated, fearing humiliation from the North, many went off to fight when they considered their honor so threatened that, without such action, all would be lost. That force also drove the same men to fight fiercely, for, as one historian concluded, "Most Confederates despised cowards and dreaded dishonor more than death." Yet not too much emphasis should be placed on that factor alone, for other places, like Kentucky, where honor remained just as highly valued as in the rest of the South, pursued a different course. Men fought for many reasons, and honor represented only one of those. Yet in the end, some men did fight—and die—because of honor.[15]

In certain ways, that code and that culture of honor became more important in explaining southern, and Kentucky, actions following the war's end. Most of those soldiers from the commonwealth who had fought in the conflict had not tasted defeat. They had been on the winning side. Some authors have suggested that, until Vietnam, only southerners had experienced defeat, among Americans, and that circumstance shaped the region's later actions and reactions to other parts of the United States. Yet even though Kentucky had not been a part of that defeated experience, it acted in similar ways. Citizens had, in a sense, selected that course after the war's end and had, in turn, incorporated those attitudes. If the war was, as one historian notes, a "holy ghost haunting the spirits and actions of post–Civil War southerners," then Kentuckians shouted, "Hallelujah!" and became baptized, not in the blood of war, but in the Reconstruction holy water of the cult of the Lost Cause. While the people had mostly *chosen* defeat—rather than experienced it—they still accepted and approved the role that honor played in their newly emerging civil religion. And even though continuity played just as much a part in that postwar world as did change, many saw challenges to their previous power and prestige. With race relations modified, with the "aristocratic ideal" under attack, with the culture of business contesting the agrarian ideal, with concern about the future everywhere, people held fast to honor as one of the last vestiges of the old antebellum world.[16]

Often that code produced relatively harmless effects. A young writer once arranged to meet Kentucky author James Lane Allen. At the expected time for Allen's arrival, the writer heard a knock and said, "Come on in." Time passed and no one entered, so the puzzled writer went to the door and saw Allen walking away. The angry Allen explained that a true gentleman would have answered the door personally and that the writer's inaction on that point had affronted Allen's sense of honor.[17]

But that same code of honor could lead to more than hurt feelings; it could cause violence. First and foremost, honor required justice, and if that could not be pursued effectively through the judicial process then it would have to occur by other means. Legal approaches and lawsuits did not safeguard honor as well as did guns, cowhides, and duels—or, regarding blacks, ropes. Honor's form of social control, built on unwritten rules, depended on an individual's force of reputation, one outside the law. Followers of the code preferred personal over impersonal justice. They wanted the satisfaction of controlling justice with their own hands. And that attitude did not just reside in an upper-class ethos; it had wide acceptance and community support. While aristocrats might deride feudists for their violent responses, incorporating sizable parts of society, those involved in that type of conflict stressed that they acted out of family loyalty and a "sense of pride." Even participants in a Mount Sterling barroom fight arising from one person calling another a liar pointed to the need to defend their honor. It might be an imperfect and flawed view, but that extralegal outlook prevailed among a wide spectrum of people. When they responded—at whatever social level—they did not necessarily react against the legal system per se, but against a particular version of the law. Their code came less from a "rational-legal" view and more from one based on community standards and beliefs about what constituted a correct response. The honorable man followed the law, but reserved a higher law unto himself. That viewpoint meant that, in the end, honor and legalism could not be compatible. Reid's society instead rewarded those who conformed to the local mores and rules and those who worshiped at honor's shrine. It also punished honor's heretics.[18]

Yet honor alone did not dictate how that society judged a man, a Reid. For intricately intertwined with the concept of honor was the equally powerful concept of American masculinity. A northern reporter for *Harper's Weekly* summarized that attitude in 1869: "The central trait of the 'chivalrous Southron' is an intense respect for virility. If you will fight, if you are strong and skillful enough to kill your antagonist, if you can govern or influence the common herd, if you can ride a dangerous horse . . . , if you are a good shot . . . , if you stand by your own opinions unflinchingly, . . . if you are a devil of a fellow with women, if, in short, you show vigorous masculine attributes, he will grant you his respect." With that respect also came the expectation that a person answered any challenge and combated any affront.[19]

The Civil War had reemphasized the importance of manly virtues, particularly courage under fire. Even those who did not fight in the conflict—the John D. Rockefellers and the J. Pierpont Morgans—earned respect in Reid's day for their toughness in business. As the era increasingly praised the self-made man, robber barons became both villains and cultural heroes. With the emergence of Darwinism and societal applications of its "survival of the fittest" idea to Gilded Age America, ambition, aggressiveness, and dominance became even more valued as male attributes. The "manly" man took action; he controlled the situation; he fought; he ruled. And that masculinity was not only expressed in business and politics, but also via male clubs, sports teams, and other outlets. As leisure time and conspicuous consumption grew, concerned critics attacked what they saw as the growing "effeminate" aspects of the age. Anxiety over masculinity came from many sources, including women's attempts to alter their status, changing aspects of the non-work world, and challenges to past patterns of dominance. One student

surveyed those attitudes and concluded that men like Richard Reid—
"reformers and cultivated men"—were, "according to influential adherents
of the manliness ethos, impatient sissies at best, sexual mutations at
worst."[20]

Yet the era tempered that extreme masculinity with another model for
the American male. In addition to their violent, starkly elemental side, men
should also be more controlled and "civilized." They must be the protectors
of women and children, of kith and kin. Manhood required not just aggression but also unselfish chivalry. Honor, after all, had many positive elements
to it, including the concept of noblesse oblige, and the idea of manhood incorporated many of these same images. The age prized the man of action
but also sought a responsible manhood as well. It demanded much.[21]

Such attitudes on masculinity permeated Reid's America. In the South,
concepts of honor may have softened some of the harshest features, in areas
such as business, but over all, the region heartily endorsed the era's masculine ideal, as it always had. When that culture of manhood combined with
the culture of honor, in the South and in Kentucky, it had produced a com-
bustible mix of violence and deaths that rent the nation. It also helped shape
an image that haunted state and region for decades.

Many observers first blamed the violence in Kentucky on the state's legal
system. The *New York Times* concluded in 1877 that "justice is rarely ad-
ministered in the courts unless the offending party is colored," and quoted
a Breathitt County sheriff the next year that the law in his community was
but a "dead letter." That same year a Chicago paper wrote of the commonwealth that "it is a frequent boast that no murderer is punished." When
traveler Warner visited the Appalachian region, he found law officers there
"as likely as not to be the worst men in the community."[22]

But the main theme that emerged from the national critics blamed the
violence not on the legal system, but on the people themselves. A New York
paper, for example, wrote of the Kentuckians as "aborigines," a people so
accustomed to murder "that they do not look upon it with the horror with
which it is regarded in civilized communities." Noting the system of honor
prevailing then, the same paper the next year satirically said that Kentucky
would be a delightful place to live if a person enjoyed "personal affrays and
private assassinations." In 1880, New Yorkers read that Kentucky's history
"is written in blood, and its best society literally streams with gore." Some
of those harsh words resulted from partisan and sectional feelings, part
from other sources—stories often originated in Cincinnati, a trade rival to

Louisville, and willing to portray the state in a negative light as a result. But the accounts, biased though they might be, were essentially correct: Kentucky *was* a violent place. Even the commonwealth's own editors admitted as much. In 1878, one declared that the people "have become saturated and satiated with blood," while another called not for more laws, but rather "a revolution in the moral sense of the community, so that the man-slayer, instead of being exalted as a sort of hero, and actually worshipped for the very qualities which ought to make men shun him" would instead be seen as a bloody killer. Four years later, another editor found the most alarming feature of the violence was the public's indifference to it and their blindness to the growing image of themselves as a "reckless, God-defying, reeking band of law-breakers and murderers." When concepts of manhood and honor united with particular local conditions, the violence grew.[23]

Perhaps the clearest presentation of that image came in an 1880 book entitled *Homicide, North and South*. Author H. V. Redfield, while proclaiming his praise for southern hospitality, generosity, and courage, stated that he wrote his work after seeing so much death in the South and so much praise for "man-slayers" there. He chose three states to represent that violence. One of them was Kentucky. Redfield pointed out that the Bluegrass State had more murders in 1878 than eight other states combined, which together had seven times the population of Kentucky. The figures showed Massachusetts, a place similar in population, had one-tenth the violent deaths Kentucky did. Then Redfield devoted an entire chapter just to the state, bringing in several Mount Sterling examples. He quoted a letter from that town which stated that in the past decade over a dozen had died in the city alone. Soon after, he noted, more had been killed. *Homicide, North and South* also included a letter from an Episcopal bishop who blamed the state's "fearful history of unpunished murder" on acts of "mistaken chivalry" and on a popular sentiment that accepted such actions. Redfield stressed the prevalence of whiskey, the tendency to have weapons at hand, and the culture itself as causes, noting that the one who kills over honor is acquitted by public opinion and his status in society is not harmed by the action. His solution? Rigid enforcement of existing law, but most of all, "an increased respect for human life."[24]

Richard Reid read widely. Whether he saw all the accounts that portrayed Kentucky in such a negative light is unlikely. But he probably perused many and, as an attorney, may well have studied *Homicide, North and South*. He knew also the force of honor in his world and the concepts of manhood all around him. Reid the reformer, the man of culture, did not meet many of the expectations of masculinity, either by physical actions or by outlook. He could certainly fulfill the protective side of Victorian era manhood by taking care of his family and friends. But his personal culture did not—and almost could not—include an aggressive, dominating masculinity. At the same time, Reid understood the role honor played in the affairs of men and women, and, in some ways, respected that viewpoint. Yet those elements also helped produce the violence that was harming his native state. And as a man of the law, he could not fully accept the extralegalism that manhood and honor produced. How, then, could he use those concepts and blend them in such a way as to support the law, not operate outside it? Indeed, what should his own course be? His solution was to live the concept of the Christian Gentleman, and be a model and example for good.

The two very different parts of manhood in Victorian America seemed to be at war with each other—the principle of the Christian Gentleman and the masculine savage ideal. Civilization's growth seemed to favor the first, but others feared that the advancement of "civilization" reduced masculinity. In one sense, the age wanted the myth—the knight of King Arthur, a person of honor, a religious figure, a respecter of women, a man in control of self, yet at the same time a warrior, a fighter, a hero. As it turned out, southerners—and Reid—saw the perfect embodiment of that ideal in one of their own.

Robert E. Lee represented, to many, the best aspects of southern honor and manhood, in a Christian Gentleman. To Reid, a man of southern sympathies, Lee meant even more. Like Dick Reid, Lee could be shy, was a loving parent, and often preferred the company of women to men. His very actions the Kentuckian repeated. After the war's end, for example, Lee had attended church service in Richmond, Virginia. When the minister invited people to come forward and receive the sacraments, a well-dressed black man did so. The white congregation remained seated. Then Lee got up and knelt by the man; his fellow worshipers followed. Reid would act similarly when confronted with a comparable situation in his own church. "Marse Robert," a biographer notes, knew that the human condition was a flawed one, yet he believed in redemption above all—a view similar to that held by Reid. But if a tragic hero in some way, Lee was still—in the end—a hero, a warrior, a person Reid believed he could never be.[25]

Dick Reid told a teacher that his highest ambition in life was to be a Christian Gentleman. Southerners who underwent conversion turned to religion as a "respectable" alternative to all that honor demanded. Evangelicalism called for self-control, self-denial, self-restraint, for humility and harmony among others. Those almost older forms of virtue vied with many of the attributes honor and manhood required. Christian modernity confronted patriarchal privilege, and while many praised the ideal of the Christian Gentleman, the question still remained chiefly unanswered: If forced to choose between the different ideals and the different responses to moral challenges, which way would people go?[26]

Reid expressed his confidence in the correctness of the Christian Gentleman. After all, in 1884, as he ran for the Court of Appeals, he felt secure at last in his life. He had the love of a wife, the support of his church, the respect of his community, and the honor of his profession. While not fully confident in all aspects of that life—as with manhood issues, for example— Reid had overcome much and had fashioned a life that both satisfied and fulfilled.

Then John Jay Cornelison asked Reid to come to his law office.

Chapter 5

A Living Death

Wednesday, 16 April 1884, dawned as a beautiful spring morning in Mount Sterling. Dick Reid, after a week of campaigning, had returned home only two days before and now welcomed friends in his law office. On stock sale day, with many people in town, various visitors spoke with him on a range of issues. It seemed a typical attorney's morning. When fellow lawyer John Jay Cornelison asked him to stop by his office to look at some legal papers, it represented the kind of request Reid had answered many times from many barristers. He patted the head of one of Cornelison's boys, who was with him, and told the father he would be there in the afternoon, since he had other things to do before then. Bettie Reid soon arrived in a buggy, and she and her husband went to a wedding ceremony at the Baptist church. Cornelison watched them from across the street. Afterwards the Reids went home for what was then called dinner, and Bettie related to him how she had been training Swiss servants, who spoke little English. Dick told his ward, his mother-in-law, and his wife about his trip to the mountains and the problems he encountered. As Reid started to return to town, Bettie Reid put her arms around him and "playfully" asked: "Stay with me for the afternoon. You are gone from home so much now that I scarcely see anything of you." He kissed her, but said, "I must go; I have an engagement."[1]

It would be an appointment with disaster. Reid walked up the stairs to Cornelison's second-floor law office in the Masonic Temple to meet a man he knew well. Cornelison had married the daughter of an influential Christian Church minister and attended the same church as did Reid. There they brought a family that consisted of the thirty-nine-year-old John, his thirty-three-year-old wife, Lissie, and their eight children, all under the age of four-teen. The household also included a white nurse and black servant. But un-like Reid, Cornelison had not known outstanding success in his chosen field. In 1870, when a young Dick Reid owned $12,000 in real estate, an even younger Cornelison had but $600. He had been appointed master commis-sioner for a time but had antagonized so many people that he had been re-moved. An abortive race for county judge had left what one attorney called "an evil sediment." Since then he had continued to practice his profession, but in the 1883 tax assessments, he was listed as owning only a town lot worth $150. The sizable family apparently lived in his father-in-law's two-story frame house on Clay Street. Partly dependent on his wife's parents, perhaps frustrated over the prospects of his own legal practice, certainly angry over recent court decisions, likely jealous of Reid's success, the two-hundred-pound Cornelison closed the door to his office behind the man who seemed his antithesis—a respected judge, a cultured man, a wealthy citizen.[2]

Reid took the chair Cornelison offered him and began reading some legal papers. Then the blows suddenly started, first from a hickory cane, then from the cowhide whip. Dazed, Reid would remember nothing of what hap-pened after that, only recalling being taken to his law office once the whip-ping had been stopped. His arm was severely bruised from wrist to elbow where he had tried to ward off blows; on the head and at the base of the neck, he had deep, dark bruises as well. Pointing to his head, Reid told a cousin, "This was the blow that hurt me." Cornelison boasted to a friend that he had struck the judge twenty-five times with his cane and seventy-five or a hundred times more with the whip as he chased him a block and a half. When a man in Bean's Store finally stopped him, he cried out, "I am thrash-ing the d____d rascal. I have not given him half enough." The assault had ended. A flushed and triumphant Cornelison walked away.[3]

But why had he done it? When the newspaper accounts appeared the next day, most included quotes from Cornelison; the injured Reid could only give a written statement. Moreover, the influential *Courier-Journal,* whose headline read "Judge Reid Cowhided," depended on its Mount Ster-ling correspondent—who also worked for a Cincinnati paper—and that man both supported Reid's opponent in the Court of Appeals race and called himself a friend of Cornelison. For the first few days, then, initial sto-ries tended to favor the assailant. Cornelison explained that he had acted because Reid had been an attorney for him in a case which had been appealed to the Superior Court: "While professing to be my friend, I had convincing, almost conclusive, evidence that he was really a traitor to my interests in the case named, and on the sly was doing all he could to defame and slander me." Three days later, Cornelison presented a long and detailed defense of his actions. Reid—his "alleged friend"—had maligned him and had shown himself instead to be a "secret enemy," a man wanting "to forever blast what little character and standing I had as a man and an attorney, and to bring disgrace and infamy upon my wife and eight little children." He sneered that this man "heralded as a pure, Christian gentleman" was a hypocrite. A few days after that, Cornelison offered still another reason for his course of action. He said that when he had been master commissioner—a job that brought him up to $800 per year—he had been asked to resign by Judge Riddell (Reid's Appellate Court opponent in 1884). At the time, said Cornelison, he had blamed Riddell for that, but recently he had discovered that Reid had secretly demanded his resignation: "I challenge him to deny it." Throughout both defenses, Cornelison's language stressed again and again how he boldly looked Reid "squarely in the face," while Reid guiltily turned away, "still not looking me in the face." Unable to submit "tamely" to such attempts to ruin him, Cornelison presented himself as the man of courage, the man wronged by Reid's ungentlemanly and unmanly actions, the forceful man protecting his family and his reputation. In short, manhood and honor dictated no other course than the one he had taken. There was only one problem with Cornelison's explanation. It was wrong.[4]

His first charge concerned Reid's supposed perfidy in the case of *Howard* v. *Cornelison*. A complicated lawsuit, it originated from an 1874 trial in Bourbon Circuit Court. There P. A. Howard sued M. M. Clay for payment of a $1,500 obligation Clay owed to Josiah Anderson, which Anderson had assigned to Howard as a payment for Anderson's debts to Howard. But to confuse matters more, should Howard win, his creditors would receive funds from any judgment, not Howard directly. Cornelison defended Clay, and he met privately with Anderson and P. A. Howard. They all agreed to a compromise, which would allow Clay to pay back—indirectly—only half the money owed, while they would get half—again indirectly—without having to turn it over to creditors. The vehicle for doing that would be attorney Cornelison. He would swear in court that the plaintiffs had told him they had no claim on Clay's funds, that would not be challenged, and the court would dismiss the suit. That, in fact, did occur. Clay paid Cornelison, as his lawyer, $250, which, then, as part of the compromise, Cornelison gave to Anderson and Howard. But the plan unraveled over the other $500, which was to go to Cornelison in the form of a note from another Howard—H. C. Howard—to him, and from Cornelison to the others. The lawyer had to bring suit to get the payment of that and, in the course of the ensuing trial, the details of the compromise emerged. The Circuit Court still ruled in Cornelison's favor, but H. C. Howard appealed. The case went to Superior Court, where Richard Reid served.[5]

In what must have been a skilled prosecution at the circuit court level, Reid had won the case for Cornelison. But, on appeal, he obviously could not defend him before the Superior Court. Reid's partner, Henry Stone, however, stepped in and enlisted William Lindsay (later a U.S. senator) to assist. Howard had on his side two prominent Mount Sterling Republicans, A. T. Wood and W. H. Holt. After hearing their arguments, the Superior Court, with Reid not sitting, overturned the earlier ruling, which had favored Cornelison, and ordered a new trial. But the court also used harsh language regarding Cornelison's actions: "The law will not enforce a contract . . . between plaintiffs and the attorney of defendant, by which the former's creditors are fraudulently deprived of the lien they have acquired." He had neither the duty nor the right to take such action, had "falsely" stated the facts of the case, and had been a part of a conspiracy to defraud, they concluded. In truth, they may have been lenient in their words, for a later Court of Appeals justice wrote that Cornelison's conduct should have been grounds for disbarment. Still, the language used clearly suggested that Cornelison had not performed honorably under the law. Such actions might receive approval in the Gilded Age world of business ethics, but would not wear well in the halls of justice.[6]

That decision was announced on 27 February 1884. About a month later, Cornelison went to Frankfort to get an order extending the time he could petition for a rehearing of the case. While there, he saw written in the margins of the court transcript, in red pencil, several comments, in what resembled Judge Reid's handwriting. Because Reid had already told his former client that he had taken no part in the deliberations, Cornelison began to question those statements and came to believe that Reid had secretly written the decision against him. He asked several people to identify the handwriting, but most could not clearly do so. Attorney James H. Hazelrigg expressed the opinion that the words were Reid's; Stone, Reid's partner and a man who knew his handwriting well, told Cornelison that they were someone else's. Political enemies of Reid's probably planted the idea that Reid had also been behind Cornelison's removal as master commissioner. His anger fermented and grew stronger. Then he had acted.[7]

But Cornelison had acted rashly and wrongly. The day the story of the assault appeared in the newspapers, Superior Judge A. E. Richards wrote Reid a public letter released to the press: "I wrote the opinion in the case. You never spoke a word to me about it before the decision. . . . The notes in the margin are exclusively in the handwriting of Judge Bowden and myself. As to the opinion, I am officially and jointly responsible with Judge Bowden; personally, I am alone responsible." Later, under oath, the other Superior Court judge, J. H. Bowden, confirmed that Reid had never mentioned or talked about the case, directly or indirectly. At the same time, the deputy clerk of the court swore that the handwritten words in question were not Reid's and that Cornelison had never asked him if they were.[8]

The other charge, regarding Cornelison's removal as master commissioner, received little attention and proved more difficult to decipher. Apparently, for some time, many members of the Mount Sterling bar had petitioned the judge to replace Cornelison. But, as one person finally revealed, "Reid & Stone and Holt, the largest and most influential lawyers, would not sign the petition for his removal," so the judge hesitated to act. While Cornelison had believed Reid his enemy in the matter, he had actually been his friend. The Christian Gentleman did not tell of acts of kindness to others; he simply did them. Reid had been innocent. Cornelison's monster of honor had devoured the wrong man, for the wrong reasons.[9]

Cornelison had first stood before the rail of public opinion. Injured, Reid waited until he had recovered somewhat before he offered his own explanation of what had occurred. His only statement in the first five days following the attack came in the newspapers, immediately after the event. He then said he had taken no part in the Howard case and had not even read the opinion. Reid acknowledged that he had heard that Cornelison held him responsible for that decision, for some reason, but he declared that he had been blameless and thought Cornelison had accepted his explanation. Reid explained how he had been totally surprised by the attack. But the people wanted to know more.[10]

On County Court Day, Monday, 21 April 1884, when the citizens of the county and city mixed, Reid gave a fuller account of what had happened and how he had acted. A reporter present described the speaker as tall, "not very strongly built," with blue eyes and a gray beard: "He looked like a gentleman and a judge." Speaking with deep emotion for a half hour to "those who know me," Reid early stated the question as clearly as he knew how: "The issue is now upon the people of Kentucky, whether the law is to be defied or obeyed; whether a judicial officer should be required to avenge a wrong done him, by taking summary vengeance in his own hands, or is it to be commended for forbearing to resort to violence and for upholding the majesty of the law." Reid briefly told how he had been invited to Cornelison's office and how the first blows had paralyzed and stunned him. Unarmed, "unable to think or reason," remembering nothing of what followed, he recovered only when back in his own law office. Then it became clear that two opinions existed: "outraged manhood" called out for vengeance against such an indignity. Family honor and the "voice of the world" cried for him to take Cornelison's life.[11]

But Reid told why he had taken, instead, another option. First of all, he did not want to be haunted by his assailant's bloody body and the knowledge that he had been responsible for producing a widow and eight fatherless children. Second, said Reid, to take personal vengeance would have gone against his whole life and character and all that it meant to be a Christian: "I never struck a human being a blow in anger, and, until this occurrence, no man ever struck me a blow." He would destroy his "Christian manhood" by shedding the blood of a fellow human. Finally, he declared, as a "lover of the law" he could not violate it, even for such a wrong. Reid looked at all that surrounded him, at the state's history, and at his vision of its future, and strongly spoke out for the law:

> There is a spirit of lawlessness abroad in the land. . . . Criminals escape punishment, and the laws are laxly administered. There is a deep disrespect—nay, almost a contempt—for law. . . . Courts are lightly esteemed. . . . In the state of Kentucky, the same demoralization prevails. Murder is rampant; assaults are frequent, and go unpunished. Society, whose fabric rests on law and the respect of its enforcement, is upheaved to its very crust. . . .
>
> What is to be the end of all this? Do we live in the dark and barbarous times when every man was his own avenger and took the law into his own hands? Or do we live in an era of Christian civilization, where the rights of the citizen are defined and should be respected? . . . Is this to be the era of lawlessness? Shall shotguns and pistols and knives rule the hour . . . ?

Reid answered with a firm "No." Very aware of the criticism by some for his inaction, cognizant that people called on him to resort to revenge and violence, he affirmed his belief that such was "a mistaken public sentiment," one that continued the lawlessness of the past. "I sound now the trumpet of the law," he concluded, "and cry aloud: Who is on the side of the law? And ask you to rally to its standard."[12]

Warm applause greeted Reid's words. They had been words of compassion, charity, and forgiveness, rather than of revenge, retribution, and vengeance. His own view of what honor should mean and of what Christianity should be, stressed the rule of law and human dignity rather than the old concept of personal justice and virulent manhood. But the question remained, after all that: Would his view, his cause, be that of the people? Reid had thrown down the gauntlet to Kentucky and the South. If they endorsed and supported his actions, then they would take a stand for an end to the culture and mindset that had brought them so much violence. His example could begin the change. On the other hand, if they castigated him for not taking the course of old traditions of honor and manhood required, then they would make it clear what they valued most. The cowhiding of Richard Reid and his response represented an important test for Kentucky and the South.

The same day that Reid spoke at the courthouse, his assailant was arraigned in city court on an assault and battery charge. With the mayor of Mount Sterling and his father-in-law, the Reverend Thomas Munnell, as his bondsmen, John Jay Cornelison went free on $200 bail, until trial before the circuit court. But his legal problems concerned Cornelison little. He had believed Reid guilty of wrongdoing, but found out that he had been in fatal error. Rather than draw attention to Reid's failed honor, as Cornelison thought, now it appeared that he was the one who had committed a dishonorable act. In fact, papers friendly to Cornelison stressed how he was a respected attorney and gentleman, in an attempt to portray him as a man of honor at the level of Reid. Cornelison sickeningly realized that he had to fight for his professional life. Instead of receiving congratulations for exposing Reid's actions, he came under criticism on all fronts. Yet he could not retreat, or that would further expose his error and compromise his honor. Cornelison—almost in a panic—struck out again and again, trying to defend a course that he likely knew was indefensible. Events had overcome any reason for them, but he did not recant; he did not apologize; he did not express regret. Cornelison had to attack or die—professionally. And so the charges against Reid, and Reid's family, went on.[13]

Defiantly walking around town, twirling the same cane with which he had beaten Reid, boasting of his actions, Cornelison continued to present reasons why he had acted. Without providing details, he suggested that Reid had "slyly" been undermining his business interests. Then on 6 May 1884, the Republican paper in Mount Sterling published another attack, not on Reid, but on his wife. Calling her "the madam," Cornelison charged that Mrs. Reid and the Christian Women's Board of Missions had said that the souls of mountain people "were not worth saving." That story would be reprinted and distributed across Appalachia by Reid's political opponents. Finally, Cornelison hinted of "a still more serious charge" in the future. It seemed never to end.[14]

Such attacks on his family hit Reid particularly hard, for the one person whose approval he sought and the one he most wanted to shield from controversy was his wife. But he could not, for her own actions had already placed her under public scrutiny and had caused both husband and wife deep distress. The first newspaper stories included an account, from the unfriendly reporter, which stated that Mrs. Reid had declared that she would kill Cornelison if her husband was not man enough to do that. Local papers spread the story, and the national press repeated it as well. The *New York Times* commented: "The wife of Judge Reid is an ambitious and courageous woman, and has threatened . . . to kill Cornelison, if her husband does not." Almost the exact words appeared in a story on the West Coast. Friends who read the account wrote to the wife asking her not to take any violent and bloody actions of vindication. Rumors quickly embellished the story, saying that Bettie Reid had taunted her husband to take revenge, and when he had declined, then she made the threat.[15]

Such stories were devastating, at several levels. First of all, while Reid had appealed for the law to take its course, the accounts presented his wife as seeking just the opposite. But more than that, in an age where male anxiety over gender boundaries had intensified, Bettie Reid seemed to be the family member taking the more traditional masculine response. Describing her as "ambitious" represented a pejorative, not a praiseworthy, response to those fears. But the most damaging effect of the report was on Richard Reid. An 1869 author had written that "a woman admires in a man true *manliness,* and is repelled by weakness and effeminacy. A womanish man awakens either the pity or the contempt of the fair sex." Though restricted in his overtly masculine activities, Reid had gained Bettie's respect in so many ways over the years and had proven to her his Christian manhood.

She, in turn, had given him the love so absent from his life before. Yet as historian Edward L. Ayers has noted of their era: "A true woman would supposedly refuse to give herself to a man who would not or could not defend her honor; no woman wanted to share in a dishonored name." Had Dick Reid, in refusing to seek out and kill Cornelison in honor-based revenge, lost Bettie's respect? Had he dishonored her? Had the very things that had attracted her as his strengths—his gentle spirit and kind ways—become weaknesses that had cost him her love and earned him, instead, her contempt? Bettie's brother wrote her that, because of the whipping, her husband now had to endure "a living death, a perpetual disgrace." Emotionally tied to Dick and living his successes and failures, Bettie had shared in what some, at least, perceived as that disgrace. But her doubts caused her husband to question how he would now answer the question posed by Lady Macbeth to her spouse: "Are you a man?"[16]

His stepson's response did not help matters. Reid Rogers at Princeton clearly believed in the code of southern honor. Writing three days after the assault, he told of his regret, anger, and humiliation when he heard the news. While admitting that his stepfather's course was that of a gentleman, "it is not enough." Cornelison must be chastised, and Reid Rogers proclaimed himself anxious to return home and avenge the indignation and blot on his own reputation: "a wrong done a family can only be righted by a member of the *family*."[17]

Mrs. Reid's words, reported in the press, suggested she was ready to be the family member to do that. But in actuality, what she said and did when she first visited her husband after the assault remains unclear. Soon after the story appeared, she denied that she had ever threatened Cornelison and repeated that denial more vehemently later. A close friend, however, remembered that she had gone to the law office armed with a pistol and became "wild with conflicting emotions" on seeing her half-conscious husband and his wounds. Mrs. Reid herself acknowledged that she had called on those present to go with her to Cornelison's office and "if need be, lay down her own life." Then, Richard Reid looked at her and said, "No, we do not want the wretch's blood upon our hands and on the future of our boy." She had agreed. Over the next weeks, she wrote many letters, defending her husband's course of action and calling for support. Exactly what occurred in that law office remains disputed. But something had happened. Stories continued to circulate, suggesting that not all was well in the Reid household. A New York paper said the "handsome and ambitious" Mrs. Reid had been mortified at Mr. Reid's "lack of courage." In St. Louis, an editorial noted how dissatisfied she was with her husband's course, and a Chicago one related that she had offered her spouse little encouragement or sympathy.[18]

Whether or not Bettie Reid had supported her husband's decision, and no matter what she said in the law office regarding Cornelison, the whole affair caused her great emotional pain, which transferred into classic physical symptoms of distress and anxiety. For most of the month after the cowhiding, she remained bedridden and "very prostrated." Hurt both by her husband's course of action and by the knowledge that all this injured his psyche as well, she incorporated both pains. She wrote that "Mr. Reid did not know that he had an enemy in the world. His sensitiveness is greatly against him." His protective shield before, she could not now be that—if she still wanted to. Reid knew his dependence on her, writing while on a campaign trip: "I feel that though all the world may desert me, you will love me still." Despite all that had happened, Richard Reid desperately continued to believe that he had the love of his wife and son, but questions that had never been there before now tortured him. He had to have the love and respect of his family.[19]

And what about the world outside his home? Both he and Cornelison claimed to be defenders of tradition and order. Did the people support Reid's view? It was judgment day.

Statue of Richard Reid, Mount Sterling Cemetery

Photograph by Russell West

Richard Reid

From Elizabeth J. Reid,
Judge Richard Reid (1886)

Richard Reid

Collection of Henry Prewitt, courtesy
of Kentucky Historical Society

Josiah Davis,
grandfather of Reid
Collection of Terry Murphy

Patsy Chandler Davis,
grandmother
Collection of Terry Murphy

Henry Prather Reid,
father of Richard Reid
Collection of Terry Murphy

J. Davis Reid,
brother
Collection of Terry Murphy

Georgetown College Magazine

Courtesy of Georgetown College Archives

Richard Reid, his stepson Reid Rogers, and wife Elizabeth Jameson Reid
Collection of Henry Prewitt, courtesy of Kentucky Historical Society

TRUSSES AND ABDOMINAL SUPPORTERS.

No. 2580.

FOR UMBILICAL HERNIA.
HARD RUBBER.

NO.		PRICE.
2580. Adult's,	. . .	$6 00
2581. Youth's,	. . .	5 00
2582. Child's,	. . .	4 00

No. 2583.

FOR UMBILICAL HERNIA.
CONTINUOUS SPRING,
LEATHER-COVERED.

2583. Adult's,	. . .	5 00
2584. Youth's,	. . .	4 50
2585. Child's,	. . .	4 00

No. 2586.

2586. Fitch's Abdominal Supporter, 4 50

No. 2587.

2587. London Supporter, . . . 3 00

No. 2588.

2588. Silk Elastic Sidestrap Belt Abdominal Supporter, . . . 5 00

☞ *25 per cent. discount to Physicians.*
The boldface numbers represent instruments illustrated.

Trusses, as advertised in the era

*From Tafel Bros.' Illustrated Catalogue, courtesy of University of
Louisville-Kornhauser Library*

Robert Riddell, Reid's chief
primary election opponent
From Notable Men of Kentucky *(1902)*

William Holt, candidate supported by Reid's allies in the
general election
From Biographical Cyclopedia of the
Commonwealth of Kentucky *(1896)*

Elizabeth J. Reid, in later life
From Elizabeth Jameson
Reid:
A Tribute *(1904)*

Elizabeth Reid Rogers,
Princess Christian of Hesse,
and daughter of Reid Rogers
Collection of Henry Prewitt,
courtesy of the Kentucky Historical Society

Blindfolded Justice, detail of Reid Memorial in cemetery

Photograph by Russell West

Chapter 6

A Seared Soul

John Jay Cornelison found few friends in the press of Kentucky and the nation. Though a Louisville editor whose niece was Cornelison's wife praised him as "kind-hearted, brave, and gentle" and a Republican paper in the same city extolled his "good moral character," they remained the exceptions. Following the publication of Cornelison's defense of his actions and its quick demolition by the Superior Court judges, most state papers echoed one in the capital city, which termed the assault unjust and unprovoked. Others attacked Cornelison's "outrageous" and disgraceful conduct, and one editor colorfully declared Cornelison's explanation "weaker than a summer-complaint baby." "When he was cowhiding the Judge, he was cowhiding the law." Nationally, newspapers ranging from the *San Francisco Examiner* to the *Atlanta Constitution* concluded that Cornelison had no grounds for his attack.[1]

But the real debate centered on Reid's response, and the reaction to that proved decidedly mixed. It showed that many still not only respected but even revered the code of honor. In nearby Bourbon County, Kentucky, where Mrs. Reid had lived with her first husband, the newspaper first justified Reid's course, saying he had been unarmed, "or he would have very properly shot Cornelison down like the ruffian deserved." The day after Reid gave his full explanation of his stand, the paper said it had spoken with attorneys, doctors, merchants, farmers, and workers, "and all agree in saying that each would have killed Cornelison had they been in Reid's place." Furthermore, most indicated that the battered man should bide his time and then "wrack it to his foe when he could be met to a better advantage"—even if through a window in the dark of night. The editorial concluded: "We haven't heard a man speak yet but who would have killed Cornelison or died in his tracks." The Owen County paper cried out: "My God, has it come to this, that our highest judicial officers have to be shot down like dogs . . . ?" But perhaps the strongest response in central Kentucky, among those who knew Reid best, came from W. P. Walton of the widely quoted *Stanford Interior Journal.* While condemning Cornelison's deed, he affirmed that the prevailing view was that Reid "showed himself the most consummate coward that ever trod shoe leather." Any person who would submit to such a disgrace did not deserve to be called a man, he confessed. Three days later another story acknowledged that the average voter in the area felt only contempt for a man such as Reid, who failed to honor the concepts of manhood.[2]

Other newspapers in the commonwealth repeated those attitudes, whether they wrote from a rural or urban perspective. In far western Kentucky, the *Hickman Courier* conceded that some correspondents had praised Reid's moral courage, but in its view, "Kentucky voters don't take to that kind of courage." A week later, after reading Reid's reasons why he did not fight, the editor responded that though the words might be brave, or even heroic, submitting to a cowhiding still "is so extremely degrading and humiliating, that it is difficult to understand how any self-respecting citizen can submit to such punishment." Self-defense, "to say nothing of true manhood," should have prompted and compelled a response. Urban newspapers often offered the same outlooks. In Covington, the press related that by failing to respond violently to the attack, Reid had lost any self-respect and had incurred the disgust of the people there. In the state's largest city, the response proved more mixed, but the *Louisville Times* determined that when Reid "waived the natural right of self-defense," he lowered himself in the estimation of 90 percent of Kentuckians. The paper asked various people what they would have done. A minister refused to answer; a judge on the high court of Kentucky only said he hoped Reid would not win election, so he would not have to sit by him on that tribunal. In a sense, by his actions Reid repudiated the traditional past of the state, with its images of a more glorious age and a noble life, and those who spoke for that culture supported author James Lane Allen's conclusion that "for one simple act of dishonor a man will pay with life-long aversion and contempt." For them, it was Richard Reid, coward.[3]

One of those newspapers had concluded that "neither law or public senti-ment" demanded a person surrender the right to defend himself. That editor correctly stated the law of Kentucky at the time, as interpreted by the courts. A year after the end of the Civil War, then-Kentucky attorney general John Marshall Harlan had defended a circuit judge's jury instructions, on appeal to the state's highest court. In the case, a man had threatened to shoot an-other. A month later, the two met on a road, one asked if he meant the threat, and when he answered affirmatively, the threatened man shot him "several times." The circuit judge had charged the jury to bring in a guilty verdict unless they determined the threatened man "had reasonable ground" to fear execution, and "*had no other apparent means of escape.*" The justices found such instructions faulty and ruled against the common-wealth, saying a "proper man" should not be expected to retreat: "The ex-ample of such humiliating and imperiling recreance would do more harm than good to the public security and peace." In short, kill rather than run.[4]

Four years later, the high court expanded that principle. In the case of *Carico* v. *Commonwealth*, a violent man, David Smith, had threatened Dr. John W. Carico, "a moral, quiet, and prudent gentleman." The physician, "without any apparent demonstration of an immediate assault" on him, had shot the unsuspecting Smith in the back, killing him. The circuit judge in that case had, as another one did earlier, instructed the jury that they should find Carico guilty unless he had been in "immediate danger." Once more, the Court of Appeals overturned the conviction and held those in-structions to be erroneous. With Justice Belvard J. Peters of Mount Sterling dissenting, the 3–1 majority ruled that such a threat, "like the sword of *Da-mocles,*" constantly hung over the person's head and an individual might never feel safe until that threat was removed: "And does either human or divine law require such prolonged agony and peril; or can the best and most prudent man suicidally forbear to strike for riddance, if they have the cour-age to defend themselves, in the only way of secure and lasting escape?" The sword should not hang over the threatened, and to remove it by killing the threat will, the court said, help ensure social order and peace.[5]

A year later, a newly constituted court threw out the Carico precedent with its extremely broad interpretation, saying that it was "not binding" and reflected the "opinion of one judge," who had influenced others to so decide. But the new decision basically reaffirmed the 1866 case and really made little change in the premise. In *Bohannon* v. *Commonwealth*, Addison Cook, "overbearing, revengeful, and vindictive," a KKK leader in Shelby

County, had assaulted Hiram Bohannon and threatened to kill him. Bohannon went back, got a shotgun, and shot Cook twice in the back. The circuit court said that the threatened person had to do "*everything* in his power" to avoid killing a foe, and Bohannon was found guilty. The Court of Appeals overturned, once more, the lower court and ruled that if the person had "reasonable ground" to believe his life in danger, then that individual need not wait to be assaulted again, and may kill his adversary, "if it is necessary." The court added that the threatened person could not go out and hunt a person down "like a wild beast," but could respond if endangered by a threat.[6]

Finally, an 1875 decision had broadened that rule even more. One man had drawn a knife on another while arguing over a prostitute, but nothing had happened. Later that evening, the same man, now drunk, had said he might kill "someone" in his drunken state. Told that, the man he had drawn a knife on earlier sought him out and shot him twice, killing him. The judges supported the view that if reasonable grounds exist, then the person could "pursue his adversary until he has secured himself from danger," though it may turn out that the appearance of a threat was actually false. Even though a mistake, such a killing, they ruled, "is excusable."[7]

Whether in self-defense or in defense of honor, a Kentuckian could seek out an assailant and kill him, and the law supported that action. While Reid spoke out that he acted to protect the majesty of the law, he could only refer to some general principle, then, for as an attorney he knew that courts would likely rule in his favor, should he kill his attacker. In a sense, his current justification came not from the courts, but from a higher law that he followed, at least for the moment.

If some newspapers found much fault with Reid's decision not to strike back, to many other people, it was Richard Reid, hero and man of courage. Several newspapers in the central part of the state praised his decision, though often in a mixed message. His hometown papers generally took no side at first and trod a cautious path editorially after that. One defended Reid but acknowledged that he had been severely criticized for not fighting. In Versailles, where Reid had once practiced law, the paper explained that the judge had the choice of slaying his assailant and wiping out his disgrace or of submitting his cause to the courts "at the risk of losing the respect of fellowmen." It called for the law and public sentiment to punish the "unmanly" Cornelison. But the strongest support for the judge came from the

Courier-Journal, where Henry Watterson, leader of the New Departure Democrats, prodded Kentucky to take the course of the New South, not the Old. Very early he wrote that Reid must be vindicated by the law, not by some vicious code of personal vengeance. After Reid's speech, an editorial praised the "manly" talk and offered: "Too long have we wandered after false gods; too long put above the law and the safety of society mere personal revenge and animosities." This incident meant more than one person versus another; it represented the law against individual justice. Revenge had long won out in that struggle, said Watterson, but "let us change it now, and change it altogether." Or as another local paper put it: "Judge Reid has put the laws of Kentucky to their highest moral test, and it behooves brave Kentuckians to uphold him."[8]

Across the nation, the attack had generally been front-page news. Interestingly, many southern newspapers said little about it editorially. Perhaps they thought it spoke for itself. But the northern and midwestern press looked on the assault as another example of southern violence and justice. The *Chicago Tribune* in a long editorial evoked the memories of Judge Elliott's assassination and said Kentuckians held justices personally accountable for their decisions by either the shotgun or whip. The worst part of all that, said the editor, was that public sentiment approved that approach. A St. Louis newspaper took the same tack and said at least whipping was better than removal via murder. It hoped that Reid's "moral courage" signaled the start of a new spirit of justice in the state.[9]

Other northern papers and periodicals printed even more specific stories. In New York, for instance, the *Times* related how the people of Kentucky regarded Reid as a coward who ran away, but then the paper applauded his actions. In stronger terms, the *Brooklyn Union* congratulated him on his "rare courage" in challenging the South's brutal, unwritten code. The *New York Mercury* termed him "A Southern Hero" and called his refusal to kill "the bravest deed Kentucky has known since the war." Over the country, the widely read *Nation* also praised Reid's bravery and honor in acting as he did. In fact, the public discourse increasingly seemed to focus on who was the coward—Cornelison by his surprise assault, or Reid by his response? Who best spoke for order—Cornelison in defense of society and honor, as he understood it, or Reid in defense of moral law that transcended the existing human code? And who best exemplified real masculinity—Cornelison by his forceful actions, or Reid as a symbol of Christian manhood? Each man represented a larger, longtime, and broadening debate that the nation was having with itself.[10]

Dick and Bettie Reid did not have to look just to the press to find out how people reacted to the whole affair, for they received hundreds of personal letters from family, friends, and strangers. While most supported Reid's course of action, some generally did so in brief notes, and a few included language that might unintentionally hurt the recipient. But virtually all focused on one of two issues—honor or manhood.

In Kentucky, various supporters praised Reid's Christian forbearance and fortitude. Reformer W. M. Beckner admitted that Reid's "mortification" must be great, but called on him to take the peaceful course dictated by reason and law. Montgomery County native and U.S. senator John S. "Cerro Gordo" Williams wrote that he knew Reid's first instinct must have been to get a shotgun and kill the ruffian on sight, but he praised Reid's Christian attitude and "higher courage." A Presbyterian minister asked Reid to continue his manly and religious course, and a Christian Church preacher encouraged his "moral heroism."[11]

Outside the commonwealth, similar letters addressed the issues and offered support as well. From Bettie's hometown of Fulton, Missouri, one person noted the "gross insult" to Reid, but advised him as an officer of the church to follow Christ's teachings and remember that moral courage stood higher than physical courage. In the same town, Reid's brother-in-law confided that he felt like shooting Cornelison, but that Reid should not so degrade himself by taking that course. He should follow the dictates of "manhood and Christianity" and trust that Kentucky would take the opportunity to redeem itself from the disgrace it—not Reid—had suffered. A St. Louis man, H. A. Redfield, extolled Reid as a brave man, "one who dares to do right," a person who did not seek the blood of his assailant to wash away the insult. Calling Reid's course "Christian-like," a stranger in Indiana told the judge that his action marked the dawning of a better civilization in Kentucky and the nation.[12]

Still others, both from Kentucky and from outside the state, focused on issues of manhood and honor in praising Reid. From Bourbon County, a friend emphasized that "manhood and heroism are immortal, while mere brutality will perish with a day. It takes more heroism to bear than to fight." A Bardstown correspondent first expressed his sympathy to Mrs. Reid, saying it must hurt her more than her husband, since the newspapers had "connected her name with the occurrence." But he praised Dick Reid, concluding that to chastise Cornelison would not prove the judge's own manliness. The most forceful support of Reid's position came from a former Mount Sterling attorney, ex-Union soldier, and onetime Republican congressman, Samuel McKee. He explained that no matter how the people clamored for blood, "true *chivalry,* true manhood" approved Reid's course as that of a man of courage.[13]

The sentiment outside the commonwealth—as expressed in letters to Reid—stressed the same themes. In Tennessee, the editor for the *Cumberland Presbyterian* stated that Reid honored Kentucky and hoped his actions would correct the "ruinious" views so long existing there. Writing from Indian Territory, one uncle declared that "the false idea of chivalry calling for revenge," so prevalent in Kentucky and the South, was rapidly vanishing as civilization advanced. Reid's own actions broke down regional barriers and would lead to a higher order of manhood, he predicted. Once more, Reid's allies praised his as the manly, courageous, honorable course.[14]

Not all agreed. Some of those who wrote—many of them relatives—presented a more mixed appraisal of his answer to Cornelison's attack. A cousin from St. Louis expressed sympathy but confessed that he would have used a pistol as his answer in return. Bettie Reid's sister, a woman with whom Dick Reid had long corresponded, wrote a letter of sympathy and told how she knew the charge was false that reported Bettie Reid would avenge the insult herself. But she also indicated that had Reid "shot the wretch down in his tracks" he would have been justified "and there would be no cause even for a regret." From western Kentucky, a former partner of one of the Superior Court judges commended Reid's legal and Christian course but agreed with others that it was "a great pity" that the judge had not punished Cornelison at the time or soon after. As an attorney, he warned Reid that his assailant might assault him again and that he owed it to his family and society to prevent that from occurring. It was not over.[15]

While the preponderance of letters to Reid supported his decision, as would be expected, a few openly called on him to reject his stated course and take another. The strongest statement of that viewpoint came from Stanford, Kentucky, where his "old friend" and college roommate simply said, "You must kill him. Nothing less can ever heal the slightest cut of that cowhide. Just the moment you read this . . . load a double-barrelled gun with buckshot, shoulder it, and never return to your house until you have riddled his carcass. Give him no chance, but kill him like a dog wherever you find him. The people will stand by you." Like the newspapers, the private letters Reid received offered various messages. He could find support or condemnation, praise or criticism, but no unanimity. Reid could accept that. But other than the acceptance from his family, he most needed the strong encouragement of his home county.[16]

That he did not have. A reporter correctly noted that "the town has never been so badly torn up over an affair as it has over this." People went outside their homes when they heard the news of the cowhiding and stood on street corners, discussing the matter, talking among themselves, taking one side or the other. Rumors abounded. People first spoke of the likelihood of a duel, then later expected some other kind of bloody outbreak in the aftermath of the assault. Harsh words came forth from partisans of each man, and fist-fights occurred. Bitterly divided, on the verge of an explosion of anger, Mount Sterling simmered with tension in the month after the cowhiding. Though not directly connected to the Reid affair, the first outward display of that pending violence came in late April, a little over a week after the whipping. A lynch mob tried to seize a convicted murderer from the city jail, but the jailer, armed with a shotgun, threatened to shoot the first man who moved to take the prisoner. The mob finally dispersed, though not before firing a symbolic, parting round into the jail, nearly hitting the jailer's wife. Many expected that lone shot to be only the first note of a bloody symphony of violence.[17]

Chords of disharmony took many forms, however, by both camps. On the night after the assault, Cornelison was hanged in effigy, with a sign on the "body" saying it had been done by the "Best Citizens." In retaliation, the next evening someone drew a picture in pencil on the courthouse wall. It portrayed Cornelison's law office and showed, according to a newspaper, two men running, "one in the lead with terrified expression, his hat flying in the air, and pursued by another with a drawn horsewhip raised in a threatening attitude." Under the Cornelison picture, the caption read "The Lawyer"; under Reid, the words "A Timid Judge."[18]

Events continued to escalate. In the late afternoon of Saturday, 19 April 1884, one day after the drawing appeared, an "Indignation Meeting" took place in that same courthouse. Chaired by former Court of Appeals chief justice Belvard J. Peters, it heard the Reverend Dr. B. T. Kavanaugh defend Reid's course as one that honored the law and the Lord. He decried the "false code of honor" that required blood to satisfy it. Speaking plainly, he said, as a Kentuckian, Kavanaugh declared that "there is a tide in this Kentucky blood that needs to be restrained." The large number of people present then adopted a series of resolutions that condemned Cornelison's "inexcusable" assault and commended Reid's "high degree of moral courage." They resolved that the issue came down to defiance of the law, or obedience to it, and praised the judge for refraining from violence. Quickly, in response, the usually pro-Cornelison *Louisville Commercial* printed a story that indicated that not everyone in the area approved those resolutions and noted the opposition, as an example, of the influential T. C. Anderson, a wealthy shorthorn cattle breeder out in the county. Divisions deepened.[19]

Local politics widened those splits. While the larger issue of the Court of Appeals race constantly loomed as a factor, another matter also created conflict. Years before, brother Davis Reid had angered some in the city by being in charge of the unpopular conscription of soldiers in the Civil War. Despite that, he had recently won election to the state legislature and came under quick local pressure to secure passage of a charter amendment affecting local officeholders. Young Mayor Richard Apperson Mitchell, though married to a Jameson—Bettie's family name—and being a cousin to Reid's earlier law partner, had provided bond for Cornelison and had sought Reid's promise to pressure Davis Reid to get the charter amendment passed. Mayor Mitchell met with Mrs. Reid when her husband was absent, and she recorded in her diary that he threatened to defeat Dick Reid if he did not cooperate. She spoke for her spouse and said he would not try to influence his brother, and then she told Mitchell that "God's retribution" would overtake him for his stance. That a woman would speak to him that way angered the mayor even more, and he remained an enemy.[20]

Like politics, like the Brothers' War, like the mountain feuds, the cowhiding divided families and faiths. In Richard Reid's church a power struggle started almost immediately. Both Cornelison and Reid attended the same services; both had friends in the congregation. Reid, as an elder, had much prestige, but Cornelison's father-in-law Thomas Munnell was also a minister in the Christian (Disciples of Christ) Church. After much internal struggle, and only after bringing in a professor and the president of the seminary for advice, Reid's church submitted its conditions for repentance to Cornelison. First, he had to acknowledge that the assault had been unjustifiable, withdraw all his charges through the press, and ask for forgiveness from the public. Next, he must acknowledge in person to Reid that "he has wickedly wronged him" and request his mercy as well. Third, the elders said Cornelison must go before the church members and repent of his "wrong-doing" and state he had sinned against his religion. Finally, they required him to plead guilty when his civil case came before the court.

Cornelison was originally given until Sunday, 4 May 1884, to respond satisfactorily or face expulsion. An elder gave him a delay of five days; during that time his last set of charges appeared, reflecting particularly on Mrs. Reid. Then on 9 May, the Reverend Mr. Munnell made the case for his son-in-law before the elders, in a five-hour meeting that ended at 1:00 A.M. He argued that Reid should be tried on the charges Cornelison had made, that to expel Cornelison would split the church, and that his son-in-law would be an "idiot" to accept the church's unconditional demands. Seeing little evidence of Cornelison's repentance from either him or his defender, the elders unanimously voted to exclude Cornelison as a member of the church, effective 11 May 1884. It had taken twenty-six days after the attack for that decision to be made, and some considered that action too hasty. But the delay and internal debate over the matter hurt Reid deeply. Of all the institutions and of all the people involved, he expected his church and its members to support his course with little discussion. After all, at every turn and throughout his life, he had followed his religion and its beliefs. He had left vengeance to the Lord; he had turned the other cheek; he had been the Christian Gentleman. While his church, in the end, had taken what he saw as the correct course regarding his assailant, it seemed only to have done so tardily and reluctantly. In the end, would they forsake him as well?[21]

While the church deliberations transpired, Reid had resumed his race for the Court of Appeals. From 23 April to 11 May 1884, he campaigned almost daily across the district, in town after small town: Paris, Winchester, Richmond, Carlisle, Flemingsburg, Maysville, Vanceburg, Grayson, Greenup, Catlettsburg, and others. Even if Reid wanted to focus on the race alone and not on the Cornelison matter, events kept such issues before the voters. The day after he restarted his canvass, a statue honoring the assassinated Judge Elliott was dedicated in Frankfort, and comments there received statewide coverage. The minister's opening prayer asked that the lawless spirit of personal vengeance be removed from the land, then principal speaker Isaac Caldwell repeated those sentiments back at the capitol. A Louisville attorney, former congressman, and student at Georgetown College some years before Reid, Caldwell called for an end to the idea that insults should result in violence. Specifically referring to the Cornelison affair, he termed it a "cowardly assault" and urged harsher penalties in such cases, so the law would not be awed by "the shotgun of the assassin, by the bludgeon and cowhide of the bully." At almost the same time, an enterprising reporter tracked down Elliott's escaped assassin, now living in Indiana, just across the river from Louisville. Elderly, weak, and poverty-stricken, Tom Buford concluded that he saw few parallels between his shooting of Elliott and Cornelison's cowhiding of Reid, which he considered a mere personal dispute. Then, a little over a week after the dedication of the Elliott memorial, news stories from Paris, Kentucky, told how a man named Sharpe had eaten at a local restaurant, gotten sick, and refused to pay. The owner, Phil Box, then began whipping him. Magistrates quickly fined Box $2.50 for breach of peace. That night, Sharpe had gone to Box's house and called him to come out and be cowhided in return. Box fired at Sharpe, who then left. Nevertheless, the response of farmer Sharpe to seek out his assailant, the interview with murderer Buford, who said he killed for honor, and the Elliott statue all reminded voters of Reid's own response.[22]

Nevertheless, people did not need these reminders, for his conduct had become the major issue of the race. Reid wanted his canvass to show that the sentiment of his Kentuckians defended his decision. He sought to make his continuing race a triumphant tour of support. He desired vindication from the people. Instead, he discovered devastating disapproval.

A more skilled political campaigner might have turned attention away from weakness and focused on strengths before voters. But Reid, in reality, did not bring a political temperament to the race. In an age of great orators, observers described him only as a "fair" speaker. His earnest words might say much, but his delivery lessened their force and emotional appeal. Beyond that, Reid's nature and personality ill-suited him for the rough infighting required to win. Little in his makeup led him to slap friends on backs, or to kiss the babies of strangers, or to laugh and tell crude jokes among male voters. Moreover, he sought to avoid conflict always and found it difficult to meet an opponent's verbal jabs with those of his own. He was too kind and too nice for nineteenth-century politics.[23]

As Reid campaigned, he quickly found that the support he enjoyed before the cowhiding had now dissipated. Even his friends divided on the matter. While some praised, others censured. But greater than the hurt inflicted by friends were the words of the general public, the people whose endorsement he most sought. He heard their judgments wherever and whenever he spoke. They could not support a man who had allowed himself to be whipped and then had not slain his betrayer, said some. Others made him feel that they despised and scorned him because of his inaction. As he walked the streets of his hometown, enemies there would raise their voices in stage whispers as he passed to make certain he heard their denunciations. Individuals in Owingsville telegraphed him saying that if he did not avenge the humiliation he had suffered, he should withdraw from the race. When he asked a Carter County supporter what people there thought of the affair, the man answered: "They think you ought to have killed Cornelison and as you did not do it they are against you." For such a proud man, one reporter noted, "the taunts of the wicked wounded and seared his soul."[24]

A discouraged and depressed Reid told his wife that he sought God's help to bring him out of the "furnace of affliction" all around him. The next day, 8 May 1884, his letter to Bettie apologized to her for all that she and the boy had to bear. He too felt that he might fall under the great burden he bore, but "I reflect that I have done right and push on" and try "to meet manfully" the crises. In return, Bettie Reid gave him detailed advice on how he should campaign and counterattack, for, in a sense, it was her campaign just as it was his. She advised him never to avoid speaking, as he had at Richmond because of "the state of things," and suggested he point out that a particularly vocal critic held deep debts to bankers unfriendly to Reid's cause.

Yet her comments could not hide the fact that Reid had lost much support and his chances of victory seemed increasingly slim. But greater than simple votes for or against him in a race was what went on around those votes. Words *did* hurt him. Despite all his years of trying to develop some toughness against the comments about his masculinity and other matters, he still heard the words, now even coming from his supposed friends. Much of his life, he had—despite his successes and honors—still been an outsider to the community. Over the years, it appeared that he had won the acceptance of those in the place he called home. But when the testing time came and he trusted in the legality and sanctity of the law, they had not. The community's norms of behavior ruled over the words as written. They once more rejected him, as did many in the larger world around him. He told his wife that, despite the problems, he proposed "to fight the matter out" to the end, contrary to rumors about his withdrawal. But the spirit behind his words disappeared. Who was he fighting for except himself?[25]

Adding to Reid's despondency were his continuing physical problems. He still suffered pain from the blows of nearly a month before; the effects still could be seen. And then the old phantoms of his childhood returned once more. Either because of the physical pain or the mental stress, or both, Reid seldom slept more than an hour or so a day, and that situation had gone on for the month after the attack. His wife continued almost bedridden during that same period, adding to his concerns. And all of that had come about because of the actions of John Jay Cornelison.[26]

On Thursday, 15 May 1884—one day short of the one-month anniversary of his caning—Richard Reid awoke as usual, at 6:00 A.M., to a bright spring day. On his way downstairs, he knocked on the doors of those still sleeping, to awaken them. His mother-in-law found him in the library praying and joined him in the personal devotion. Then they went in for breakfast, where Reid spoke cheerfully of his prospects to those assembled. The women at the table talked of household costs, new dresses, and ways to aid Reid's campaign. A comment about surplus butter brought laughter from all. Then Dick went to his wife's room, where she had breakfast in her sickbed. He kissed her, she stroked his beard, and they each inquired about the other's health. As he prepared to depart, Bettie asked if he had to leave so soon, and he answered that business called. In town, he met various friends on the street and in his law office, and they discussed the upcoming election. At 9:00 A.M., he crossed the courthouse square to go to another attorney's office to discuss a pending case. On the way, Reid met a blind woman, led by an orphan boy, and they asked for his charity. He gave liberally and spoke words to the woman that caused the child to remember how beautiful he thought they were: "Though you can not see in this life, when your eyes are first opened, it may be that you will behold the light of heaven." Then he moved on.[27]

It seemed a typical day in the life of Richard Reid. But his routine had differed in one very significant way that morning. Richard Reid was carrying a gun.

EVENTS OF 16 APRIL–15 MAY 1884

April 16 Reid goes to Cornelison's law office, cowhiding begins
17 Stories in newspapers; Cornelison hanged in effigy at night; Judge Richards writes letter attacking Cornelison explanation
18 Drawing on courthouse in night
19 Indignation Meeting and resolution
20 Cornelison's first lengthy defense written
21 Reid speech in courthouse defending his actions; Cornelison arraigned, posts bond
22 Second part of Cornelison defense printed
23 Reid electioneering—Richmond
24 Reid in Paris; Elliott monument dedicated; mob turned back in Mount Sterling
25 Paris, then on to other counties
26 Paris speech
27 Christian Church ultimatum to Cornelison
28 Reid in Winchester
29 Richmond
30 Carlisle

May 1 Flemingsburg; cowhiding in Paris that day
3 Maysville
4 Bracken County
5 Reid in Robertson County; Cornelison's later charges
6 Maysville
7 Vanceburg
8 Greenup
9 Grayson
10 Grayson, Catlettsburg
11 Church expels Cornelison
13 Reid back in office
15 Goes to Judge Brock's law office

Chapter 7

A Madman

After leaving the blind woman, Richard Reid continued to Judge Calvin Brock's law office, on Maysville Street, about a block from Cornelison's place of business. They discussed a case of theirs just decided in federal court, and Dick Reid sighed, "Well, that ends that suit." After some casual conversation, Brock said he had to leave to attend to some other clients, and Reid, complaining of a severe headache, asked if he could stay for a moment and rest on the bed Judge Brock had on the second floor. Brock replied that he certainly could and then departed around 10:00 A.M., leaving the front door unlocked so Reid could leave when he wanted. About an hour later, Brock returned with an acquaintance, and they talked for some thirty minutes. With the dinner hour approaching, Brock went upstairs to wash.[1]

He found Richard Reid dead of a gunshot wound to the head.

Brock yelled for help, and doctors and others soon crowded in the small room. Reid's body lay on its back, his left arm on his chest, his right at his side. Blood pooled by his head. On the floor was his .38 caliber Smith and Wesson revolver with one spent shell. The physicians found the bullet had entered behind the right ear and had exited back of the left one. The only entrances to the room had been through Brock's office or via an outside staircase, but that door had remained locked from the inside. Someone discovered a handwritten card on the bureau. In pencil, Reid had scrawled the words, "Mad! mad! Forgive me, dear wife, and love to the boy." He had not signed the piece of paper. But the situation seemed clear to those present.[2]

Judge Reid had committed suicide.

Word of his death spread rapidly and soon reached Cornelison. Ashen and shakened by the news, he said in a faltering voice, "I am sorry." Then at night he boarded an eastbound train, leaving behind his wife and children. He feared for his life—and well he might. As he headed to the depot, someone cried out, "There goes the wretch; hang him." The next day a newspaper reported that men in Mount Sterling sought mob justice for Cornelison; another called him "Judge Reid's real murderer." When Cornelison finally got off the train in the relative safety of Ashland, he reportedly paced the floor and looked like a haunted man.[3]

Back in Mount Sterling, Mrs. Reid was entertaining several women visitors she had invited to join her in her bedroom that day, when a servant announced the arrival of a friend. Thinking he was there to discuss politics, she asked, "Do you bring good news?" His face, then his words, quickly told her he did not. Absolutely distraught "with almost unbearable grief," she and other family members could hardly accept this latest and cruelest news. Friends feared for Bettie's life as well. Her own ghosts of memory stalked her.[4]

A coroner's jury of six men quickly met, examined the evidence, and concluded: "We, the jury, find the deceased, Richard Reid, came to his death by a pistol shot from his own hand, between 9 and 11 A. M., May 15th, 1884." But that formal statement only gave closure to the official process. So many other questions remained unanswered and begged for explanation.[5]

Why had he done it? Why had Reid determined that death would be better than life, that his problems could not be solved except by suicide? On the day before Reid's death, one of the local papers had reprinted a *New York Sun* story entitled "Insane Moments" and subtitled "Homicidal and Suicidal Impulses That Spring Up Involuntarily." While Reid likely read that story, it is unknown whether it influenced his decision. In fact, as a friend of Reid's told that same newspaper a week after the suicide, "What occurred in that room God only knows. . . . But something did occur."[6]

That remains a great mystery, one without any certain answers. Just what did occur and, most of all, why? No historian could re-create with certainty what happened after Reid walked up those stairs. Yet unless that final mystery is unraveled, his whole life can never be completely explained. And so to understand the life and death of Richard Reid fully, his personal past must be compared with what is known about the action that ended that history—his suicide.

In Reid's era, suicide carried with it a tremendous stigma, yet historically that had not always been the case. As a student and onetime teacher of Greek and Roman culture, Reid had read of what people of those eras considered noble suicides—Cato, Socrates, and Lucretia, for instance. In the Homeric poems, most such deaths resulted from a heroic rather than a melancholy reason. Cicero had written that actors need not remain on the stage of life until the play's end, if they have had applause enough. Roman philosopher Seneca stressed the quality of one's life over its quantity. But Plato and Aristotle had both condemned suicide, one because it went against basic nature, and the other because it threatened the authority of the state. Those views gained force when St. Augustine proclaimed that the murder of self absolutely sinned against God. A church council in A.D. 452 pronounced suicide the work of the devil. But some twelve hundred years later, such authors as John Donne, David Hume, and Charles Louis de Secondat Montesquieu all defended, to some degree, the right of the individual to take his or her own life, while Immanuel Kant and others continued to see that action as a violation of moral law. The debate continued over the centuries. Legally, the state supported those who saw it as a crime against the nation and a sin against the community. Into the early 1800s, the French hanged suicides upside down on the gallows; the British pounded a stake through their hearts and confiscated their property. The law blamed the victims of the act, and the suicide taboo ran strong. But Reid knew that authors and philosophers throughout history had given different answers as well.[7]

He may have been less knowledgeable about the scientific thought of his era regarding suicide, though not necessarily so. Reid likely had not read one of the major authorities on the subject, published three years earlier in Vienna in 1881. *Der Selbstmord als sociale Massenerscheinung der modernen Civilisation,* written by Thomas G. Masaryk (later president of the Czech state), found close correlations between suicide and level of education, and suicide and mental illness. Masaryk argued that taking one's life indicated a lack of moral courage. He blamed the growing suicide rates on the decline in religious faith and called for a revival of church-inspired moral discipline.

But if he did not see that work, Reid may well have read two shorter studies, one by William Knighton in the 1881 *Littell's Living Age* and the other by M. G. Mulhall in the 1883 *Contemporary Review,* both widely circulated journals. Noting the increasing prevalence of suicide, as "men are everywhere becoming more weary of the burden of life," Knighton presented various reasons for that, but closed by suggesting that "want of sleep usually plays an important part in the tragedy," particularly in combination with mental disorders. Mulhall found the same situation—a growing number of self-inflicted deaths—and traced that to insanity, grief, drink, and various other causes. He discussed the fact that three-fourths of the suicides were men and concluded that though "the female intellect [is] less powerful than man's, it is at the same time better balanced." His solution to the problem of suicide included increased use of coffee (and less liquor), better homes (and less crowding), fewer marriages of cousins, reduced pressure in schools on children, higher religious training, more weddings, and greater sense "of the duties that each of us owes to society." Few of those seemed to apply to the teetotaler, married, well-to-do, and religious Reid, and such articles likely meant little to him and his decision.[8]

Much more crucial to Reid's thought process—if indeed one did take place—may have been religious thinking on the issue of suicide. Reading his Bible itself provided him no explicit prohibition, for it contained over a half-dozen examples of suicides, including those of Saul falling on his sword and Sampson pulling the temple down. Despite the mass suicide at Masada, the Jewish tradition had developed strong prohibitions against suicide, based on biblical readings. But in the early Christian era, many martyrs died for the faith and with the expectation of entering a better world. Out of that background came St. Augustine's forceful stand against suicide, based on the commandment "Thou shall not kill." Only through God's expressed will should a person take his or her life, said St. Augustine. Yet later religious thought, as offered by Donne, for instance, affirmed that "whensoever I may justly depart with this life, it is by a summons from God." Other arguments grew up to support St. Augustine's basic conclusion, however. Thomas Aquinas suggested that since God gave life and controlled it, then those who took their own life sinned against the Lord. John Locke in his *Second Treatise on Government* used the religious arguments that humans, as servants to a higher being, must do that master's bidding; to commit suicide and remove that servant opposed the master's will. Others considered the taking of one's life as an action against the "natural" will to live and thus antagonistic to the covenant established by God in the beginning of the world. By Reid's time, then, most religious thought, and the philosophers he had long respected, condemned suicide.[9]

But not all. Religious beliefs both inhibited suicide and facilitated it. Elements in Western theological teaching viewed death as the release of the soul from the corrupt world, freeing it to go to a better place where deceased loved ones could reunite at last. It also valued self-sacrifice for morally good causes, as, for example, when a physician courted death by entering plague areas to provide relief and treat victims. In those instances, although the actions seemed suicidal, they earned subsequent approval as heroic. People applauded such men and women as Christ-like martyrs who then passed to a world beyond. As a deeply religious man, Reid knew those elements of his religion, just as he understood the strong and more prevalent prohibitions against suicide. Did he act *because* of his religion, or *despite* it?[10]

Even if Richard Reid knew the various dimensions of the historical, scientific, and religious aspects of the debate on suicide, of course, that still fails to explain fully why he acted as he did. To solve the mystery of Reid's death requires looking at it through a modern-day psychological lens and subjecting it to scrutiny based on current understandings of suicide.

While much has been learned about why people kill themselves in the nearly 120 years since Reid's death, even more remains unknown. As a textbook recently noted: "The truth is that we do not fully understand why people commit suicide." A few generalizations do hold true: suicide rates go up in the spring and continue to be much higher for males than females. Women tend to use gas or pills, men guns or hanging. In short, the typical person who successfully kills self is an older male who, in a state of despair, ends his life in the spring by a pistol shot—in other words, a Richard Reid.[11]

But if Reid fits the profile of the person who dies, that still does not explain why he killed himself—or why others do. Over the years, various studies have offered answers, usually falling into one of two categories, psychological or sociological. One psychological view, for instance, suggests that attempts at suicide represent not a real desire to die, but rather a "cry for help," a calling out by the desperate for aid and attention. But that applies more to those who do not succeed in their attempt and who subconsciously do not really want to die. Reid did.[12]

Another common psychoanalytic theory emphasizes the idea of displacement. In a 1910 meeting in Sigmund Freud's Vienna apartment, one person present stated that "No one kills himself who did not want to kill another, or at best, wish death to another." Subsequent Freudian theory suggests that individuals then unconsciously turn such aggressive feelings inward and murder themselves instead. They may do so to induce guilt in others as well. Some part of Reid may have wanted to do what the crowd sought and kill his assailant, just as another part of him, his better self, said he must not.

Faced with that dilemma, his inner voices produced his suicide. Or perhaps it went beyond that and represented something else entirely.[13]

But the Freudian approach, by itself, ignores almost totally any societal factors. Yet sociological theories regarding suicide had long existed as well, with one of the most influential emerging not long after Reid's death. In 1897, French sociologist Emile Durkheim's *Le Suicide* used statistics to show causes for the growing suicide rates in "civilized" countries and suggested various catagories of suicide. He described individuals who took their own lives for the good of society or to meet societal demands—such as the Japanese hara-kiri, or the soldier who falls on a hand grenade to save his comrades—or suicides that occurred when an individual's relation to the society all around changed so suddenly that the person could no longer adapt, or deaths of people who felt alienated from both the individuals and the society around them, who no longer considered themselves integrated into that life, and who had few social supports from family or community. His understanding of suicide stressed that it came more from social forces outside a person's control and represented an extreme reaction to them. As another said, suicide thus stood as a "vote of no confidence in the social order." Writing thirteen years after Reid's death, sociologist Durkheim could have been easily describing the Kentuckian, for—as Reid saw it—his support group, his community, had not accepted him, and he had become alienated from them. Few cared for him any longer; he had little to live for; he died. Or so that theory suggested.[14]

But no single theory satisfactorily explains Reid's decision. As one author argued, "Individuals kill themselves for a number and variety of psychologically felt motives." Others have stressed that the social and psychopathological explanations complement each other and both have worth in the attempt to try to detail why human self-destruction occurs. Both the mind of the man and the social forces that are—or are not—part of his being constitute the mix that makes up the totality of an existence. A combination of answers unlocks the Reid mystery.[15]

Perhaps the cause of Reid's suicide, then, is not to be found solely in such issues as community but rather in Cornelison's cane. In one sense, the people may have been more correct than they knew when they blamed Cornelison for Reid's death, for brain trauma can produce the symptoms that create suicide. Cornelison had caned the judge so hard that he tore and cut the hat Reid wore. The day after the assault Reid had a massive, swollen bruise behind his ear, near the base of the brain, that did not go away quickly. In the month after the attack, Reid suffered from severe and frequent headaches. When given a detailed description of Reid's wounds and the possible effects on him, a modern-day physician concluded that Reid had likely suffered traumatic brain injury to the occipital or temporal areas. Such an injury can produce not only intense and unabating headaches, but also "irritability, depression, or . . . alteration in personality." As Reid's note said, perhaps the pain did drive him "mad," or at least cause him to fear for his future sanity. His pistol had been aimed at the spot where the pain had been greatest, where his shame most showed.[16]

The headaches also contributed to Reid's sleeplessness, which may have been a possible—though somewhat more unlikely—factor as well. Following lack of sleep, in a time of extreme stress, and "when adequate coping mechanisms are lacking," sleepwalking or arousal parasomnias can result. Reid had exhibited such sleep disturbances early in life, but less so since his marriage. Circumstances related to his case once more caused his night demons to rise up. Moreover, while the literature remains cautionary, many recent studies suggest that males in particular can engage in serious aggression while sleepwalking. Plato noted that situation centuries ago, when he wrote:

> In all of us, even in good men,
> there is a lawless, wild-beast nature
> which peers out in sleep

Unaware of, and unable to control, their "wild-beast" behavior, men commit violent acts—including murder or possibly self-murder. Even in Reid's time that condition was recognized. In an 1879 case, the Court of Appeals supported the use of sleepwalking as a proper defense in a murder case where a sleeping man shot a porter who was trying to wake him. The justices noted that "loss of sleep and mental anxiety" helped create that state, and once in it, a man would be free from legal responsibility for his actions. Some modern studies question such interpretations as misreading the evidence, though most agree that violence can occur. But suicide while sleepwalking remains more problematical. Would Reid have written a note while sleepwalking? Probably not. Though unlikely, it should not be completely dismissed that Reid killed himself while sleepwalking.[17]

But if that effect of his injuries remains highly speculative, clearly the physical damage to his brain joined with sociological and psychological causes as being factors in producing depression. And virtually all studies indicate that somewhere between one-half and three-fourths of suicides result from some form of clinical depression. Edwin S. Shneidman's longtime psychological study of that condition led him to regard suicide, in the words of others, "as a conscious effort to seek a solution to a problem that is causing intense suffering. To the sufferer, this solution ends consciousness and unendurable pain—what Melville in *Moby Dick* termed an 'insufferable anguish.' All hope and sense of constructive action are gone." Different studies have also noted that such depression clouds normally rational thinking, so that while the leap into the oblivion of suicide may seem the most reasonable course to the victim, a more rational mind would come up with alternatives that would be more reasonable still.[18]

But depression emerges not just from such physical causes as the injuries Reid suffered and their effects. A sudden change in a relationship may create depression as well. If caring others suddenly withhold their support, then hopelessness and helplessness grow, and the decision for death becomes stronger. In Reid's case, he believed in and lived a romantic love, where a spouse's affection lay at the center of happiness. His compassionate marriage meant that each member of the union respected and honored the other, and each depended on the other. Yet husband and wife also each had duties in marriage, and even Mrs. Reid, in her more equality-oriented marriage, still expected her husband to display such virtues of manhood as courage, generosity, and dignity. And Reid had done that, in the ways he could. He had never put himself in a position where physical courage would be demanded, but instead had taken strong public stances on various issues. In gaining Bettie's admiration, he had shown himself to be the perfect Christian Gentleman. But to do so, Reid had to maintain a careful balance in his life. He desperately needed the nurturing and love his wife provided and had to have her esteem. This nurturing and love was called into question when, after his cowhiding, in his law office, she seemed to suggest that a real man would go out and kill Cornelison for what he had done. Though she soon retreated from that stand—and probably quickly regretted it—the memory remained with Reid and the words echoed within. Furthermore, the newspaper version spread the story, and enemies taunted him with it, again and again. Her words may have cut even deeper than almost anyone suspected, for she knew Reid's hidden secret, another great mystery of his life.[19]

It was a secret he revealed to almost no one, and very few outside his family had ever been aware of it. While a birth defect may have been present, when his nurse had "sportively seized" the fifteen-month-old Reid, she had inflicted a "serious injury." In the language of the time, he had suffered a "violent rupture"—or what modern physicians would likely label a bilateral (double) hernia. In that condition, the weakness in the abdominal wall can result in a protrusion of the contents of the abdomen. Any strain or increase in pressure—a cough, bowel movement, or even a strong hug—can cause a reemergence of the hernia, which would then have to be pushed back. If the hernia almost always protrudes, then some device may be used to restrict it. That apparently characterized Reid's situation, for his doctor later wrote that Reid "was a victim to the torture of rude instruments." He wore a harsh steel contraption until he was at least seventeen years old. Richard Reid remembered few times when he did not live with pain. The steel truss constantly reminded him of his bodily limitations. But then so did his whole world of childhood. While all around him his friends played sports or engaged in the activities of children, he had to avoid physical exertion and only watch. He even had to shun overt displays of affection from his family, for a forceful hug could add to his suffering. That lack of physical intimacy made him appear reserved or even cold in manner to some of those he knew. His father, among others, had figuratively never embraced the son who could not perform as he expected or sought. Classmates would consider him effeminate because he did not engage in the manly activities, never knowing that he could not. In many ways, Reid had shown real courage in bearing his pain as he did and not letting it keep him from success. But those all around him never knew that. Instead, their responses made him grow up mostly lonely, as something of an outcast. Necessity forced him to transfer his energies and talents to intellectual achievements, where he won some of their approval as a result. And over time, step-by-step, he had become integrated into the community around him. But his infirmities always held him back. When others went off to fight in the Civil War, he had sought to join them and had asked a doctor if he could physically perform the duties of a soldier. When told that would be impossible, Reid swore the physician to keep his condition a "profound secret." And so it remained.[20]

Because of his physical problems, Reid had never fought a fight. When Cornelison began hitting him, it likely shocked his system, and his body probably reacted in such a way that Reid remembered nothing of what followed. He could not have easily fought back, even he had wanted to, because of his condition. In fact, the efforts made to try to escape the blows may have aggravated the hernia and added even more pain to the episode. After the assault, Reid could not tell people that was why he did not respond. For to acknowledge such physical infirmity would mean admitting that he was—to that era's thinking—really something less of a man, after all. He could have salvaged a part of honor had he told people why he could not have responded, but at the cost of manhood. Reid lost either way—and remained silent.

The issue of manhood figured prominently in one other result of a severe inguinal hernia, such as Reid likely had. In some of those cases, the testes may intermittently retract back into the abdominal cavity, or in some cases may not descend at all. Either way, they can atrophy, which, as a doctor notes, "would emasculate the individual." Infertility would usually result. A hernia could also make normal sexual relations painful as well. That situation may have been the reason Reid doubted that he would ever marry. When his romantic love for Sallie, then for Bettie later, overcame those concerns, his words at the time suggest that he also feared marriage for what it might reveal about himself to those he loved. Had Mrs. Reid never been married before, she might not have known, or concluded, that her husband differed from others in that way. But she had been married before Reid. Yet she loved him and, as the scant evidence suggests, carefully initiated him on their wedding night. It was a fragile matter, however. A quarter century before, a "Southern Physician" had written in a national journal that "in men, real or fancied impotence is very apt to induce self-destruction," but Reid had displaced such concerns by raising Reid Rogers as his son. Still, sexual intimacy in the Reid household revealed Richard Reid at his most vulnerable. Any change could upset that sensitive equation of trust, one that had produced much happiness over time.[21]

Bettie Reid's words after the whipping ripped apart Reid's carefully crafted domestic world. To him, she had been accepting of his limitation, had loved him, had made him feel manly in their home. If he had sexual self-doubts and feelings of inadequacy, she had calmed them, as well as many of his old fears. Moreover, when he did give love he did so fiercely: "He clung to those he loved . . . with an intensity amounting almost to worship." At one level, then, when the angry words of Bettie Reid came, they tore at his psyche and struck down the fragile manhood she had helped create. When she became ill soon thereafter—whether because of psychosomatic causes or real grief over what was happening to her husband, and the image of him she honored—all that caused Reid greater mental pain, for his course of action seemed to be the source of her distress. Manhood, even the definition of Christian manhood, placed the honor, care, and responsibility of wives with their husbands. Now he seemed to have failed her there as well. As the bedridden Bettie and the forsaken Dick Reid slept in their separate rooms, it symbolized the increasing distance that suddenly had divided their marriage. If he had lost the respect and love of the person he most cared about, then he had little left.[22]

What, then, drove Richard Reid to suicide? A 1968 survey concluded that the typical suicide exhibited one or more of several characteristics: "(1) Ambivalence—the desire . . . to live and to die, present at the same time; (2) feelings of hopelessness and helplessness, futility, and inadequacy to handle problems; (3) feelings of either physical or psychological exhaustion . . . ; (4) marked feelings of unrelieved anxiety or tension, depression, anger, and/ or guilt; (5) feelings of chaos and . . . inability to restore order; (6) mood swings . . . ; (7) . . . inability to see alternatives . . . ; (8) loss of interest in usual activities, such as sex, hobbies, and work; (9) physical distress, such as insomnia. . . ." A more recent study similarly summarized the many motives as "aggression directed inward . . . ; efforts to force love from others; efforts to make amends for perceived past wrongs; . . . the desire for reincarnation; the desire to rejoin a dead loved one; and the desire or need to escape from stress . . . [or] pain." In both instances, virtually all those could apply to Reid's case. But in their brevity, those abstract words do not convey the complexity and the pain in Reid's decision.[23]

For everywhere Reid looked, few appeared to care. And the hurt increased and the despair intensified. People seemed to forget the Richard Reid who had been a good public servant, a fine scholar, a loyal churchman, a devoted husband, a loving stepfather, a kind man. The better angels of those around him had been overwhelmed by the darker demons within. Reid had spoken of the frailty and falterings of his race, but had also said that, in the end, goodness would prevail. But it had not. His very view of human nature appeared flawed, or even wrong. The people—his people— had not praised his actions very much, and the court of public opinion had ruled that the judge had dishonored not only himself but also his community, thus dishonoring them all. They would shun him for that insult. Increasingly, he was losing most of the support groups that had so long allowed him to cope and achieve, and with that came his loss of all sense of community. He had tried to live the perfect life, but it proved not perfect enough because it failed to incorporate a key element of his society's historical and violent culture. The things he valued most, the truths he held most dear, now disappeared, one by one, chiefly destroyed by the words of his friends and those he loved.[24]

How could he regain their hope and respect, and his own sense of honor and manhood? Or could he ever? In the first century B.C., Publilius Syrus had asked, "What is left when honor is lost?" What indeed? Reid could not—would not—take the course the masses cried for, by killing another. His own code did not allow that, nor did his personal beliefs about the sanctity of life. Yet that decision left him hopeless for future redemption. His fire and passion for life disappeared, as honor departed. Like the Romantic poets, the isolated and lonely Reid had wandered from human society in search of redemption and, finding none, become more "enamored of eternity." As he sought answers, his religion offered solutions, at least as he interpreted them.[25]

Reid did not fear death. Hamlet had hesitated before the great unknown as he spoke of "the dread of something after death":

> The undiscover'd country, from whose bourn
> No traveller returns—puzzles the will,
> And makes us rather bear those ills we have
> Than fly to others that we know not of . . .
> Thus conscience does make cowards of us all.

But to Reid, he considered the afterlife known territory, a place to which he could bravely go and leave the ills behind. When in college he had written that "death comes clothed in no artificial terrors." Understanding the hidden ways of God, believers saw life's end, he said, as a mere change of state. They could look back and say: " 'I have done my duty. The world has been the theatre of my actions, humanity my audience, and heaven shall be my home.' " He welcomed an end to earthly consciousness, but, like the early Christian martyrs, did not consider himself a suicide victim. Rather, in his conceptualizations and rationalization of the act, he may well have viewed his death as a self-sacrifice. Like Christ, he too would die for the sins of others, a martyr to the cause of the law and Christian morality.[26]

In his state of mind that last day, Reid perhaps also believed he honored manhood by his death. "Real Men" in Reid's society killed, often other men. The judge, however, could not hurt others without hurting his own sense of self. But he did have courage, honor, and manhood, as he defined it and lived it. He would show his wife and his world that he was indeed a man. He could kill. He would have the courage to kill himself.

When Reid went to Judge Brock's office that morning in May, he probably had been contemplating suicide more and more each day, as his depression grew and grew, as his internal voices debated life or death. But he likely had not planned to end his life in that particular place and at that time. As he said then, he simply had a headache. Perhaps when he woke from what had become rare sleep, the pain remained, or had grown worse. For a man whose whole life had depended on reason, that may have, once more, caused him to fear for his sanity. He had already endured so much in life, for so long, that he could endure little more. While Bettie Reid had not physically died—a frequent cause of suicide—Reid had suffered a sense of loss, wondered if he had lost her love, and feared that he had forfeited her respect. He knew that he no longer commanded the strong support of his community and worried that even his loyal church members had turned against him; he believed that his personal faith would take him to a better place after death, a place where Sallie awaited, as did a painless new life and ultimate vindication.

When they found Reid's body, it appeared to have been facing the mirror in the room when it fell. On 15 May 1884, Richard Reid awoke from his brief sleep and looked at himself in the mirror. What he saw before him, no one knows. But it was not hope. He felt the pistol in his pocket, made his decision, and wrote his hurried note. No internal voices called to him loud enough to cause him to stop. To his mind, death offered the only answer. He pulled the trigger.[27]

Reid may have been alone in that room, but by their harsh words, inaction, and lack of support, the people had also killed him, just as if they had held the gun in their hands. His blood stained them all. Reid himself may have believed, in that time of his "madness," that he had shown his detractors that he had courage, when he took his own life. Yet in so doing, he also admitted that, in one way, they had been right. He had been a coward, in that he could now no longer daily bear to face his wife and the world. Ironically, while he voiced the higher ideals, in truth he really did accept key parts of the code he so publicly attacked. The southern cult of honor and the American definition of manhood had been more a part of his being than he had realized. Reid may have been baptized in a Christian, religious, legal code of honor, but he had also been washed in the blood of the Lost Cause mentality that he so honored and whose hero, Robert E. Lee, he so admired. Shakespeare had written, "Take honour from me, and my life is done." Reid had lost the respect of almost everyone, but he still could have gone on with life had his own conscience told him that his state of honor, as he defined it, remained intact. If Reid considered himself right and above reproach in his own judgment, then he could remain more indifferent to the arrows of contempt. All would not be lost if he had preserved real honor as he understood it. But Reid could not live if he also lost his own self-respect—and he had. That was his tragedy. In the end, he could not break free of the past that had formed him. Reid lived in a prison of his own history, and it destroyed him. He had died on the altar of honor.[28]

Chapter 8

A Matter of Vengeance and Victims

When people take their own lives, they often do so because, to their own thinking, they have no alternative, no other way out of the problem they see themselves confronting. Depressed and despondent, they may filter out the positives around them and see, more and more, only their difficulties. Reasonable answers to their situations may not be seen clearly through their glasses of desperation. When Richard Reid put the pistol to his head, he forfeited all the good that could be his future on the Earth. He would never again see the stepson he loved or all the other young men and women he and Bettie had raised as their own in his house. No more would he hear the laughter of children in the streets, or offer kind thoughts, such as to the blind woman, as heard by the orphan boy. Never again would he receive heartfelt thanks from an innocent client, who had received justice because of Reid's work. The jurist would never have the opportunity to influence someone in the years ahead and perhaps turn around a life; he would not be able to comfort those in need. Reid would not be able to advance black rights or women's rights; he would never again be able to share his deep love for humanity on this earth. Nor would he ever know just how many friends he really did have. The mind that caused his suicide robbed Reid of hope.[1]

The kind of visual and vocal support so lacking while Reid lived was displayed in guilty force at his funeral, "one of the largest ever held in the State." On a bright, cloudless Saturday afternoon, on 17 May 1884, the Christian church in Mount Sterling quickly filled. The pallbearers bringing in the silver-trimmed casket included Governor Proctor Knott, Chief Justice

Tom Hargis, two other Court of Appeals judges, both of the Superior Court justices, and fellow Mount Sterling attorney W. H. Holt. The Reverend John W. McGarvey, professor of sacred history at the College of the Bible in Lexington, delivered a sermon stressing that Reid's "madness" resulted from the false articles and the wrong voices of the people: "It was echoed in his ears from every side; it was hurled in his teeth, and he was led to believe it." By such "vile slanders," Reid's insanity developed. As a people, Kentuckians continued to live by the rule of avenging every wrong by lawless action and not by the church's law. Because of that, concluded the Reverend Mr. McGarvey, "I fearlessly declare that this was not a suicide, but a murder—a murder beginning in a treacherous assault and continued by slow tortures until the end was reached."[2]

Next, French-born Christian Church minister and Kentucky University president Charles Louis Loos offered a few words about an event where "Christianity was on one side and brutality on the other." He told those assembled that what had occurred affected not just Mount Sterling but the nation. Reid had shown America that through his "unquestioned manhood" he would rather suffer than violate the law. His life—and his death—must thus not be forgotten, and his "heroic Christian fortitude" must stand as a model for future generations. Finally, a church elder arose and told of his lifelong friend, now dead before him: "As I stand here to-day, I ask myself, 'Am I guiltless of this man's blood?' 'Are you?' I fear not." Reid's "sensitive soul" needed sympathy from his friends, but found little: "His great heart could bear no more, and so it broke." For himself, said Elder Shouse, he simply hoped to meet Reid in the place of no tears, "where thy spirit, too noble to be comprehended by grosser natures of earth, shall be fully understood." It then ended. The men and women filed out of the church, and a mile-long procession went to the Machpelah Cemetery, where the society of Odd Fellows performed their special funeral rites over the mortal remains of Richard Reid. As a newspaper concluded: "And thus closed the last act of a tragedy which for sadness has never been equaled in the state." But in reality, more scenes remained to be played out in the Reid controversy.[3]

A few days later, numerous attorneys gathered in the capitol to honor one of their own. Reid's former mentors Porter and Duvall, classmate J. Q. A. Ward, and many others assembled to hear comments from the "silver-tongued orator" W. C. P. Breckinridge, and six others, including Chief Justice Hargis. Reid's onetime opponent and then friend, Hargis recalled

Reid's good humor and calm demeanor: "Such was the man who was sacrificed by a false public opinion, which waited and condemned, while envy and slander slaughtered him." The outgoing court justice now called the code duello "ignorant and brutal," something that deserved no respect from intelligent people. Instead, argued Hargis, "It is the coward's refuge, the bully's boast, and a wart upon the fair name of Kentucky." Let this day, he intoned, see the start of a better public opinion, one born out of "the grave of a martyr for the noblest principle of humanity." Very quickly, Reid's friends had now made his course the one of honor, heroism, and manhood.[4]

The state and national press took up that theme, to a degree, but also emphasized Reid's insanity, his Christian example, and his death as the triumph of the code of violence. And a few still proclaimed that he should have killed Cornelison or that the assailant should now die violently. Outside of Kentucky, for example, papers in Baltimore, New York, Cleveland, and St. Louis, among others, noted how depression and disgrace caused Reid's madness, though the *New York Times* reporter suggested that Reid only pretended to have a headache to foster the illusion of mental illness and really killed himself because of shame and cowardice. But most focused, in either front-page stories or editorials, on the southern code of honor as a cause of his death. In a lengthy editorial, for instance, the *St. Louis Post-Dispatch* declared that "while he had the nerve to die by his own hand, he had not the courage to bear the suspicion of personal cowardice to which the affair had exposed him." They stated that "the traditional and ineradicable sentiment of his State called for personal vengeance, quick and deadly," an idea they found to be "a relic of barbarianism." A San Francisco newspaper said Reid had the choice of either killing or submitting to the indignity, and had done neither by killing himself. The *Chicago Tribune*, shocked by Reid's suicide, asked, "How many more victims must fall before the people of Kentucky will demand that this code of cowardice shall be abolished . . . ?" In New York, editors considered Reid's death to be evidence of the South's "medieval society," where the coward who assaults is praised and the victim of the attack criticized. E. L. Godkin, writing in *The Nation,* called the self-murder pathetic and tragic. It showed, he said, that Kentucky's social code required a judge to take revenge in his own hands, "exactly as if he were a . . . New Guinea savage."[5]

As more than one Kentucky paper noted, it was well that the stock market crashed the same day as Reid's suicide, diverting attention from his action, or the denunciations from the national press might have been even greater in volume. Not so distracted, newspapers in the commonwealth devoted much attention to the whole issue. Some simply saw Reid's suicide as the act of a madman. The *Catlettsburg Central Methodist* said that such must be the case, for "no man while in his right mind ever took his own life." Emphasizing Reid's personal and political problems, a Paris editor termed his action that of a "temporarily deranged" man. An often-critical *Louisville Post* appraised the death as "the most melancholy and unfortunate event in the history of Kentucky" and melodramatically told how Reid, without sleep and "deserted by former friends," peered into his wife's eyes and saw only despair. Then, "he looks in the face of his boy only to realize that the shame of the father will be visited upon the son," and thus decided, in a fit of insanity, to die. (The one problem with that colorful and widely quoted re-creation was that stepson Reid Rogers had not seen Dick Reid since the attack, had remained at college, and because of the measles had not even been able to attend the funeral. He had returned home only the next day.) But to some, the death meant only that it had been Richard Reid, the madman.[6]

Some newspaper accounts, more charitably, stressed Reid's Christian spirit. The same *Louisville Post* editorial concluded that "Reid represented the right. He represented humanity. He represented the law. He represented the cause of God." Others noted his "high-toned Christian principles" and how they caused him to kill himself rather than bloody his hands with the life of another human. The *Paris True Kentuckian* affirmed that Reid considered God stronger than man and his Christian duty greater than personal cries for vengeance. Yet, said the editor, that course brought "the Devil's crew, the vanguard of vice and crime," and all the "blackguards and bullies" to denounce him and hound him. They murdered a Christian leader, concluded the paper.[7]

But most commentators concentrated not on the religious Reid or the "insane" one, but rather on what all this meant for justice and the law in Kentucky. Unable to provide any other answer, several simply held "society" responsible for Reid's death and said little beyond that. The *Winchester Democrat* averred that only when public sentiment sustained Reid's moral principles would the methods of Cornelison end. Watterson's *Courier-Journal* similarly attacked the "vitiated" public view that endorsed a code calling for the death of the assailant. As a result, people questioned Reid's motives and stands, and "in a State of brave men, few men were brave enough to stand with or for him." In short, he had not been the coward;

Kentucky had. That newspaper's companion sheet, the *Evening Times,* confessed that a cowhide whipping represented "an ineffaceable stigma, a degradation utter and unmentionable" that ruled Kentucky. A death must result, or total shame. Under the code, said the paper, "our record is stained with much blood." When Reid forgave as a Christian and followed his oath as a judge, he stood for a new civilization for the commonwealth, one less savage and barbarous. But he could not convert the people to his "higher type of manhood" and died as a martyr to their sentiment. And what of Cornelison? The Vanceburg paper suggested he would be a victim as well. His children would live in "deep and damning infamy" while their father—"unfit for heaven, unwanted in hell"—would be forever haunted by Reid's ghost, constantly sounding "the knell of doom to his diseased and crime-stained soul." In one way at least, then, justice would win out. But too late for Reid.[8]

Amazingly, a few papers still criticized Reid for not trying to kill Cornelison. From different ends of the state, in Hickman and Newport, papers said 90 percent of the people demanded that Reid avenge himself, and he could not stand their rebukes: "Judge Reid killed the wrong man." But perhaps the greatest irony came from an editorial in the formerly critical *Interior Journal.* The paper now praised Reid's moral courage and religious forbearance, and said he did right in following the course of the law. Then, in the next paragraph, in the same editorial, the paper argued that "if there ever was a case which demanded the prompt action of Judge Lynch the present is one." Calling himself a "law-loving" man, the editor nevertheless concluded that Cornelison "has forfeited his neck. Let him pay the penalty." That sentiment showed that, for some of least, Reid's death taught them nothing. A powerful tide continued to flow against all that Reid had lived—and died—for. The regeneration of Kentucky sentiment seemed a still-distant dream.[9]

If in life Richard Reid had not sought revenge against those who had wronged him, after his death, his friends worked very hard to wreak political retribution on those they held responsible for his demise. In a sense, *they* would defend Reid's honor and do their duty to him, as an obligation, even after death. Their attentions centered, most immediately, on Circuit Judge Robert Riddell, principal candidate against Reid for the court seat in the primary. Once Cornelison's various "defenses" appeared, allies of Reid came to believe that Cornelison had just been an unknowing dupe in the political race. As the assailant provided details of how he had "discovered" that Reid had betrayed him in the master commissioner imbroglio, it began to appear that Riddell had fed him those "facts" and that motive. Others suggested that Riddell supporters had planted the seed of distrust about the *Howard* case in Cornelison's mind as well, hoping all of that would cause a confrontation, which, given Reid's personality, might not reflect well on him. If that had been part of a political strategy, then it succeeded more than Reid's enemies had hoped. As the *New York Times* reported soon after the attack, "It is thought politics had something to do with the trouble since, in Reid's district, the proof that a man will not fight is equivalent to his death as a politician." Whether coincidental or not, quickly after the assault, Riddell began to campaign in his opponent's home county, normally a breach of political etiquette at the time. Nor did Riddell ever express condolences to Reid or his personal regrets and sympathy after the attack. Had politics started the process that ended in Reid's death? The idea infuriated Reid's allies.[10]

Supporters determined that they would do all they could to ensure Riddell's defeat. The day following the funeral, Justice Hargis and Reid's partner Henry Stone met most of the afternoon, planning their strategy against their common enemy, Riddell. The next day, County Court Day in Mount Sterling, Stone—who had wept openly when he had seen Reid's body—fired the opening shots of the political attack. In a speech at the courthouse, after bitterly criticizing Riddell's course, he called on Montgomery County Democrats to give their delegate votes to the other chief candidate, Laban T. Moore, instead, adding that should Riddell receive the nomination, "he can not be elected." Moreover, said Stone, he "ought to be defeated." Not long after that, newspaper stories appeared, quoting Hargis as saying that should Riddell win the nomination, the Democratic justice would "vote for and stump the district" for a Republican instead. In early June Hargis confirmed that he had spoken those words, "and I have no idea now that it will ever be regretted." Party divisions appeared beyond repair.[11]

In early June 1884, the Democratic convention to select the party's nominee for the appellate judgeship convened in Winchester. Stone, Hargis, and other Reid supporters did all they could to refuse compromise and defeat Riddell. The first ballot ended with 63½ for Riddell, 56 for Moore, and 47½ divided between two minor candidates. By day's end, 72 more ballots had changed nothing. A week and 150 votes later, despite what one paper called "bribery and bulldozing," the convention still had no nominee. Finally, late that day, after over 175 ballots, Robert Riddell won the nomination, 92–75, over Moore. The *Yeoman,* party organ for the Democrats, predicted that the candidate "cannot be beaten by any man in that Appellate district."[12]

William H. Holt was not so certain of that. In late June the former Republican candidate for the seat announced that he would run as an independent. A Mount Sterling attorney, Holt had been a close friend of Reid's. He had been Grand Marshal of the Odd Fellows lodge where Reid belonged; he had been one of the first people in the room where Reid lay dead; he had been a pallbearer at the funeral; he had eulogized his friend before the Montgomery County bar. Born in a log cabin in the same county (Bath) and in the same year as Stone, Holt quickly gained the support of Democrats Stone and Hargis. He also had other powerful allies outside his normal Republican circles. A paper noted that the "entire influence" of the Christian Church—to which Holt, Hargis, Stone, and Mrs. Reid all belonged—had gone against Riddell and for Holt. A story indicated that $25,000 in campaign funds had been gathered (a huge sum for the time) and that Bettie Reid had reportedly given $1,000 to Holt's race. Key Democratic leaders, such as Senator Cerro Gordo Williams, refused to speak for the candidate, and the *Courier-Journal* drew fire for its "mean and treacherous" attacks on Riddell. In return, the Democrats loyal to the nominee took up long-successful tactics and printed stories which indicated that Holt had referred to Jefferson Davis as an "arch traitor" and had instead praised black voters. The independent candidate hotly denied saying such words, and ex-Confederates Hargis and Stone supported him, taking away much of the sting of the attack. But the district the year before had given the Democrats a sizable 6,300 majority. Could Holt overcome that?[13]

As the 4 August 1884 results trickled in from across the forty-county district, it became clear that the race would be very close. Reid's Montgomery County showed how deep the divisions ran there, for native son Holt carried that usually Democratic area by 17 votes out of 2,450 cast. Riddell, in turn, barely won his home county of Estill by but 18 ballots. It went that way county by county, with Holt doing well in Republican areas, Riddell in Democratic ones, but by a much reduced margin. The Reid men had left the party and gone to Holt. Two weeks after the voting ended, two Appalachian counties still had not been recorded and Holt held a 42-vote margin, out of over 62,000 cast. One of the counties remaining to be counted, Lawrence, usually went Democratic; the other, Owsley, went heavily Republican as a rule. When the results finally arrived, Holt, with a large victory in Owsley, overcame Riddell's smaller one in Lawrence and won the election by a 620-vote margin, 33,603 to 32,983. He became the first Republican elected to the highest court of Kentucky and would be named chief justice four years later. But an ex-Confederate, Reid-trained Mount Sterling attorney James H. Hazelrigg, defeated him for reelection, in a race marked by racial arguments. Nevertheless, Holt had done what the Reid supporters wanted; he had beaten Riddell. Vengeance was theirs. The two men most responsible for that—Hargis and Stone—both soon moved to Louisville to practice law, for they had made serious enemies in their home areas. Henry Stone became city attorney there, then general counsel for the L&N Railroad. His only daughter, May Stone, helped found Hindman Settlement School in the mountains of eastern Kentucky and gained wide acclaim for her work. But by then, the political fallout of Reid's race had long ended.[14]

The legal ramifications of Cornelison's assault on Reid reverberated much longer than the political machinations, however. Soon after the attack, the assailant had been arraigned on the charge of "willful and malicious battery" and had been released on bond. Friendly newspapers quickly called for Cornelison to be tried for mere battery, a minor charge punishable by a small fine. But Reid's suicide changed the legal equation, for his friends sought to punish Cornelison as harshly as possible. When the case went before the circuit court in December 1884, the charge had been amended to read that Cornelison—"willfully and maliciously, and with the intent to wound and kill"—had assaulted him, had "cruelly and dangerously" beaten him, and had "greatly endangered" his life. Despite the descriptive words, the case remained one of assault and battery. Defending Cornelison of those charges was wealthy attorney and former congressman Thomas Turner, and future gubernatorial candidate A. T. Wood, among others. The commonwealth's attorney prosecuting the case had powerful help, in this very visible instance. Former state attorney general John Rodman and a future holder of that office, William J. Hendrick, joined attorneys W. R. Patterson and Henry L. Stone in the attempt to convict. Stone, in particular, made the prosecution and conviction of Cornelison his personal vendetta to avenge Reid. With such experienced and respected counsel on both sides, this clearly would not be a routine trial for simple assault.[15]

Cornelison sought to do everything he could to avoid having the jury hear the prosecution's witnesses against him, or, failing that, to keep the opposition attorneys from delivering their summaries and attacks on him.

Accordingly, once the jury was impaneled, Cornelison began a bizarre series of legal moves regarding his plea before the court. First, he offered to file a written response admitting the assault—but not the attempt to injure seriously—and requesting mercy. Prosecutors opposed that, and the judge agreed. Then the defense offered to plead guilty to a straight charge of assault and battery, but that too the prosecution refused, so a "not guilty" plea went into the books once more. Then, suddenly, Cornelison's lawyers pled guilty to the charge as read. However, the commonwealth's attorney sought, and received, the court's permission to introduce testimony to aid the jury in its deliberation regarding punishment. At that Cornelison now arose, said he had been improperly advised by his counsel, and asked to withdraw the guilty plea. His attempt to place the case in the jury's hands without arguments had failed. The judge overruled that motion to change the plea and permitted witnesses to be called. As expected, they swore to facts that painted a damning picture of Cornelison and mainly supported Reid's earlier version. As summarized by the court, Cornelison had struck an unsuspecting Reid several times with his cane and then some seventy-five more times with the cowhide whip, injuring him severely. Both Superior Court judges swore that Reid had nothing to do with the case that Cornelison said caused his assault on the judge; testimony showed that numerous attorneys had petitioned for Cornelison's removal as master commissioner and that Reid should be held blameless for that. In short, little emerged that supported Cornelison or provided mitigating circumstances for him, just as his defense feared. It became clear that he was doomed; the only question was what level of legal hell they would assign him to. Before final arguments began, Cornelison once more asked to change his plea to "not guilty," and the court allowed that, which gave his lawyers the opportunity to defend, but also allowed prosecution to attack.[16]

Cornelison's attorneys praised the code of honor, with Turner saying he would have killed rather than be degraded by the whip. They called for forgiveness to the father of eight small children and asked for minor punishment. A statement from the defendant was read in which he admitted guilt and requested mercy. The prosecution then concluded with a series of closing arguments by various attorneys, as was the accepted custom. Going first, Patterson noted that while even Judas had showed remorse over his betrayal, Cornelison had displayed no sense of repentance; he should be viewed by the jury as the murderer of an innocent man. Next, Hendrick asked that no mercy be given, for the defendant had sacrificed his family's happiness by his "devilish malevolence." Moreover, the twelve men judging Cornelison must, he declared, perform their duty and defend the law. All too often, Kentucky's soil had been "stained with the blood of innocent victims," by demanding private vengeance for a personal insult. It required cleansing with a new spirit of the law. General Rodman followed those words with similar sentiments, but also noted that one of the defense counsel, Turner, despite all the sworn sentiments, still had the gall to say that the handwriting on the margin of the disputed case was Reid's. Even now, he stressed, Cornelison and his supporters yielded not on the facts. Finally, Stone addressed the jury. His comments would later fill twenty-eight printed pages, as he detailed each point against Cornelison. He began by saying that it would have been better had the assailant shot Reid, for what he did only tortured the victim into a slow death. Stone recited Cornelison's "extraordinary vacillation" regarding his plea, summarized the damaging evidence in the *Howard* case, reiterated the master commissioner testimony, hinted that Riddell formulated the plot for political purposes, emphasized the harshness of the assault, and declared that Cornelison, "in the eyes of God," killed Reid. He called on the jury to vindicate Reid's trust in the law and stop "this violent spirit terrorizing our courts." Confine Cornelison, he concluded: "Dare to do your duty like men."[17]

As those jurors deliberated Cornelison's fate in the jury room, ten of the twelve wanted to sentence him to ten to twenty years for his crime. Another sought a five-year jail term. But one juror favored only thirty days in jail and, as was often the situation when that one person might hang the jury, his views heavily influenced the eventual findings. A decision was reached and the verdict read: "We of the jury find the defendant guilty, and fix his punishment at a fine of one cent and cost and imprisonment in the county jail for three years."[18]

Cornelison immediately appealed, and the case, ironically, first went before the Superior Court. All three sitting judges had to recuse themselves because of their ties to Reid, so the governor appointed three others to hear the arguments from Stone, Hendrick, Rodman, recently retired Judge Tom Hargis, and Attorney General P. Wat Hardin, for the commonwealth. Prominent attorney William Lindsay (who had defended him in the now-infamous *Howard* case) joined Cornelison's previous lawyers in arguing his side. The court announced its decision on 14 November 1885. First, it did not support Cornelison's claim that the judges had been illegally appointed or the argument that his family situation could be emphasized as mitigating testimony. However, by a two-to-one vote, the Superior Court overturned Cornelison's conviction. They found that regarding assault and battery, the common law as construed in Kentucky limited punishment on that charge to a fine only. His three-year jail term thus caused them to remand the case back to the circuit court for a new trial. That decision devastated Reid's supporters, but in one sense, it would have delighted Reid himself. For the court, which called the assault "one of unparalleled atrocity," had not taken legal revenge, but had instead followed the law as they interpreted it. In a strict sense, the law had ruled supreme. At the same time, however, that ruling also supported the arguments of those who defended the code of honor, for freeing Cornelison showed them that only personal actions could adequately satisfy the desire for vengeance.[19]

But it had not ended, for the case now went to the state's highest tribunal, the Court of Appeals. There new justice William H. Holt of Mount Sterling declined to sit on the case, and the three remaining judges heard arguments from basically the same set of attorneys as before. The 11 December 1886 decision announced that by a two-to-one margin the court had overturned the Superior Court and upheld the original circuit court verdict. They based their decision on the old English system of common law, which still had validity in state legal circles. The justices argued that the Kentucky statutes limiting punishment in such cases did not supersede "the common-law right of the jury to punish with fine and imprisonment to any amount, or for any time, in its discretion." The only limitation on such discretionary powers would be that they could not adopt "cruel and excessive punishment," and they did not find that so in this instance. "Neither the court nor the jurors," said the justices, "could have closed their eyes to the cruelty and enormity of the offense committed. None more humiliating or degrading could have been inflicted." Saying that such actions struck "at the very existence of society," the Court of Appeals stated that the punishment must deter such assaults. They thus affirmed the judgment in Mount Sterling. In dissent, one judge argued that Kentucky had no statute for aggravated assault and that assault and battery had always been treated as a misdemeanor. He found the jury's punishment had been one reserved for felonies and further criticized the majority ruling regarding the "unlimited discretion" of jurors. And in truth, he, and the Superior Court majority, may have had the better of the arguments. But courts, before then and since, have bent the constitution to find judgments that properly sway before the prevailing political breezes. In *Cornelison* v. *Commonwealth,* the justices—like the jurors in Mount Sterling—sought to sentence Cornelison not just on the stated charges, but rather for what he had done to cause Reid's suicide. A minister visiting Mount Sterling at the time found "the sentiment is strong against Cornelison." Though the law could be interpreted to support the justices' decision, it could not be done so easily; their pronouncement did satisfy local mores and desires. In that sense, and in still another irony surrounding Reid, the court did legally what Reid would not do illegally: ignore the law in order to punish Cornelison.[20]

And after all that, it still had not ended. Cornelison began serving his term in 1887, and within a month got a sympathetic local justice of the peace to turn him loose on a writ of habeas corpus. As soon as the news became known, the circuit judge returned him to the county jail. An angry Bettie Reid engaged an attorney and tried to get the justice of the peace indicted for his illegal act, but nothing resulted. Some time thereafter, however, she and her lawyer convinced the county judge that local citizens might try to free Cornelison by violent means, and he ordered him transferred to jail in Louisville (where, coincidentally or not, Stone and Hargis both practiced). The 19 July 1888 issue of the *Louisville Times* reported how Cornelison had just made his seventh attempt to be released on a writ. That started another public furor, four years after Reid's death, for the friendly *Times* described Cornelison not as a "ruffian" but a "cultivated, mild-mannered," well-dressed gentleman who should be freed to care for his wife and children. Then the paper editorialized that the punishment had been too severe: "Had Judge Reid defended himself like a man . . . as the law authorized him to do, a fine of $5 and costs would have been the extent of the punishment. . . . Cornelison is the victim . . . of Reid's wrong-doing." Honor still ruled.[21]

That proved more than Henry Stone could stand. Quickly, his published letter reminded people just what Cornelison had done and how he had been trying to get out of jail on one pretext or another ever since. The subject of public debate once more, a defiant Cornelison responded with a public statement of his own, and a much-modified account of what happened years before. Now, in his appeal for support from the people, he said Reid had entered his office "uninvited and unwanted" (both statements contradicted in sworn trial testimony). As he spoke with him, Reid had threateningly "got up with a hickory cane in his hand" and Cornelison had raised his own cane in self-defense. Only then had he drawn his small whip, which he used for "about twenty-five licks," not the seventy-five the court had declared. Nor had Reid been injured, as stated in the trial: "He was not dazed, he was not hurt, nor was he bewildered." In fact, said Cornelison, the story that he struck Reid with a cane originated only after the suicide. He concluded by saying that Reid "sold out my interests for his own private benefit" in the court case and for that treachery he had whipped him.[22]

Perhaps Cornelison believed his own lies; possibly he imagined that all those who had sworn differently under oath had done so falsely; conceivably, he hoped that the new tactic of the wronged gentleman would win him support from a populace with a short memory—and perhaps it did. In the next month, August 1888, the judge of the Court of Common Pleas in Louisville confirmed that Cornelison was properly incarcerated, but did conclude that the order sending him from Mount Sterling to Louisville had been illegal. He ordered him returned to that county. Cornelison's attorneys promised to appeal that decision as well. But as it turned out, they did not need to do so. With a new governor, ex-Confederate general Simon B. Buckner, in office, Cornelison's allies had asked for a pardon. The Governor's Executive Journal for 8 October 1888 read: "The Governor this day respited for nine months the unsatisfied portion of a Judgment for one cent and three years imprisonment in the County jail . . . against Jno. J. Cornelison for assault and battery." Often in such instances, the request for pardons only offered the view of one party, in this case Cornelison. It may be that Governor Buckner became one more victim of Cornelison, for his pardon suggested that the attorney had only nine months left on his sentence, which would mean it would end in July 1889. However, in the earlier decision ordering Cornelison returned from Louisville to Mount Sterling, the judge had explicitly said that Cornelison's term would conclude on 3 April 1890. Apparently, Governor Buckner, or one of his aides, either miscalculated the months or was—more likely—misinformed in the pardon request. Either way, Cornelison went free, though "broken in mind and body."[23]

But like Reid, he could not break free of the past. Cornelison returned to Mount Sterling and by 1890 had formed a partnership with H. Clay McKee, with offices near where the assault had occurred. But an attorney who knew him recalled later that Cornelison by then had become "a much broken man." An unworthy defender of the Code of Honor, he found few supported his actions and many shunned him for them. At the time of Reid's suicide, a newspaper had predicted that the assailant's future would be one of horror and remorse. Little in Cornelison's public statements indicated such emotions, but he too, at last, may have become a victim of the tragedy as well. Cornelison went to Lexington, living at 109 North Limestone, and there he died in February 1899, not yet fifty-five years old. During the trial Stone had asked, "What shall be John J. Cornelison's place in history?" Of the many answers that could be given perhaps the best was the conclusion offered by a later Court of Appeals judge from Mount Sterling. He ended his sketch of Cornelison's life, saying, "Not many years after that he removed to Lexington. His position there seems to have been obscure."[24]

Suicide not only kills the person committing the act, but it also destroys a part of the people who knew the victim well. Family members not only experience a deep sense of loss, but they may also react with feelings of anger for somehow being responsible or feelings of guilt and shame. They may endure emotions of inadequacy at not having been able to meet the victim's needs, or even deny the suicide's occurrence altogether. Bettie Reid suffered all those reactions. The pistol that Reid used to end his life had been one which he had given her for protection when he was away, but which she had urged him to carry because of all the threats around him. He had killed with her gun. Bettie also began to think that if she had not been ill and had been more cheerful, she might have prevented the death. Various newspapers had openly suggested that her illness had contributed to his "madness." None of those sources, nor her friends, nor Mrs. Reid herself, suggested that her words may have been a factor, but she well may have felt guilty over what she said to her husband, in his office that day of the caning. When the day of his funeral came, a distraught Bettie Reid had been too prostrated and weak to go to the church, and had a private service for him in their home. She, too, had become a victim.[25]

A resilient and strong woman, though, Bettie Reid faced a world without her husband and went on into a new life. In his will, written four months before the attack, her husband had bequeathed $500 to the Kentucky Female Orphan School at Midway and the same amount to the Christian Gospel Missions, to perpetuate his father's name. A thousand dollars went "to my boy," Richard Reid Rogers, and the rest of the estate—later valued at over $50,000—he gave to his "loving and faithful wife." That, together with the funds from her first husband's estate, allowed Mrs. Reid to live comfortably as an independent woman the rest of her life. Attractive and young-looking—a reporter said she was thirty-five when he described her, while she was in fact forty-four at the time—Bettie Reid apparently did not encourage the later attention of men in her community. She never remarried, stayed in the home with its memories that she and her husband had shared, and lived the rest of her life as the widow of Richard Reid.[26]

But she did not retreat into some gloomy seclusion from the world. She had too much vitality and energy to do that. Bettie made certain Cornelison would be prosecuted fully, first, then later continued to be active in political matters. In 1895, for example, she advised a gubernatorial candidate to send two hundred dollars to a particular person in the county, who would "urge the farmers to put in their appearance"—a possible reference to vote buying. However, most of her immediate attention in the two years after the suicide focused on writing. Mrs. Reid wanted to tell her husband's story, so she began a book on his life.[27]

Actually, three books appeared about Richard Reid between 1884, the year of his death, and 1886, and Bettie Reid was directly or indirectly involved in each. The first, privately printed and edited without attribution by Kentucky University president C. L. Loos and his wife, was simply entitled *Letters*. That accurately described its contents. The first part—about 60 percent of the 150-page book—included verbatim letters to and from Reid, his wife and son, and others. Subdivided into sections on correspondence from ministers, "ladies," and "other friends," it began with a March letter from Dick to Bettie and continued to the day of his death. In a shorter, second section, Loos selected postsuicide letters to Mrs. Reid, separated into similar divisions. Overall, the book included full texts of some 250 letters and noted that the originals would be preserved by the widow. Because not all those letters printed in the work would be included in later publications, it represents a key source on Reid's life.[28]

The last item cited in *Letters* was dated October 1884, so the book appeared after that. A second work bore an 1884 copyright date, but included news of Cornelison's December trial on its last page, so if it appeared in 1884, it did so very late. More likely it came out in early 1885. Entitled *Richard Reid: A Memorial* and published commercially in Louisville, the 110-page book had been anonymously edited by Judge Hargis for Bettie Reid. Beginning with the suicide, then resolutions about it, the book included press reactions to all that, followed by newspaper responses to the original assault. At least twenty-one Kentucky papers were quoted, often in extensive length. While not so valuable as the *Letters* volume with its private correspondence, the *Memorial* did include material from some papers no longer extant. Like its predecessor, it did not choose comments extremely critical of Reid, but did incorporate some less-than-positive analysis by certain newspapers.[29]

But those two very friendly works did not satisfy Bettie Reid. She began working on a full biography, which would use those books heavily, but would go far beyond them. In 1886, Standard Publishing Company of Cincinnati produced her *Judge Richard Reid: A Biography*. Although reflecting the way biography was written in Victorian America, it remains an excellent book and shows the talents Mrs. Reid possessed. While the introduction began by proclaiming that "this book is the modest history of the quiet life of a scholar and a Christian gentleman," the six-hundred-page work reflected what she called "the complex original" that was Richard Reid. Isaac Errett, editor of the *Christian Standard,* critiqued and helped write the manuscript, and Stone, Hendrick, and Loos aided as well, but the book in its essence was Bettie Reid's, heart and soul. She also worked hard to market it, preparing a sixteen-page "Agents Wanted" brochure, with excepts of favorable quotes, while personally wooing booksellers to put the work on their shelves.[30]

In the book itself, Reid incorporated most of what had previously appeared in the *Letters* and *Memorial* volumes. Of the 225 non-family letters already printed, 210 were republished in the biography; of the 21 newspapers in the *Memorial,* 15 resurfaced in Reid's book. But together those works make up under half of the pages in *Judge Richard Reid*. Bettie Reid added a dozen earlier letters that her husband had written to her, two dozen that he had sent stepson Reid Rogers, another two dozen he had penned to other family members, and ten new letters others had mailed to her. Additionally, the Reverend Daniel Potter had preserved nine valuable letters from his student to him in the 1857–74 period and now gave those for her use as well. Even more importantly, she used a journal she had written after his death in order to record her memories, since she believed "that she would not live to see this book completed," as well as a diary she kept. Reid did note, however that she used the diary sparingly, for its pages "are too heavily freighted with anguish." When her experiences and memories, and the recollections of those who had known Richard Reid when young, were added to all that, an almost new book emerged. Bettie Reid had done her historical homework.[31]

The first five of the book's thirty chapters took Dick Reid through the Civil War and his first love, and included much fresh material. When Elizabeth Jameson appears on the scene, Bettie Reid asked editor Errett to prepare that chapter, as a disinterested third party. Though the work would be far from unbiased overall, Mrs. Reid sought to free it from some of that bias. After the chapter on their marriage, she reappears as author, to tell of his reading habits, religious character, and legal practice. Various speeches—on temperance and women's rights—emerged in full. New accounts from the press filled the chapter on Reid's first court race, followed by much of the already printed material on the assault, suicide, and reaction to those. Bettie added information, from her retrospective, on the local situation—the political infighting, the religious controversy, and the personalities involved. She detailed his last few days on this earth, wrote a "Retrospective" which noted that Reid, "almost alone of Kentuckians, . . . could stand up and advocate all that was most advanced in the rights of women," and prepared a detailed index. President Loos wrote a five-page conclusion. At the end of the work, in an appendix, the Cornelison trial accounts and prosecution speeches—no defense ones—were included. Disappointingly for the author, the book culminates with the note that the Superior Court had overturned the decision, but says that it will be appealed where "there is every reason to believe that the judgment of the Montgomery Circuit Court will be affirmed." And so the biography ended.[32]

Had the book included only those elements, it would have been received for what it was—a well-documented, if selective, life of Reid, one worthy of praise. But Bettie Reid also included one chapter that added even more intrigue and controversy to the tragedy of Richard Reid. In it, she suggested that Reid had not committed suicide at all, but had been murdered, probably by Cornelison.

"Did Judge Reid take his own life?" her chapter asked. She attacked those who said he was depressed, and wrote that his political outlook had brightened. Mrs. Reid quoted those who said that he had seemed, to them, to be in good spirits. She also questioned whether he would have killed himself anyway: "He would not have left her [his wife] the suffering to bear alone . . . nor would he have given her the additional sorrow for his loss. He would not have left the young manhood of the boy he loved unguarded and unprotected." Next, she cast doubt on the suicide note, written in such a "frenzied hand" that only parts of it resembled Reid's. Finally, she argued that no powder-marks were visible on the body, as they should have been if the pistol had been held near the head. Mrs. Reid mentioned, almost in passing, that one witness thought he saw Cornelison near Brock's law office that day, and she thus planted that seed of doubt. She also, to her credit, provided facts and arguments to suggest the suicide theory, and ended the chapter as if that had been the cause of his death. But by raising the murder question, she once more brought out another mystery in Reid's life, and death.[33]

Was she correct? Was Reid murdered? Some of the reasons she gave reflected the era's lack of understanding of suicide itself. Depressed people do not always act despondently. In fact, if they have made the decision to die they may appear happy and at peace with themselves, for their troubles soon will be ended, as they see it. Furthermore, the mindset of those who take their own lives may consider that by suicide they are making the lives better for a son and wife left behind, by removing the source of *their* unhappiness.[34]

Much more of an issue was the question of the powder burns. The French government introduced smokeless gunpowder the year Reid died, and such powder did not become commonly manufactured for a decade after that. Reid had thus used black powder, which would have, at close range, left significant tearing of the skin and noticeable residue. Unfortunately, no coroner's report apparently remains, but the coroner's jury at the time found no reason to question that a suicide had occurred. Yet one newspaper reporter—who may or may not have seen the body—indicated that "the closest scrutiny failed to show that even a hair of his head was scorched." Was she correct on that point, which offered support for the claim of murder? Was this another mystery in the Reid story? However, some other factors tend to refute her murder theory. First of all, the outside door was locked from inside, so any killer would have come in and left by the front door to Brock's law office, a door on the busiest street in town, across from the courthouse. While it would be possible for Cornelison to enter and leave without being seen, his notoriety at that time makes that more unlikely. But even if someone did enter and exit without being observed, that does not explain away the suicide note. Mrs. Reid admitted that parts of it appeared very much to be in Reid's handwriting. And even, in a more far-fetched scenario, had Cornelison somehow forced Reid to write the note before killing him, he would have dictated very different words than the ones which ended with "love to the boy." The note supports the suicide, as does much more. As she sat down to write, it is likely someone told Bettie Reid that no powder marks had been seen and she had seized on that to add to her "proof." But in the end, much of what she considered evidence does not hold up under scrutiny. In her society, it would be a man of weakness who killed himself over a failure of honor, even though the act itself might appear an honorable one. Reid would be more manly had he been cowardly murdered, as she hinted. Moreover, murder freed her of guilt. She tried to do what is commonplace in suicides—deny it was a suicide at all. But most evidence suggests it was.[35]

That chapter and all three books represented an attempt to shape the history of the affair from the beginning. No books came from Cornelison's pen or those of his supporters. The Reid works presented few missives or editorials that defended Cornelison or portrayed Reid negatively. Some of those can be uncovered through historical research, but the evidence leans heavily to Reid's side through Bettie's efforts. In her way, she continued to protect the man she loved, long after his death and hers.

Elizabeth Jameson Rogers "Bettie" Reid lived for sixteen more years after the publication of the biography. During that time, she reportedly stood up in church in one instance and "confessed blame for his death." His shadow was always there, and she could see his distant grave from her second-floor bedroom window. She died at her home in Mount Sterling on 2 July 1902.

In that time she had seen her son Reid Rogers become very successful. He had graduated from Princeton two years after his stepfather's death, and then had received a law degree from the University of Virginia in 1889. Reid Rogers practiced under family friend Henry Stone in Louisville, then joined William J. Hendrick in Frankfort as an assistant attorney general. In the early 1890s, he returned to Mount Sterling for a time as a lawyer, went to Jackson, Tennessee, and married "a noted Southern beauty" and then moved to New York City, just before the twentieth century began. In 1907, Rogers headed the Department of Law and Government in the Panama Canal Zone and served as general counsel for the railroad company there. Two years later, he went back to New York and became the attorney for the city's streetcar system for the next forty years. During that time, he kept his ties to Mount Sterling, owning a controlling interest in a bank there and visiting relatives. People in the area still remember him as a slender, "down-to-earth" man who "looked like a Kentucky Colonel" and dressed differently from the locals, always sporting a bowtie. They liked him. In 1920, he sold his mother's estate Belle Vista for some $30,000, and by the 1940s, it furnished land for a subdivision. The old Reid house went through various owners and became surrounded by newer homes, but generally remained in a good state of repair. Richard Reid Rogers, age eighty-one, died on 11 November 1949.[36]

Years before, prior to World War I, his daughter Elizabeth Reid Rogers had been traveling in Europe with her parents when she met German prince Christian of Hesse, and they later married in Berlin. After the war, they had a home in Schleswig-Holstein and a villa at Cannes, but traveled a great deal as well. In 1923, for example, the royal couple visited the central Bluegrass and attended the Kentucky Derby, before returning overseas. They had four children, two of whom were living in Texas at the time of Reid Rogers' death, and two residing in France. But the family's overseas connection may have, unintentionally, also helped protect Richard Reid's memory. Bettie Reid had in her possession hundreds of personal letters, many of them published in the various books. They apparently went to her son, on her death, but after that their trail becomes unclear. Did they go to Europe with his daughter? Did they reside in America in still-unknown hands? Since those originals have not surfaced, there remains no way to compare them with what Mrs. Reid published. An examination of materials published in the *Letters* book and the same ones that appeared in the biography shows little difference in the two, but occasionally some lines were omitted in the later version. How much overall and hidden editing took place? What did letters not published say? And what intimate details were recorded in the journal and the diary she mentioned? In short, how did she shape the historical record to support her version of it? Without those letters the chief portrayal of the past remains the one fashioned by Bettie Reid. She and other allies assuaged their guilt and got their revenge on Riddell in the court race and on Cornelison in the courtroom, but she also tried very hard to make certain that Richard Reid received vindication from those who would write his history. And in large part, she succeeded.[37]

Epilogue: A Failed Hero

While the death of Richard Reid itself represented a massive tragedy, it seemed that his death meant little to history—and even to historians. Over the years, state and southern scholars ignored the Reid-Cornelison controversy.[1] Only three exceptions occurred. In 1916, Frankfort attorney L. F. Johnson's *Famous Kentucky Tragedies and Trials* devoted 11 of its 336 pages of text to the tragedy. His straightforward account presented the bare outline and made few judgments. It also had little impact, apparently, on the historical writing that followed. That remained the situation for over six decades, until Jerry Lee Butcher's dissertation on southern violence discussed Reid briefly. Twenty years afterwards, University of Kentucky history professor Robert M. Ireland published an excellent article on the subject in 1997. A student of constitutional law, Ireland chiefly focused on the legal aspects of the controversy. For well over a century, then, only Bettie Reid's book told the story in full detail. Dick Reid remained almost lost to history.[2]

That situation could be overlooked, in one sense, if his death itself had changed subsequent history. It did not. Historian Gerda Lerner, in stressing that history represents a people's collective memory, notes that "collective forgetting of the dark side of events is hurtful . . . to the whole society, because one cannot heal nor can one make better decisions in the future, if one evades responsibility for the consequences of past actions." At virtually every level, Reid's memory faded while the sins of the past continued and, in some cases, intensified. Violence grew and respect for formal law declined over the next several decades. Community and regional standards of honor and manhood continued to dominate. Before his death, letters to Reid told him how his example would mean change. One explained to the judge that his heroic course would live "long after the present generation has passed from earth"; another said Reid's model would mold sentiment for years to come. After Reid's suicide, a newspaper predicted that his death had planted a seed of good from which would spring the regeneration of Kentucky. They all erred. The seed died.[3]

At the local level, where his example should have been most felt, little changed, as the decade after his death continued to be filled with violence and lawless acts in Mount Sterling. In 1888, some seventy-five African Americans in the city organized to protect a man they feared was going to be seized by a lynch mob. Some three hundred whites turned them away, but no mob "justice" followed. Three years after that, a man named Lee Wigginton and his son were arrested for poisoning two men. A mob took Wigginton's wife from her home "and hung her up for a while" to extract a confession. Getting what they sought, they stormed the jail for Wigginton, but the jailer kept them out. Three weeks later, some forty masked members of another mob tried once more to take Wigginton, but again failed. A year after that, another mob hanged a man on the railroad trestle near town. In 1894, attorney and councilman Henry Watson caned and badly beat the city's fifty-eight-year-old mayor, Adam Baum. Lawyer Watson, who had killed a black man "some years ago," claimed the mayor had taken "indecent liberties" with his ten-year-old daughter. Baum, a merchant, said he had patted her on the shoulder as she left his store, and that had been all. Cornelison's idea of honor and his caning example apparently lived on, if Reid's did not.[4]

The next six months after that incident proved particularly violent and showed the continuing unrest in Mount Sterling. On the last night of 1894, a lynching took place, on the ever-popular railroad trestle. Earlier that year, J. L. Bomar had begun shooting at three men, right in front of the courthouse. They fired back, killing Bomar. One of the men involved in that affray had been Thomas Blair. On 31 December 1884, ten months later, he had been in a "disreputable house," had shot at a man there, and had been subsequently arrested, to sober up. A few masked men took him from the jail, joined a dozen or so others, and lynched him. On New Year's Day, the citizens of Mount Sterling awoke to find the body, with the sign on it reading "Friends of Capt. J. L. Bomar." Two supposed mob members and the jailer, who had helped them, were arrested, but the newspaper suggested they were but scapegoats, since the two town factions "each was doing all it could to protect its own scoundrels." No indictments resulted. Then in June 1895, John Johnson, the African American son of the man Watson had killed earlier, resisted arrest and, in the confused events that followed, was wounded and a policeman killed. The dead law officer had been married ten days—to a woman whose first husband had been murdered five years earlier. This time the lynch mob kept away, but a "legal lynching" quickly took place in August. The killing kept going on in Reid's Mount Sterling.[5]

All of which took its toll on the town. During the 1895 events, the local newspaper cried out that the "dangerous spirit" of mob violence had again disgraced the city. That had to end, it editorialized: "Business is stagnant. We are advertised to the world as a lawless community." And in fact, the rapidly expanding city and county of Reid's time had stopped growing. By 1920, the population had actually fallen below its 1890 level. The "Gateway to the Mountains" had lost that economic leverage, and in 1920 no business employed more than seven people. In the 1960s, the area made something of a comeback due, in part, to the completion of an interstate highway nearby. Montgomery County's population rose by 1980 to over 20,000, but fell once more over the next decade. While a modified court day continued to draw people to town, by 1986 rail service had completely ended. The city still grew and still offered many strengths as a community for the people who lived there. But it had learned only slowly from Reid's death just how exacting the cost of violence could be, and it had never really recovered from what had taken place in that second-floor law office that day in May 1884.[6]

Kentucky learned even less. Ironically, a month after Reid's death, Thomas Buford, the escaped assassin of Judge Elliott, voluntarily returned to the Central Lunatic Asylum, for he had almost starved living in the woods of Indiana. He died in the asylum the next year. But tragedy struck that family again, for his brother, ex-Confederate general Abe Buford, at almost the same time as Reid, committed suicide by copying Reid's actions and shooting himself in the head, due to financial worries. Two months later, a newspaper reported that Kentucky congressman William Wirt Culbertson had attempted suicide in his Washington hotel room but had not succeeded. That prompted a story a week later that told how two Kentuckians, Speaker of the U. S. House John White (in 1845) and Congressman Elijah Hise (in 1867), had committed suicide while serving, and how ex-congressman

James L. Johnson had killed himself in 1877. In Kentucky political circles, death by suicide somehow seemed almost commonplace.[7]

But unfortunately, so too did death in personal controversies. Individual violence abounded. For example, in November 1889, two prominent Republican leaders met in the Lexington post office. William Cassius Goodloe, a nephew of the fiery old antislavery advocate Cassius Marcellus Clay, had recently been given a bowie knife by "Old Cash," with the admonition that if he was insulted and did not fight, "You're no Clay. I never want to see you again." When he met Armistead Swope in the post office, Goodloe told Swope to quit blocking his way; Swope declared that those words insulted him and both drew weapons. Swope fired two shots into Goodloe; he in return inflicted at least thirteen wounds with his blade. Swope died instantly, while Goodloe lingered on for forty-eight hours and then suffered death as Cassius Clay had sought, as a Clay should. The words of newspaper stories said much about how society viewed the matter. One noted: "Mr. Shelby says that he never thought he would ever witness such a magnificent display of manly courage and bravery. Colonel Swope, . . . the very picture of manly symmetry, and Colonel Goodloe, . . . as handsome a man as one could find any where, stood facing each other like two gladiators." Both died in an arena still governed by the code of honor.[8]

The next year an earlier chain of events also culminated in death. Some eighteen months before, a Louisville reporter filed a story about Kentucky congressman William Preston Taulbee, a former Methodist minister and schoolteacher now turned politician. In it he revealed how "the mountain orator" had been found "in a compromising way" with a young woman who worked in the patent office. That story wrecked Taulbee's marriage and ended his congressional career. When he saw reporter Charles E. Kincaid, they fought; now on the last day of February 1890, they met again, and the still-angry Taulbee spoke harshly to the newspaperman. Two hours later, in the U.S. Capitol stairwell, Kincaid encountered Taulbee, pulled a pistol, and shot the unarmed man. He died twelve days later. The *Courier-Journal* defended the blood on the Capitol walls, saying, "Kincaid was right." He argued in his defense that he had been verbally abused and threatened and, unable to accept the insults anymore, had reacted as honor dictated a gentleman should. The District of Columbia's code apparently differed little from Kentucky's—Kincaid went free.[9]

Personal disagreements ending in death continued. In 1895, the "unwritten law" made its appearance once more when Kentucky governor John

Young Brown's son was killed by Fulton Gordon. Brown and Gordon's wife of ten years had been found in a state of undress in a Louisville room and Gordon had killed both, shooting his wife, the daughter of the former state librarian, once, and Brown seven times. Again, no conviction followed.[10] The most famous incident of personal violence centered on William Goebel. An ambitious state senator from northern Kentucky, he and a Democratic rival, banker John Sanford, had openly argued over various public issues. Purchasing a newspaper, Goebel had written in it of "Gon____h____ea John." On 11 April 1895, the two enemies met outside a Covington bank. When Sanford asked if he had written the offensive article, Goebel admitted that he had. Quickly, two shots rang out, one from Goebel's pistol, one from Sanford's. The banker fell forward with a bullet in his head and soon died. His widow had to be placed in an insane asylum. Goebel had a bullet hole in his coat and was unharmed. Since no one could say which man drew his weapon first, Goebel went free because of "reasonable doubt." The next year Goebel easily won reelection as his party's senate leader. In 1899, he ran for governor in a race that was so close it had to be decided by the legislature. While those deliberations ensued, Goebel was shot as he walked to the state capitol. The General Assembly quickly threw out enough disputed votes to make him governor and swore him in. He died three days later, the only governor in American history to die in office as the result of an assassination. Trials, which included the Republican secretary of state and mountain feudists as principals, went on for seven years, further placing Kentucky violence and state justice before a national audience in a very negative way. When Kentucky had adopted a new constitution in the early 1890s, delegate Goebel had remarked that "the age of dueling is as dead as the age of chivalry." But in modified form, duels and affairs of honor had lived on.[11]

And on and on. In 1937, Henry H. Denhardt, a former lieutenant governor and adjutant general, went on trial for allegedly killing his fiancée. Much evidence supported that charge, but the judicial proceeding ended in a hung jury. While awaiting retrial, Denhardt was walking down the streets of Shelbyville when the dead woman's three brothers started shooting at him. He was hit three times in the back, then received a bullet, at close range, to the back of the head. An attorney with Denhardt fell to the ground, looked up, and saw one of the brothers pointing a gun at him as well. But another brother yelled, "Oh hell, don't bother with him; he ain't nothing but a lawyer." The community endorsed the assassination of Denhardt, and the brothers were found "not guilty." But all those examples had included such people as a former congressman, a reporter, a governor's son, a state senator, a banker, a gubernatorial candidate, a secretary of state, and a lieutenant governor. The supposed "best men," those who fashioned and executed the laws, continually presented the example to Kentucky and the nation that the personal vengeance that Reid had so abhorred still won out, in the end.[12]

But group violence in that same era affected more people, claimed more victims, and attracted more attention. Lynching and racial killings continued across Kentucky, as they had when Reid had lived. The most infamous example, which reached an international audience through a story in a Paris, France, newspaper, concerned a 1911 murder in Livermore, Kentucky. The mob seized Will Porter and placed the black man on the stage of the local opera house. Some sources said admission was charged to the spectacle. Those present emptied their pistols at the man on the stage and then filed out of the theater. No one wore masks, and indictments followed. But all defendants won an acquittal. From 1890 to 1910, in Kentucky, at least a hundred blacks and nearly thirty whites died through extralegal executions, mostly lynching.[13]

Feud violence continued into the early years of the twentieth century as well. In the decade of Reid's death, the virus of family "vendettas" seemed to infect almost all of eastern Kentucky. Besides the well-known Hatfield-McCoy feud, more violent ones occurred, and dozens died in each. During the Clay County conflict, a minister concluded, "It is a small thing here to kill a man. It is so common." At the beginning of the twentieth century, the last of the great feuds gave "Bloody Breathitt" its name, and again involved leading families. On one side of the Hargis-Marcum "troubles" stood the Democratic county judge and the sheriff, while the other included the town marshal and the town's most prominent attorney, both Republicans. That lawyer, James B. Marcum, so feared for his life that he went outdoors only with a child in his arms, for he knew that the peculiar code of honor in the mountains meant that no one would shoot and risk hitting a baby. But one day, he did not do that and was shot in the back, while his two main enemies passively watched. One of them, the county judge, would later be killed by his drunken son; the other, the sheriff, was shot in 1912, as he stood near an open window in his barricaded house. In a two-year period, over thirty had perished before the feudal fires. Finally, it ended, but the legacy and the stereotypes persisted into the twenty-first century.[14]

The message that violence could achieve desired ends continued to echo across the commonwealth. First the tollgate raiders,[15] then the tobacco farmers, had problems that they could not solve, they believed, through legal means. The American Tobacco Company, for example, had formed agreements with foreign buyers of tobacco, so that each had their own territory from which to purchase "the weed," thus giving them a monopoly—and farmers very low prices. By 1904, prices had fallen below the cost of production, and desperate agrarians in Kentucky and Tennessee agreed to form a cooperative, "pool" their tobacco, and hold it off the market until prices rose. They wanted to counter a trust and monopoly with one of their own. Success followed, but one problem remained. Not all joined the pool. By selling their tobacco to the so-called trust, such farmers undercut the cooperative. To remedy that, the "Silent Brigade"—or more commonly the "Night Riders"—organized to fight in what became known as the Black Patch War (named for the "dark" tobacco of western Kentucky). Called the largest mass agricultural protest in American history, the Night Riders formed irregular armies across the region, with some ten thousand men armed to fight. They terrorized individual, recalcitrant farmers by first burning their crops and barns, and then, if that failed, by beating or even killing those who resisted. Huge Night Rider bands seized whole towns and torched massive trust warehouses filled with tobacco. Oaths of secrecy, masks, and military-like precision marked the raids, but they succeeded chiefly because the populace approved. Local officials turned their backs on illegality; juries failed to convict. Powerless farmers fought an enemy they argued that they could not control in legal ways. And they achieved success. Prices did rise, and eventually a U.S. Supreme Court decision struck down the tobacco trust. Desperate farm families had collectively earned a needed victory but, once more, had done so in such a way that the lesson taught that success could best be achieved through violence, outside the law.[16]

Approved extralegal actions continued in the 1920s. With Prohibition, Kentucky moonshiners—who had a long and storied history of illegal operations—suddenly found their product in greater demand. Agricultural depression and economic want caused their numbers to grow as well. Reportedly, Al Capone used western Kentucky stills to help fill his Chicago needs; more certainly, once-wet communities across the commonwealth now turned to local bootleggers to supply their wants, outside the law. And in the next decade, the nation's attention turned once more to Kentucky, as the story of "Bloody Harlan" emerged. Like farmers earlier, coal miners in

Appalachia faced economic disaster now, as the Great Depression raged. Thrown out of work and, if unemployed, then evicted from their rented home in the company-owned towns, jobless miners and their homeless and increasingly hungry families formed an explosive mix in the mountains. Those who tried to form unions for worker security found themselves fired. Company-paid "gun thugs," operating as official deputies, ensured that justice would serve only one side. One-third of the mines closed completely; wages fell 60 percent for those who still went into the dark earth daily. On 5 May 1931, the so-called Battle of Evarts left three company men killed and two more wounded, and at least one worker dead. Over the next half-decade, more died. Nationally known writers came to tell the miners' story but were often beaten or indicted for their efforts. What a state official called a "virtual reign of terror" existed, and a woman remembered it as a time when "Harlan County blood ran like water." Finally, the unions received recognition, relative prosperity opened up the mines once more, and temporary industrial peace came at least. Once more, the system had given the dispossessed little hope that justice could be found under the law. Generation after generation of Kentuckians had listened not to Reid's example but to the gun's voice as the answer.[17]

Feuds, lynching, the Goebel assassination, the Black Patch War, moonshining, "Bloody Harlan," the killing of Denhardt—all those came one after the other, constantly adding to the image of violence surrounding Kentucky. Some observers in the commonwealth worried over that continuing trend. In 1889, the adjutant general, after investigating one feud, had concluded that troops should be sent in to ensure the presence of real justice: "The people have grown to believe that the machinery of the law has been used to protect favorites and to punish enemies, and distrust of the law prevails." The next year, the *Courier-Journal* blamed the lawlessness on the inefficiency of the courts.[18]

But the greatest condemnation of the Bluegrass State came from the national press. In an editorial entitled "The Shame of Kentucky," the *New York Times* blamed the situation on the fact that communities there still clung "to the barbarous theory that human life may be properly taken to resent an insult or avenge the death of a relative." People in the area needed to be educated in what humanity meant, it concluded. *The Nation,* two years later, compared Kentucky civilization to that of fifteenth-century Ireland and declared that such "barbarianism" killed the best leaders or caused good people to turn away from migrating there. After Goebel's assassination, the *American Monthly Review of Reviews* wrote of the "temporary insanity" of the commonwealth's whole population. That same event caused a *Century Magazine* writer in 1900 to call the Kentuckian "a man of war, quick to take affront and ever ready for a personal test of courage." The Bluegrass gentleman, he affirmed, had become "careless of life," while the "wild and semi-savage" mountain people defied all laws. By the turn of the century, then, a Kentucky stereotype had become well developed.[19]

Statistics suggested that such images had all too much basis in fact. Unreliable numbers by a Chicago paper in 1885 reported that the "Dark and Bloody Ground" stood behind only frontier Texas in the number of people murdered. Five years after that, the census recorded that Kentucky had more homicides than any state except populous New York. A decade later, another newspaper study ranked Kentucky sixth in murder rate. A third of a century later, in 1933, amid the Coal Wars, the commonwealth counted 602 homicides, 526 by firearms, and that number ranked it eighth nationally. At the same time, violence also slowed the state's development, as the newspapers suggested. Plants went elsewhere, where it was safer; capital did not go to bloody places. The commonwealth had been first in the South in the value of its manufactured products as late as 1900, but the growing stereotype began to take its toll. Looking back a quarter century, on the eve of the Great Depression in 1929, one study showed that Kentucky manufacturing volume had grown 65 percent in that timeframe but the South's had increased over 170 percent. Of all the states in the region, Kentucky tied for last in rate of growth. Part of that resulted from the price extracted from the state's industry by Prohibition, but part came because businesses did not want to go to places of violence, which Kentucky was in the national mind.[20]

Ironically, at almost that same time, the stereotype and the reality began to diverge. From over 600 murders in 1933, the number of homicides thirty years later had fallen to 200, in a much larger population. The murder rate went from 14.5 to 6.0 in 1960, placing it fifteenth nationally. By the beginning of the last decade of the twentieth century, it had declined to twenty-first in murder rate and twenty-fifth in the number of homicides. With a low violent crime rate (thirtieth in 1993), and very low property crime rate (forty-sixth of all states surveyed), Kentucky by the twenty-first century, comparatively, had become a very safe American place in which to live. But decades of killing, beginning before Reid's time and continuing long after it, could not be easily discarded from the national consciousness. The legacy of violence lived a prolonged life, long after it should have died in Kentucky.[21]

Reid's stance had given Kentucky and the South an opportunity to begin rejecting the lawless image that the nation so criticized. Significant praise and support of Reid and criticism of a code that demanded personal vengeance could have shown others that they could take similar stands for humanity and not suffer the scorn of their communities. It was a testing time for state and region. But Kentucky failed that test, and so too did the South. In the post–Civil War world, as "the Old South dueled with the New in the hearts and minds of southerners," those whites who sought to preserve traditional ways of life often found themselves powerless to do so in a rapidly changing America. Frustrated, they became aggressive and struck out at those they held responsible for their situation, or those they feared. At one level, angry agrarians in the late nineteenth century, opposing railroads, monopolies, banks, and other institutions, channeled their rage into political protest. At another level, the presence of blacks now freed from the shackles of slavery created another kind of concern in the white South. While segregation resulted from that, so too did massive racial conflicts and lynching. When those societal responses combined with an existing culture of honor, southern violence began to be seen, increasingly, as a phenomenon important in understanding the region and its emerging history.[22]

Like Kentucky, the South continued to be a violent place. An 1896 article on southern homicide showed the "Wild West" to have a high murder rate in regard to population, but of the long-established states, the South remained a very dangerous place in comparison to the rest of the United States. East of the Mississippi River, eight southern states (including Kentucky) exceeded the national rates; no northern one did. As many homicides occurred in the extended South as in all the rest of the nation, even though it had less than half the population. The author blamed all that on the justice system and the attitude that human life was considered cheap. A decade later, a Louisiana lawyer pointed to unwritten "laws" which made convictions difficult and violence more commonplace. Survivors of street duels would be automatically acquitted, he noted, and epithets, "which constitute moral insult . . . justif[y] an assault." By 1920, western rates of violence had declined, so that the South had an unfortunately unchallenged lead as a place of homicide. An *American Sociological Review* study took that discussion through the World War II era. Its statistics showed that over the past decades, every single southern state's serious crime rate exceeded the national figures and usually ranked in the highest percentiles in the United States.[23]

The national violence of the 1960s brought a whole series of investigations into violence, and many focused on the still deadly South. Firing the first scholarly salvo in that discussion was Sheldon Hackney, whose article was reprinted and widely distributed as part of the official report by the National Commission on the Causes and Prevention of Violence. He simply wondered why the South had been more violent. Noting that one southerner, when asked the question, had replied "that he reckoned there was just more folks in the South that needed killing," Hackney turned to other answers. He rejected class structure and ruralness and instead pointed to history as the best indicator. Not present-day influences, but past cultural patterns need to be examined, Hackney argued. Like W. J. Cash, he stressed that the absence of legal institutions created personal vengeance as the prevailing way to settle disputes. A similar conclusion came from sociologist Raymond D. Gastil. In articles and a book, he too emphasized the regional culture and the degree of "southernness" in a state as the best predictors of higher homicide rates. Of the fifteen states with the highest murder rate in 1960, twelve were southern, for example. At almost the same time, John Shelton Reed used opinion poll data to show large regional differences regarding attitudes on violence, above and below the "Smith and Wesson Line." While an occasional study thereafter countered those arguments by affirming that poverty, not culture, best explained the prevalence of violence in the South, most works continued to support the subculture thesis.[24]

From the 1980s on, authors found new answers and focused on honor as the key ingredient in that cultural mix. Both Bertram Wyatt-Brown's work, chiefly on the era before the Civil War, and Edward L. Ayers's study of late-nineteenth-century southern crime and punishment explained regional violence chiefly as an outgrowth of a deeply ingrained code of honor. Psychologists, led by Richard E. Nisbett and Dov Cohen, accepted those historical arguments, as well as ones focusing on the Celtic origins of violence, and combined them with modern-day experiments to fashion the same general conclusion: honor mattered, then and now. In a 1993 *American Psychologist* piece, Nisbett quoted an earlier southern juror's conclusion why a man who shot another was found not guilty: "He wouldn't of been much of a man if he hadn't shot them fellows." Finding little support that poverty or the onetime presence of slavery had any effect on murder rates, Nisbett instead stressed that southerners tend more to endorse violence as a suitable response when insulted. Cohen, Nisbett, and two other coauthors also noted that the South exceeds northern homicide rates not in felony-related murders, but in "argument- or conflict-related" ones. Such cultural norms of honor, they concluded, have became part of the social expectations and definitions of what being a man in the South is.[25]

Expanding those findings in a brief book, *Culture of Honor,* Nisbett and Cohen repeated the arguments that southerners continue to react to insults in ways that demonstrate a culturally based rule of retaliation. They also used some field experiments, perhaps less successfully, to conclude that people from the South respond "cognitively, emotionally, physiologically, and behaviorally" in very different ways than northerners when confronted with potentially violent, honor-based situations. Their surveys found that on abstract questions on general violence, few differences existed between the sections. But when the questions involved honor and protection of family and home, southerners then endorsed lethal violence more than northerners. Taking that a step further, the authors conducted controlled experiments where they asked subjects to complete a scenario involving an insult to a man's fiancée. Three-fourths of southerners ended the story with threats or an injury to the person who had insulted the woman; only one-fifth of the non-southerners so responded. The two psychologists concluded that the South still had a different ideology regarding violence and the acceptance of it. Not all agreed with those studies. But if, as John Shelton Reed has argued, the culture of violence is a learned trait, then southerners learned it very well indeed.[26]

The continued presence of violence in Kentucky and the South seemed to indicate that the Reid example had made little impact on the culture of honor over the years. But in certain ways his controversy, along with similar situations later, did have a subtle, and long-term, effect on that issue. As the years passed, the legal system that had once supported personal acts of revenge gradually changed, so that individual vengeance became less accepted. While the case law advanced more rapidly than did a jury's willingness to follow newer judicial guidelines, over time "not guilty" findings on personal retribution for a supposed insult to honor become much more legally problematic. Appropriately, the law that Richard Reid had been a part of led the way toward a new view of what honor should be, and what human life should mean.

In the two decades after Reid's death, two conflicting concepts competed in the courts. Increasingly, Kentucky's rulings began to depart from earlier decisions supporting a person's right to kill, even under the weakest of excuses. In an 1889 case, with Reid's friend Judge Holt now sitting on the court, the justices refused to overturn the conviction of a man who had waited in ambush to kill a man he claimed had insulted and wronged him. A dozen years later, with still another Mount Sterling attorney on the high court, the justices expanded their ruling even more. Railroad agent J. B. Rudert had gotten into a late-night argument in the train depot with a man named Harrison, who threatened him. The agent tried to shoot Harrison, but the bullets did not fire. Re-armed, he then followed Harrison, who did not have a weapon, and shot him in the back, killing him. The Court of Appeals overturned Rudert's original acquittal, saying that a veiled threat of danger at some possible future time could not justify murder. Instead, there had to exist real danger of "great bodily harm" or death before a person could respond violently and receive the approval of the law.[27]

Yet Kentucky's rule of law did not represent the prevailing interpretation, for two concepts of the law still warred with each other, as two out-of-state cases illustrated. An 1892 Alabama case showed the changing legal views in parts of the South, for it moved far from the code of honor. There, the judges ruled that a threatened person must have "a reasonable belief" that only by killing an assailant could he save his own life. To justify a homicide, the person involved had to try to avoid provoking an argument and could not willingly be a part of one. Moreover, violence could occur with impunity only when the appearance of "imperious, impending necessity" would impress a prudent person that he could repel the danger no other way. "Wounded pride" and a sense of shame gave no defense to kill: "Such thoughts are trash, as compared with the inestimable right to live." Yet a Missouri case a decade later revealed the conflicting views. In *State* v. *Bartlett,* déjà vu seemed everywhere. William D. Edwards had threatened a frail, "badly ruptured" man, E. Russell Bartlett. The two met, and Edwards took out a rawhide whip and started striking Bartlett on the head and shoulders. Partially stunned by the blows, Bartlett ran toward his office, but Edwards continued to hit him. Finally, Bartlett called him to stop or be killed. When Edwards did not cease, Bartlett shot and killed him. The Missouri court supported Bartlett's action as an "unavoidable necessity," stating that a person under the "humiliating indignation" of an assault should be under no obligation to retreat: "It is true, human life is sacred, but so is human liberty."[28]

All those cases had been decided when a 1903 *Harvard Law Review* article surveyed the issue in "Retreat from a Murderous Assault." At that time, it found the two views, as represented in the Alabama and Missouri decisions, to be the rule of law. In 1895, the U.S. Supreme Court had argued that a person was not obliged to flee if under attack and could respond with violence in such cases. Then two years later, the same court had also upheld a case supporting the doctrine that a person had to retreat "as far as he can" before resorting to killing an assailant. Author Joseph H. Beale Jr. made his own feelings very clear on which doctrine he advocated, in words that could have been Richard Reid's two decades before:

> The feeling at the bottom of the argument is one beyond all law; it is the feeling, which is responsible for the duel, for war, for lynching. . . . We have outlived dueling, and we deprecate war and lynching. . . . In all these cases sober reflection would lead us to realize that the remedy is really worse than the disease. So it is in the case of killing to avoid a stain on one's honor. A really honorable man . . . would perhaps always regret the apparent cowardice of a retreat, but he would regret ten times more . . . the thought that he had the blood of a fellow-being on his hands. It is undoubtedly distasteful to retreat; but it is ten times more distasteful to kill.[29]

Retreat or kill? That debate went on, despite the arguments in the *Harvard Law Review*. By 1931, Kentucky law itself retreated somewhat on the question, for in that year, the state's high court ruled that flight was not necessary: "It is the tradition that a Kentuckian never runs. He does not have to." That "no retreat" concept remains the prevailing doctrine in Kentucky. However, the Model Penal Code does require retreat, noting that the protection of life is greater than "the sacrifices of the much smaller value that inheres standing up to an aggressor." But the Kentucky legislature refused to incorporate that particular provision in the state's revised penal code. Yet across the nation, more and more, the issue of preserving life has won out over the issue of honor.[30]

Finally, the state's law changed as well, providing a more appropriate penalty for beatings such as Reid's. In his era, the courts had to jump through the tricky common law legal hoop to achieve a sentence befitting the crime, since simple assault and battery was only a misdemeanor, punishable by a small fine—and it remained that for almost a century in Kentucky. Now, the widely copied Model Penal Code, which forms the basis for the statutes of at least thirty-four states, including Kentucky, provides the category of aggravated assault. That results when the attacker uses a deadly weapon and shows "extreme indifference to the value of human life." A felony, it brings with it a much harsher sentence than assault did in Reid's time, and thus makes it less necessary for honor to be satisfied properly by personal means. That statute and the changing constitutional interpretations have brought the law much closer to Reid's view of what it should be and should do. And perhaps that change in the law did gradually have an effect on community standards. While other factors obviously had an influence, still Kentucky's homicide rate fell drastically after World War II; the South's, which stood half again as high as the national average in 1970, had fallen to only 25 percent greater a decade later. At long last, Reid's voice crying out for the value and dignity of human life may finally have been heard.[31]

If honor fought a vigorous rearguard action as it slowly retreated from its position of prominence in southern and Kentucky life, its companion force—manhood—began a strong advance for several decades after Reid's death. Leading that movement would be Theodore Roosevelt. In 1884, Roosevelt's wife and mother had both died on the same day, in the year of Reid's suicide. Transforming himself in the West from a man of "effete dudeism" to a masculine cowboy, he also soon penned his multivolume *The Winning of the West*. In its pages Teddy Roosevelt told his readers how American manhood had been forged in the forests of Kentucky and then refined in other frontiers across the new nation. Out of that violence and struggle, a strong people emerged, in TR's version. With Darwinian concern that "modern" civilization might produce decadence and effeminacy, instead of masculinity, Roosevelt found eager auditors in his call for Americans to be the dominant race through a superior manhood, "the strenuous life," and nationalistic fervor. Sports offered one way to achieve such virility, with its competitiveness, energy, and teamwork. Strenuous exercise, muscular bodies, violent clashes on the playing field—these represented the new ideal for men of Roosevelt's class and generation. Even President Charles W. Eliot of TR's Harvard defended the growing sport of (helmetless) football from its critics, arguing that "effeminacy and luxury are worse evils than brutality." Religion became a part of the era's answer as well. A "muscular Christianity" stressed strength of body as well as spirit, and the YMCA's athletic emphasis grew. Evangelist Billy Sunday would later personify the epitome of that with his combative virility. Once when preaching, he was assaulted by a man lashing him with a whip. Sunday promptly hit his assailant twice, knocking him down. The Christian Gentleman had transformed into the manly Christian.[32]

War provided another way American men could prove their manhood. Conflict would give them an opportunity to develop fighting virtues and show that they were the equals of those who had tamed the nation's early frontiers. The *Maine*'s sinking boosted such needs. With American honor, chivalry, and manhood now demanding intervention, the Spanish-American War put TR and others happily in the middle. That conflict caused many to call it a needed war, a good war, a conflict that gave what the nation had to have. Louisville's Henry Watterson praised it, for "the Anglo-Saxon species in America has had its downward course toward emasculation arrested." After the killing, and the glory, had ended and the issue of imperialism arose, the *Courier-Journal*'s editor framed that issue in similar terms, saying that the president had "the young manhood of the country—yea, and excepting a few old grannies and aunties—behind him." Through war, Americans—northerners, southerners, and westerners alike—had demonstrated their manhood, and now imperialism allowed them to take up the white man's burden and dominate on the world's stage.[33]

But the glow of that "splendid little war" and the colonies that came from it soon faded. The insurrection in the Philippines that killed more men than the Spanish-American War, and lasted far longer, created more debate on the American mission. Then came the Great War and those who experienced its trench warfare, shelling, gassing, and deaths returned home with little sense of being better because of the slaughter. Honor and manhood suffered serious wounds in the mire and blood of the Western Front. The subsequent disillusionment of the 1920s, followed by the economic want of the Depression decade, gave little opportunity for such an expansive manhood to flower as before. Such attitudes may have been partially sublimated into a growing love for sports, business rivalries, clubs, and fraternal organizations, but the strong antiwar views—which would end only after Pearl Harbor—demonstrated the reaction against that aggressive spirit as well.[34]

However, by the last part of the twentieth century, conditions that reflected those present in Reid's time began to bring forth similar debates on what being a man meant. A century earlier, Gilded Age Americans worried and wrote excessively about changing gender roles and how "modern" women would affect that society. They faced issues of race relations and massive immigration; they agonized over large businesses, the disparity between rich and poor, and the costs that trusts and monopolies brought; they debated, almost endlessly, whether tariffs should chiefly protect businesses in America or be low enough to bring in cheap goods to make workers' lives better in that way. People in that era lived in fear of violence, watched bombings increase, and constantly complained of the need for more law and order. They deplored the state of politics and considered many of the leaders morally corrupt. Individuals argued over whether the nation should be more involved in the world scene or retreat from it. Some decried the widespread availability of drugs, alcohol, and gambling, and criticized the morality of the era. And virtually all had to adapt to rapid change, new inventions, and different outlooks. While much had changed a century later, many of those same issues continued to be debated, in modified form. Those who lived in the ending decades of the twentieth century had many similar fears and concerns—and often reacted in similar ways.[35]

Janus-like, justice, honor, and manhood continued to show two contradictory faces. Neither visage represented total good or total evil; each had strong elements as well as weak. In justice, for example, at one extreme stood totally abstract justice, with no input of community mores, or compassion or humanity. Farthest from that view was a justice interpreted almost completely by the community's definition of what that entailed, with little recognition of the neutrality or the majesty of a formal law. In Reid's era, the second face of justice dominated.

Similarly, manhood presented two differing concepts of what it meant to be male. One end of the scale offered the kinder, gentler man; on the other the aggressive, dominating one. One author noted that twentieth-century individuals moved "from self-discipline to self-expression, from self-denial to self-enjoyment." Beyond that, one group defines modern masculinity by showing acts of kindness, earning the respect of peers, and being a good father and husband. But far distant from that view stands one nearer to the Gilded Age's "strenuous life" manhood. Contemporary advocates now cheer the hard-hitting football player or the very competitive figure in any sport. Modern-day Darwinists may praise the ruthless CEO in a corporate boardroom or the "tough" politician who will do almost anything to survive and win. And as Vietnam becomes more removed, as history in a textbook, chronologically closer and almost bloodless later conflicts offer new models for those enamored with the violence of the warrior. Attempts to capture a part of that martial spirit may surface by joining a paramilitary unit, or by becoming a battlefield reenactor, or by playing at paintball war, or through various rituals. Others may do their "killing" on a computer screen. In one way, society has channeled those urges into relatively non-violent ends, but the violent means used reflects still that aspect of masculinity, alive and well. Yet each differing concept of manhood has validity. Society may, at various times, require compassion and quiet strength, but at others toughness and fortitude as well. If each generation defines and then redefines what manhood means, then the current debate reflects that continuing confusion, in much the way it did in Reid's time.[36]

Finally, honor had its own extremes as well. One interpretation, in Reid's era, required gentlemen to show control, restraint, and forgiveness, to remain above the fray, even in the face of justifiable violence, while in the opposite view, the code called for vengeance to answer even the slightest offense. But where does honor now dwell? While respected when used as the basis of honor codes in military academies and universities, it often is associated with more negative images. Lyndon Johnson partially defended American involvement in the Vietnam War by saying, "Our course is charted always by the compass of honor." The mafia may call itself "the honorable society" and other criminal elements may praise honor among thieves. Honor may be present as part of some ill-formed "code of the streets," where respect, once won, must be guarded and defended, even with violence. As one historian concluded, "Honor has found new breeding grounds in cities." But in reality, it hides everywhere. As people continue to question a system of law that they argue favors one class over another, or does not punish properly—concerns of Reid's time—then they still look to a personal sense of justice to redeem honor. Films in the Rambo or Dirty Harry tradition praise violence, vigilantism, and personal revenge as solutions. Acceptance of extralegal retribution reflects disrespect of the ability of the legal system to bring justice to those who seek it.[37]

Yet that extreme of honor can include positive elements as well. It is true that some of those results may come partly because of less noble aspects of the code. For example, John Shelton Reed noted that southerners "will be polite until they're angry enough to kill you." The courtesy and hospitality that characterize parts of the South might have grown to help avoid conflict, which, with a sense of honor present, might otherwise escalate into violence. Similarly, politicians from the South, from Henry Clay to LBJ, used civility and compromise—with just the right threat of force—to forge compromises and fashion constructive legislation. Again, that ability may have partially grown out of their living in a society, where, without compromises, the code would claim even more lives. But honor has another side. Restraint and forgiveness should be more important than the often-senseless violence of the nineteenth-century honor system, but, at the same time, there *are* causes worth dying for. A rechanneled honor can motivate individuals of integrity not to forgive a Hitler or ignore racism, but, instead, to grow angry over injustice, oppose the dishonorable act, and show zeal for the right. At a time when media talk shows, political "attack ads," and other forums often wage war on honor and any sense of civility, a new century must move from the extremes of honor and redefine it into a new, individualized notion of honoring personal obligations, of showing greater respect of others, of valuing human life and dignity. As Susan Faludi has suggested, a rapidly changing world offers the opportunity for "a new paradigm of human progress," where the best parts of justice, honor, and manhood combine to open a new frontier of human dignity and "to act in the service of a brotherhood that includes us all."38

In his era, Richard Reid had sought to bring about just such a place of progress by calling on the people to support a fresh frontier of thinking for a new Kentucky, a new South, a new America. But the reaction to his nonviolent response and then later to his violent suicide showed just how deep-seated those attitudes were and how difficult change would be. In his time, each area—justice, honor, and manhood—seemed to be at the extreme. Community justice brought vigilantism and lack of respect for the law; the code of honor brought untold violence; masculinity brought an aggressive manhood. But Reid, in a sense, stood at the other end of the cultural spectrum in each of those areas and extremism in the defense of that view proved no virtue. Legalism, forgiveness, compassion—they represented his vision of a future too far removed from that time, and too extreme for that society. Reid tried to cause a reevaluation of the old ways, but it would take many more deaths and many more lives uselessly ended—like his—before those views faded.

But if they did modify in certain ways over time, they also continued to live on. His dilemma, his choices, his options remain before us. He faced the ageless question of choosing between forgiveness and forbearance on the one hand, and revenge and retribution on the other. But the debate—his debate and later ones—intensifies when justice clearly demands that certain acts *must* be punished. Yet in doing that, how does a society, or a Reid in it, temper that response with actions that represent as well the values and ideals they have articulated and the future they have sought? In his era, Reid refused to descend to the level of Cornelison, but it cost him almost everything to take that course. He may have lost his way as he spoke for a higher and brighter future, one to be always sought, if perhaps never achieved. Reid's life reminds both of the better nature that he called on people to follow and also the darker side of the human soul. Reid fought that fight within himself, and his life, his history, still leaves its lessons for new generations, as they face the same struggles.

In his time, Reid should have been at his personal summit, for he had climbed the high mountains of his fears and physical problems, but then, after the caning, he had peered out and seen even higher challenges now before him. When he looked at the faces of his people and his America, he saw revealed back to him parts of his own tortured soul. He had lived for the law, and died for it; he had lived for his love, and departed when he feared the loss of love; he had lived with hope in the future, and died without it.

Yet he had lived, had shown the rare courage to try to effect change, had achieved much, and had done right for his fellow humans. That they did not return his devotion cut deeply, and a life filled with the scars of so many pains could not endure the new, cruel wounds to the psyche. And so Richard Reid died a failed hero—but a person who, above all else, had tried to be a hero for others. The man of many mysteries ended his life, facing the ultimate mystery.

In the cemetery at Mount Sterling, Richard Reid lies beside his wife and stepson. His tall bronze and granite monument, situated on a high hill, shows a man with a book in one hand and a pen in the other. A plaque on the front presents blindfolded justice with a broken sword and serpent nearby. Part of the inscription reads, "Martyr to law." The four angels once surrounding the sculpture have been stolen. Whether by design or not, the statue of Reid has its back to the town that he believed had turned its back on his cause. He instead faces the other graves, the dead past. Yet as he looks out, his eyes sweep beyond all that, perhaps still searching for the better future that he never found, and for which he died.

Notes

INTRODUCTION

1. Robin W. Winks, ed., *The Historian as Detective: Essays on Evidence* (1968); Winthrop D. Jordan, *White over Black: American Attitudes toward the Negro, 1550–1812* (1968), ix.

2. Scott Reed, introduction to *Famous Kentucky Tragedies and Trials*, by L. F. Johnson, (1916; 1972), [ix]. I wish to thank Christopher Waldrep and Bertram Wyatt-Brown for suggestions on some of these points.

PROLOGUE

1. *Louisville Courier-Journal*, 17 April 1884; *Cornelison v. Commonwealth* 2 S.W. 237; Elizabeth Jameson Reid, *Judge Richard Reid: A Biography* (1886), 180, 503 (this work hereinafter cited as *Judge Reid*); *Mount Sterling Daily Sentinel-Democrat*, 17 April 1884; *Paris Semi-Weekly Bourbon News*, 18, 29 April 1884. Another version has Cornelison saying "that is an infamous thing." See *Louisville Commercial*, 17 April 1884.

Cornelison's name was frequently misspelled. Those errors have been corrected without comment throughout.

2. *Judge Reid*, 177 n, 177–81, 561–62; *Cornelison v. Commonwealth* 2 S.W. 237; *Paris Kentuckian*, 23 April 1884; *Louisville Courier-Journal*, 22 April 1884; *Paris Semi-Weekly Bourbon News*, 29, 18 April 1884; *Louisville Commercial*, 17 April 1884, 29 July 1888; *Mount Sterling Daily Sentinel-Democrat*, 17 April 1884. *Judge Reid*, 562, has a different quote from Cornelison: "I am thrashing the d——d rascal."

CHAPTER 1

1. *Judge Reid*, 1–2; "Mr. Richard Reid," *Kentucky Law Journal* 2 (1882): 3. The Reid biography is generally a collection of letters, remembrances, and recollections, and includes

much primary material. Another branch of the Reid family is described in Thomas Marshall Green, *Historic Families of Kentucky* (1889), 160–61, 99–100.

2. *Judge Reid,* 3–5; Richard Reid, *Historical Sketches of Montgomery County* (1882; 1926), 51; Arthur K. Moore, *The Frontier Mind: A Cultural Analysis of the Kentucky Frontiersman* (1957), 23; Richard A. Prewitt, *Michael Prewitt Sr. and his Descendents, 1720–1977* (1977), 353–54; Hazel M. Boyd, *Some Marriages in Montgomery County, Kentucky, before 1864* (1961), 26. On the non-political aspects of early Kentucky, see also Stephen Aron, *How the West Was Lost: The Transformation of Kentucky from Daniel Boone to Henry Clay* (1996), Elizabeth A. Perkins, *Border Life: Experience and Memory in the Revolutionary Ohio Valley* (1998), and Craig T. Friend, ed., *The Buzzell about Kentuck: Settling the Promised Land* (1999).

3. *Judge Reid,* 5.

4. Ibid., 3–5; R. Reid, *Historical Sketches,* 51.

5. *Judge Reid,* 5; Rowena Lawson, *Montgomery County Kentucky 1850 Census* (1986), n.p.; Prewitt, *Prewitt Descendants,* 358.

6. *Judge Reid,* 4–5; Montgomery County Deeds, County Clerk's Office, Mount Sterling, Kentucky, Deed Book 20–21: 278–79.

7. *Judge Reid,* 6–7; E. Anthony Rotundo, *American Manhood: Transformations in Masculinity from the Revolution to the Modern Era* (1993), 42.

8. *Judge Reid,* 7.

9. Ibid., 6–9; Emmy E. Werner and Ruth S. Smith, *Vulnerable but Invincible: A Longitudinal Study of Resilient Children and Youth* (1982), 153–60. The literature on sleepwalking (arousal parasomnias) is sizable and evolving. Samples of the literature include A. N. Vgontzas and A. Kales, "Sleep and Its Disorders," *Annual Review of Medicine* 50 (1999): 387–400; and Maurice M. Ohayon, Christian Guilleminault, and R. G. Priest, "Night Terrors, Sleepwalking, and Confusional Arousals in the General Population," *Journal of Clinical Psychiatry* 60 (1999): 268–76.

10. *Judge Reid,* 12–15; D. S. C. M. Potter to Richard Reid Rogers, 5 July 1884, in *Letters* (n.d.), 94; Carl B. Boyd Jr. and Hazel M. Boyd, *A History of Mount Sterling, Kentucky, 1792–1918* (1984), 265. On the school system see the overview in Lowell H. Harrison and James C. Klotter, *A New History of Kentucky* (1997), 148–51, and broader surveys such as Moses Ligon, *A History of Public Education in Kentucky* (1942), Frank McVey, *The Gates Open Slowly: A History of Education in Kentucky* (1949), and Frank F. Mathias, "Kentucky's Struggle for Common Schools, 1820–1850," *Register of the Kentucky Historical Society* 82 (1984): 214–34. The *Letters* volume referenced above likely appeared in 1885. It contained full texts of letters about Reid, sent mostly to his wife after his death. Often fuller texts appeared there than in her later biography, cited in n. 1.

11. D. S. C. M. Potter to Richard Reid Rogers, 5 July 1884, in *Letters,* 94, 99–100; *Judge Reid,* 14. On Guerrant, see William C. Davis and Meredith L. Swentor, eds., *Bluegrass Confederate: The Headquarters Diary of Edward O. Guerrant* (1999), 1–13; J. Gray McAllister and Grace O. Guerrant, *Edward O. Guerrant* (1950).

12. Potter to Rogers, 5 June 1884, in *Letters,* 96; *Judge Reid,* 13.

13. Fredrick Rudolph, *The American College and University: A History* (1962); Alvin F. Lewis, *History of Higher Education in Kentucky* (1899); McVey, *Gates Open Slowly,* 78–105;

Harrison and Klotter, *New History,* 152–53; John D. Wright Jr., *Transylvania: Tutor to the West* (1975), 65–184.

14. Robert Snyder, *A History of Georgetown College* (1979), 1–14, 29; Lindsey Apple, Frederick A. Johnston, and Ann Bolton Bevins, eds., *Scott County, Kentucky: A History* (1993), 40, 55, 75, 81 (quotation), 154, 115. See also Carl R. Fields, *A Sesquicentennial History of Georgetown College* (1979), 1; Leland W. Meyer, *Georgetown College* (1929), 36–74; and Samuel S. Hill, "Outline Sketch of Georgetown College," *Filson Club History Quarterly* 26 (1952): 166–71.

15. Snyder, *Georgetown College,* 10, 14, 16–22, 34; Hill, "Outline Sketch," 169–71.

16. *Catalogue of the Students of Georgetown College,* (n.d.); *Catalogue of the Officers and Students of Georgetown College, Kentucky, 1855–1856* (1856), 14.

17. Apple, Johnston, and Bevins, *Scott County,* 33–35; Stuart S. Sprague, "The Death of Tecumseh and the Rise of Rumpsey Dumpsey: The Making of a Vice President," *Filson Club History Quarterly* 59 (1985): 455–61; Jonathan M. Jones, "The Making of a Vice President: The National Political Career of Richard M. Johnson of Kentucky" (Ph.D. diss., University of Memphis, 1998); Ella W. Drake, "Choctaw Academy: Richard M. Johnson and the Business of Indian Education," *Register of the Kentucky Historical Society* 91 (1993): 260–97.

18. Leland W. Meyer, *The Life and Times of Colonel Richard M. Johnson of Kentucky* (1932), 317–21; Apple, Johnston, and Bevins, *Scott County,* 37, 49, 116, 113, 124–26.

19. Thelma Dunn, transcriber, *Montgomery County, Kentucky, County Clerk Tax Assessment Records 1806–1807–1808–1809–1810 and the 1810 Census Record* (1996), 66, 110, 137, 1; Apple, Johnston, and Bevins, *Scott County,* 113.

20. Snyder, *Georgetown College,* 27, 38–41; Apple, Johnston, and Bevins, *Scott County,* 156, 158, 160, 145; *Catalogue, 1855–56,* 13, 15–16; *Catalogue of the Officers and Students of Georgetown College, Kentucky, 1856–1857* (1857), [14]; Fields, *Sesquicentennial History,* 5; entries of 21 December 1859, 25 January 1860, 30 May 1860, Records of Georgetown College, 1859–1887, College Archives, Georgetown College.

21. John L. Peak to Elizabeth Reid, September 1885, quoted in *Judge Reid,* 24; *Catalogue, 1855–56,* 5–8. On Cantrill, see *Biographical Encyclopaedia of Kentucky* (1878), 765; on Ward, H. Levin, ed., *Lawyers and Lawmakers of Kentucky* (1897), 141; on Atherton, E. Polk Johnson, *A History of Kentucky and Kentuckians,* 3 vols. (1912), 2: 805–806.

22. *Catalogue, 1855–56,* [4], 11–12.

23. Edward C. O'Rear, *History of the Montgomery County (Ky.) Bar* (1945), 55; Peak to Reid, September 1885, William G. Welch to Elizabeth Reid, 18 December 1884, both quoted in *Judge Reid,* 23, 20.

24. [Richard Reid], "The Martyr to Science," *Georgetown College Magazine* 1 (1857): 197–99.

25. Apple, Johnston, and Bevins, *Scott County,* 156, 193; Fields, *Sesquicentennial History,* 12; Snyder, *Georgetown College,* 27, 37; *Catalogue, 1855–56,* 14–15. The activities of another member of the Ciceronian Society, who attended Georgetown College just before Reid, can be followed in the James Tevis Diary, 1852–53, College Archives, Georgetown College.

26. [Richard Reid], "Music," 67–71, and Richard Reid, "Unity of Purpose in Life," 216–19, both in *Ciceronian Magazine* 1 (1856).

27. Richard Reid, "The Old Age of the Scholar," *Ciceronian Magazine* 1 (1857): 388–91.

28. Ibid., 391–93.

29. Richard Reid to D. S. C. M. Potter, 26 February 1857, 29 October 1858, quoted in *Judge Reid*, 24–26, 29.

30. William G. Welch to Elizabeth Reid, 18 December 1884, John L. Peak to Elizabeth Reid, September 1885, J. A. Chambliss to Elizabeth Reid, 31 December 1884, quoted in *Judge Reid*, 19–24; Atherton, quoted in *Richard Reid: A Memorial* (1884), 106–107. The latter source is a collection mostly of newspaper quotes.

31. *Catalogue of the Officers and Students of Georgetown College, Kentucky 1857–1858* (1858), [5]; entry of 26 May 1858 Records of the Faculty, vol. 1, College Archives, Georgetown College; "Richard Reid" entry, "Catalogue of the Students of Georgetown College with a List of Academic Honors Conferred by the College," College Archives, Georgetown College; *Seventeenth Annual Commencement of Georgetown College* (n.d.).

32. Entry of 22 June 1858, Records of the Trustees of Georgetown College from 1837 to 1865, College Archives, Georgetown College; *Catalogue of the Officers and Students of Georgetown College, Kentucky 1858–1859* (1859), 4, 10; *Catalogue of Georgetown College, Kentucky 1859–1860* (1860), 4, 12; Snyder, *Georgetown College*, 36; Richard Reid to D. S. C. M. Potter, 15 July 1860, quoted in *Judge Reid*, 30, 26.

33. Richard Reid to D. S. C. M. Potter, 15 July 1860, quoted in *Judge Reid*, 20–21, 30; *Paris True Kentuckian*, 16 April 1879; *Georgetown Times*, 21 May 1884; Levin, ed., *Lawyers and Lawmakers*, 86; *Biographical Encyclopaedia*, 163–64; unidentified clipping, 1891, in James M. Saffell Scrapbooks, Southern Historical Collection, University of North Carolina; Sallie E. M. Hardy, "Some Kentucky Lawyers of the Past and Present," *Green Bag* 9 (1897): 308–309.

34. Richard Reid to D. S. C. M. Potter, 15 July 1860, quoted in *Judge Reid*, 31; G. Glenn Clift, *Governors of Kentucky, 1792–1942* (1942), 198–99; *Biographical Encyclopaedia*, 260–63.

35. Lewis Collins and Richard H. Collins, *History of Kentucky*, 2 vols. (1874), 1:59; Lowell H. Harrison, *The Civil War in Kentucky* (1975), 5; Lebanon [pseud.], "Suggested Thoughts," *Ciceronian Magazine* 1 (1856): 269–71; Snyder, *Georgetown College*, 42; entry of 23 April 1861, Records of Georgetown College, 1859–1887; James C. Klotter, *The Breckinridges of Kentucky, 1760–1981* (1986), 80; Will D. Gilliam Jr., "Family Friends and Foes," *Louisville Courier-Journal Magazine*, 20 November 1960; John Fox Jr., *The Little Shepherd of Kingdom Come* (1903; 1973), 153–54.

36. For the first year of the conflict of Kentucky generally, see L. H. Harrison, *Civil War in Kentucky*, 6–13; Lowell H. Harrison, *Lincoln and Kentucky* (2000), 111–50; Steven E. Woodworth, " 'The Indeterminable Quantities': Jefferson Davis, Leonidas Polk, and the End of Kentucky's Neutrality, September 1861," *Civil War History* 38 (1992): 289–97; E. Merton Coulter, *The Civil War and Readjustment in Kentucky* (1926), 18–124; Edward C. Smith, *The Borderland in the Civil War* (1927), 263–312; Timothy Russell, "Neutrality and Ideological Conflict in Kentucky During the First Year of the American Civil War" (Ph.D. diss., University of New Mexico, 1989); John A. Boyd, "Neutrality and Peace: Kentucky and the Secession Crisis of 1861" (Ph.D. diss., University of Kentucky, 1999).

37. *Judge Reid*, 34, 10, 13, 22, 35; *Christian Standard*, 31 May 1884, quoted in *Richard Reid: A Memorial*, 92; *Biographical Encyclopaedia*, 263; Richard Reid to D. S. C. M. Potter,

February 1863, quoted in *Judge Reid*, 36. On the general health of Kentucky soldiers, see John David Smith, "Kentucky Civil War Recruits: A Medical Profile," *Medical History* 24 (1980): 185–96.

CHAPTER 2

1. Richard Reid to D. S. C. M. Potter, 29 October 1858, quoted in *Judge Reid*, 29.

2. *Judge Reid*, 32, 27, 47; John L. Peak to Elizabeth Reid, September 1885, quoted in *Judge Reid*, 21.

3. *Judge Reid*, 20–23, 42–43, 117, 125; *Richard Reid: A Memorial*, 29, 22, 18, 106; *Paris True Kentuckian*, 30 April 1879; Reid to D. S. C. M. Potter, 29 October 1858, quoted in *Judge Reid*, 29.

4. *Biographical Directory of the American Congress, 1774–1949* (1950), 1367; *Judge Reid*, 32–33.

5. *Judge Reid*, 32, 37; *Georgetown Times*, 2 July 1884.

6. Richard Reid to Linda Jameson, 18 August 1863, quoted in *Judge Reid*, 37, 39.

7. *Ibid.*, 36–40; *Fulton (Mo.) Telegraph*, 27 November 1863; *Paris Kentuckian*, 16 May 1884; *Memorial*, 10. The exact date of her death became confused over the years. The *Paris Kentuckian*, 16 May 1884, said Sallie Jameson died the day before the wedding, which was also the time given in one of the sources in *Richard Reid: A Memorial*, 10. The *Georgetown Times*, 21 May 1884, places her death at the day of the wedding, a time reported in another source in *Richard Reid: A Memorial*, 70. See also *Judge Reid*, 386. However, the Fulton paper clearly places the date on the eleventh, and Jameson's sister gave the wedding date as the twenty-fifth, both of which are likely correct. Had her death occurred so close to the wedding, Reid would already have been there, rather than back in Kentucky.

8. *Fulton (Mo.) Telegraph*, 27 November 1863; John I. Rogers, quoted in *Judge Reid*, 39–40; Richard Reid to Reid Rogers, 16 April 1883, quoted in *Judge Reid*, 159; *Georgetown Times*, 2 July 1884; *Judge Reid*, 485.

9. Richard Reid to D. S. C. M. Potter, 13 September 1864, quoted in *Judge Reid*, 41, 45; O'Rear, *Montgomery County Bar*, 55; "Mr. Richard Reid," 3; *Louisville Courier-Journal*, 15 June 1882.

10. *Mount Sterling Kentucky Sentinel*, 28, 21 July 1865; Deed Book 28–29, Montgomery County Deeds, County Clerk's Office, Mount Sterling; *Judge Reid*, 47 n, 47.

11. *Judge Reid*, 52–53; deed dated 18 January 1869 between Richard Reid and J. D. Reid, and C. Brock, executor, Montgomery County Deed Book 30–31, pp. 304–305; Prewitt, *Prewitt Descendants*, 358; Richard Reid to Elizabeth Rogers, 29, 30 July 1872; Reid to Linda Jameson, 12 August 1872, quoted in *Judge Reid*, 53.

12. Richard Reid to Linda Jameson, 25 May, 29 December 1869, quoted in *Judge Reid*, 49; Prewitt, *Prewitt Descendants*, 354; *Mount Sterling Kentucky Sentinel*, 3 November 1865; Caswell Lane, interview by author, Mount Sterling, 1 October 1999. The house still stands, and the comments on the Hood house and countryside come from personal observation.

13. Richard Reid to Linda Jameson, 25 May, 29 December 1869, quoted in *Judge Reid*, 49–50. On Apperson, see R. Reid, *Historical Sketches*, 57–60; *Biographical Encyclopaedia*,

26; William E. Connelley and E. Merton Coulter, *History of Kentucky,* 5 vols. (1922), 4:615; O'Rear, *Montgomery County Bar,* 38–41, 56.

14. Collins and Collins, *History of Kentucky,* 2:631–33; Boyd and Boyd, *Mount Sterling,* 1, 5, 48–50, 103; Frank F. Mathias, ed., *Incidents and Experiences in the Life of Thomas W. Parsons* (1975), 121, 192 n; James A. Ramage, *Rebel Raider: The Life of General John Hunt Morgan* (1986), 218, 208, 225; Davis and Swentor, eds., *Bluegrass Confederate,* 464. The city was supposed to be called Mount Stirling, but the spelling was somehow corrupted to the present spelling. See Robert M. Rennick, *Kentucky Place Names* (1984), 205.

15. Richard Reid to D. S. C. M. Potter, undated [late 1864–early 1865], Reid to Elizabeth Rogers, 17 January 1865; Reid to Linda Jameson, 6 January 1865, all quoted in *Judge Reid,* 45–47; Davis and Swentor, eds., *Bluegrass Confederate,* 689; "Kentucky," in *Appleton's Annual Cyclopedia and Register of Important Events* (1866), 461; Harrison, *Civil War in Kentucky,* 95.

16. Clipping dated 10 May 1877, "Clippings from the 'Looking Backward' Column of *Mount Sterling Sentinel-Democrat,*" Mount Sterling Public Library; James Lane Allen, *The Blue Grass Region of Kentucky* (1892), 203, 207, 36; Edward L. Ayers, *The Promise of the New South: Life after Reconstruction* (1992), 213.

17. W. T. Price, *Without Scrip or Purse; or, The "Mountain Evangelist," George O. Barnes* (1883), 60; Harrison and Klotter, *New History,* 239–43. On the urban South in this era, see, for example, Lawrence H. Larson, *The Urban South: A History* (1990); Larson, *The Rise of the Urban South* (1985); David Goldfield, *Cotton Fields and Skyscrapers: Southern City and Region, 1607–1980* (1982); Howard N. Rabinowitz, "Continuity and Change: Southern Urban Development, 1860–1900," in *The City in Southern History* ed. Blaine A. Brownell and David R. Goldfield, (1977).

18. Boyd and Boyd, *Mount Sterling,* 31; Harrison and Klotter, *New History,* 235; Marion B. Lucas, *From Slavery to Segregation, 1760–1891* vol. 1 of *A History of Blacks in Kentucky,* by Marion B. Lucas and George C. Wright, (1992), 158–60, 166, 185.

19. *Mount Sterling Kentucky Sentinel,* 29 September 1865; Lucas, *From Slavery to Segregation,* 1: 185–201; George C. Wright, *Racial Violence in Kentucky, 1865–1940* (1990), 19–60; Peter C. Smith and Karl B. Raitz, "Negro Hamlets and Agricultural Estates in Kentucky's Inner Bluegrass," *Geographical Review* 64 (1974): 217–34. See also Victor B. Howard, *Black Liberation in Kentucky: Emancipation and Freedom, 1862–1884* (1983), and Marion B. Lucas, "Kentucky Blacks: The Transition from Slavery to Freedom," *Register of the Kentucky Historical Society* 91 (1993): 403–19.

20. *Mount Sterling Democrat,* 2 July 1880; *Montgomery County, Kentucky, Bicentennial, 1774–1974* (n.d.), 17; *Mount Sterling Democrat,* 20 January 1882; Boyd and Boyd, *Mount Sterling,* 55–58, 63.

21. Boyd and Boyd, *Mount Sterling,* 54, 58, 61, 79; Collins and Collins, *History of Kentucky,* 2:261. Mount Sterling, like Kentucky generally, had a very small immigrant population, compared to the overall American average. In 1870, the city contained forty-four foreign born, under 1 percent of its population. Mount Sterling grew from thirty-first in size among the state's cities in 1870 to seventeenth twenty years later. *Mount Sterling Democrat,* 2 July 1880; Collins and Collins, *History of Kentucky,* 2:263–65.

22. Collins and Collins, *History of Kentucky,* 2:631; A. B. Lipscomb, ed., *The Commercial*

History of the Southern States: Kentucky (1903), 99; *Mount Sterling Advocate,* 13 November 1894; Boyd and Boyd, *Mount Sterling,* 123, 118, 61; *Mount Sterling Democrat,* 7 March 1881; Richard Reid to William Lindsay, 19 June 1878, Lindsay Papers, Special Collections, University of Kentucky.

23. Price, *Without Scrip,* 246; Lane interview; *Montgomery County Bicentennial,* 111–12. The presence of women at Mount Sterling Court Day may not have been the norm in Kentucky. See Pattie French Witherspoon, *Through Two Administrations: Character Sketches of Kentucky* (1897), 62.

24. *Kentucky State Directory, Travelers and Shippers Guide for 1870–1871* (1870), 148–49; Boyd and Boyd, *Mount Sterling,* 61, 244, 67, 103; *Montgomery County Bicentennial,* 44; *Courier-Journal* article reprinted in *Mount Sterling Democrat,* 9 December 1881; *Louisville Courier-Journal,* 1 June 1882. Ronald D Eller, *Miners, Millhands, and Mountaineers: Industrialization of the Appalachian South, 1880–1930* (1982), 66, 142, has maps showing railroad expansion into the mountains.

25. Klotter, *Breckinridges of Kentucky,* 6; Boyd and Boyd, *Mount Sterling,* 59–60, 259–62; Richard Reid to Linda Jameson, 22 June 1871, quoted in *Judge Reid,* 55.

26. Richard Reid to Linda Atkinson, 1 January 1873, quoted in *Judge Reid,* 55.

27. Fannie Payne to Elizabeth Reid, 23 April 1884, quoted in *Letters,* 55, 61; *Elizabeth Jameson Reid: A Tribute* (1904), 11–13; *Mount Sterling Advocate,* 8 July 1902; O'Rear, *Montgomery County Bar,* 56; Eric C. Nagle, *Vital Records from Newspapers of Paris, Kentucky, 1813–1870* (1999), 206, 237; Kenney Roseberry Family Files, Paris, Ky.; *Bourbon County, Kentucky, Tombstone Inscriptions* (n.d.), 52; *Judge Reid,* 57–58. Most of the "colleges" more resembled today's secondary schools. See Jo Della Alband, "A History of the Education of Women in Kentucky" (master's thesis, University of Kentucky, 1954), 157.

28. *Fulton (Mo.) Telegraph,* 14 November 1873; *Judge Reid,* 56–58.

29. Richard Reid to Elizabeth Rogers, 1873, Reid to C. O. Atkinson, 26 November 1873; Reid to D. S. C. M. Potter, 1 January 1874, all quoted in *Judge Reid,* 62, 58, 59.

30. *Judge Reid,* 48, 56; *Richard Reid: A Memorial,* 107; Bourbon County Will Book S, pp. 33–35, 52–58, 82–83, 95–99, Bourbon County Order Book T, pp. 150, 172, 185, 197, 242, 423, Bourbon County Deed Book 70, pp. 630–32, Bourbon County Clerk's Office, Paris, Ky.; Montgomery County Deed Book 36–37, pp. 636–37; "Clippings from the 'Looking Backward' Column," 7 June 1877; Paul E. Fuller, *Laura Clay and the Woman's Rights Movement* (1975), 39; Nancy M. Theriot, *Mothers and Daughters in Nineteenth-Century America* (1996), 34; Montgomery County Deed Book 40–41, pp. 24–26; Lane interview and personal observations. In good condition, the house, now divided into two dwellings, still stands, in the middle of a subdivision. Ann and Curt Steger, interview by author, Mount Sterling, 15 June 2001.

31. Charles E. Rosenberg, "Sexuality, Class, and Role in Nineteenth-Century America," *American Quarterly* 25 (1973): 140; *Judge Reid,* 62, 58; Stephen M. Frank, *Life with Father: Parenthood and Masculinity in the Nineteenth-Century North* (1998), 51, 2, 87; *Compendium of the Ninth Census (June 1, 1870),* (1870), 541.

32. *Judge Reid,* 76, 72–73; O'Rear, *Montgomery County Bar,* 85; *Mount Sterling Daily Sentinel-Democrat,* 17 May 1884; *Mount Sterling Democrat,* 19 August 1881; Eleanor Breckinridge Chalkley, *"Magic Casements"* (1982), 70; Klotter, *Breckinridges of Kentucky,* 198, 213.

33. *Judge Reid,* 65–66; *Richard Reid: A Memorial,* 39; *Mount Sterling Democrat,* 10 September, 16 April 1880.

34. *Judge Reid,* 66–67; Tenth Census of the United States, 1880: 1st Ward, Mount Sterling, Montgomery County, Kentucky (microfilm, Kentucky Historical Society). The Hortons were sometimes referred to as Mrs. Reid's nieces, but that likely results from their addressing the Reids as "Uncle" and "Aunt." *Louisville Courier-Journal,* 15 June 1882.

35. Carl N. Degler, *At Odds: Women and the Family in America from the Revolution to the Present* (1980), 77; *Mount Sterling Democrat,* 8 October 1880; *Elizabeth Jameson Reid,* 6; Richard Reid to Elizabeth Reid, 7 March, 8 April 1884, quoted in *Letters,* 5–6; Reid to Elizabeth Reid, 18 May 1875, quoted in *Judge Reid,* 62–64.

36. Bertram Wyatt-Brown, "Church, Honor, and Secession," in *Religion in the American Civil War* ed. Randall M. Miller, Harry S. Stout, and Charles Reagan Wilson (1998), 97; Wyatt-Brown, "God and Honor in the Old South," *Southern Review* 25 (1989): 290; Ted Ownby, *Subduing Satan: Religion, Recreation, and Manhood in the Rural South, 1865–1920* (1990), 129; *Paris Semi-Weekly Bourbon News,* 29 April 1884; *Richard Reid: A Memorial,* 6, 14, 102; *Letters,* 97–98; *Judge Reid,* 82, 85; Richard L. Harrison Jr., *From Camp Meeting to Church: A History of the Christian Church (Disciples of Christ) in Kentucky* (1992), 180–84; Richard Reid to Reid Rogers, 12 November 1882, Reid to Jno. D. Harris, 20 July 1883, both quoted in *Judge Reid,* 150, 99. See also Price, *Without Scrip,* 242. In 1870, the Christian Church ranked third in the state, with 141,585 members, behind the Baptists and Methodists. *Ninth Census: Population* (1870): 539.

37. Gail Bederman, *Manliness and Civilization: A Cultural History of Gender and Race in the United States, 1880–1917* (1995), 16; Mark C. Carnes, *Secret Ritual and Manhood in Victorian America* (1989), 1–3, 14, 25–26; Michael Kimmel, *Manhood in America: A Cultural History* (1996), 117, 171; Rotundo, *American Manhood,* 64; *Mount Sterling Democrat,* 23 April 1880.

38. Susan Curtis, "The Son of Man and God the Father: The Social Gospel and Victorian Masculinity," in *Meanings for Manhood: Constructions of Masculinity in Victorian America,* ed. Mark C. Carnes and Clyde Griffen (1990), 67–71; Ownby, *Subduing Satan,* 208–209; Richard Reid, "Temperance Address," quoted in *Judge Reid,* 118–24;

39. Bederman, *Manliness and Civilization,* 170, 13; *Lexington Daily Press,* 3 February 1874, <http://www.uky.edu/~dolph>; John W. Stevenson to "Mr. McChesney," 8 May 1878, in 1877–78 Letterbook, John White Stevenson Collection, Special Collections, University of Kentucky; *Frankfort Daily Kentucky Yeoman,* 27 April 1880.

40. R. L. Harrison, *Camp Meeting to Church,* 184–85; Richard Reid, "Address to Young Ladies," quoted in *Judge Reid,* 129–34, 489.

41. Preston Taylor to Elizabeth Reid, 20 November 1885, quoted in *Judge Reid,* 463–64.

42. *Mount Sterling Democrat,* 21 October 1881, 21, 28 March 1882, 21 January 1881; Richard Reid to May Horton, 18, 23 August 1882, quoted in *Judge Reid,* 142–45. Mrs. Bardell, in the *Pickwick Papers,* is the landlady who sues Pickwick for breach of promise. See Margaret Drabble, ed., *The Oxford Companion to English Literature,* 5th ed. (1985), 66.

43. *Paris Kentuckian,* 21 May 1884; *Judge Reid,* 100–106; R. Reid, *Historical Sketches,* passim; Elizabeth Reid to Mrs. Cornelius Bush, 20 March 1882, in Mrs. Richard Reid Collection, Kentucky Historical Society. An image of the library appears in the *Christian Standard,* 1891, clipping in Everett Donaldson Papers, Mount Sterling, Ky.

44. Rotundo, *American Manhood,* 115, 111, 130–32; John D'Emilio and Estelle B. Freedman, *Intimate Matters: A History of Sexuality in America* (1988), 75, 78; Karen Lystra, *Searching the Heart: Women, Men, and Romantic Love in Nineteenth-Century America* (1989), 233, 124, 149, 7; Degler, *At Odds,* 42; Theriot, *Mothers and Daughters,* 35. See also J. A. Mangan and James Walvin, eds., *Manliness and Morality: Middle-Class Masculinity in Britain and America, 1800–1940* (1987); Peter T. Cominos, "Late-Victorian Sexual Respectability and the Social System," *International Review of Social History* 8 (1963): 18–48, 216–50; and Peter W. Bardaglio, *Reconstructing the Household: Families, Sex, and the Law in the Nineteenth-Century South* (1995), 224–25.

45. *Georgetown Times,* 2 July 1884; Kate G. Reid to Elizabeth Reid, 31 May 1884, in *Letters,* 133.

CHAPTER 3

1. Henry Lane Stone, *"Morgan's Men": A Narrative of Personal Experiences* (1919), 3–35; *Judge Reid,* 115–16, 150–51. Sketches of Stone's life appear in O'Rear, *Montgomery County Bar,* 60–65; J. A. Richards, *History of Bath County* (1961), 297–98; J. Stoddard Johnston, ed., *Memorial History of Louisville,* 2 vols. (1896), 2: 402–405; E. P. Johnson, *History of Kentucky,* 2:647–49; Levin, ed., *Lawyers and Lawmakers,* 212–15.

2. *Majority and Minority Reports and Testimony Taken by the Rowan County Investigating Committee* (1888), 5–7, 427, 228; *Louisville Courier-Journal,* 6 August 1885; Robert M. Ireland, "Law and Disorder in Nineteenth-Century Kentucky," *Vanderbilt Law Review* 32 (1979): 281, 288, 291; Ireland, "Violence," in *Our Kentucky: A Study of the Bluegrass State,* ed. James C. Klotter (rev. ed., 2000), 157; Ireland, "The Buford-Elliott Tragedy and the Traditions of Kentucky Criminal Justice," *Filson Club History Quarterly* 66 (1992): 402; Ireland, *Little Kingdoms: The Counties of Kentucky, 1850–1891* (1977), 82; Hambleton Tapp and James C. Klotter, *Kentucky: Decades of Discord, 1865–1900* (1977), 177.

3. Ireland, "Law and Disorder," 287, 283, 292; Ireland, "Violence," 158; Robert M. Ireland, "The Nineteenth-Century Criminal Jury: Kentucky in the Context of the American Experience," *Kentucky Review* 4 (1983): 56; Ireland, "Buford-Elliott," 402–403.

4. Robert M. Ireland, "The Politics of the Elective Judiciary during the Period of Kentucky's Third Constitution," *Register of the Kentucky Historical Society* 93 (1995): 399; *Kentucky Law Journal* 1 (1881): 151; John W. Stevenson to C. E. Sears, 10 January 1882, Stevenson Collection.

5. Ireland, "Law and Disorder," 294–97; Ireland, "Violence," 158–59; Nancy Disher Baird, *Luke Pryor Blackburn: Physician, Governor, Reformer* (1979), 107; *New York Times,* quoted in Ireland, *Little Kingdoms,* 82. Numerous such petitions exist in the papers of various governors, Kentucky Department for Libraries and Archives.

6. Ireland, *Little Kingdoms,* 78–80; James C. Klotter, "Feuds in Appalachia: An Overview," *Filson Club History Quarterly* 56 (1982): 311–13; Ireland, "Criminal Jury," 54. See also Mary K. Bonsteel Tachau, "Comment," *Vanderbilt Law Review* 32 (1979): 301–303, and Timothy S. Huebner, *The Southern Judicial Tradition: State Judges and Sectional Distinctiveness, 1790–1890* (1999).

7. *Ninth Census: Wealth and Industry,* 3:392, 81: Harrison and Klotter, *New History,*

220–21, 234, 240; *Lexington Kentucky Gazette,* 7 July 1866; Joseph F. Wall, *Henry Watterson: Reconstructed Rebel* (1956), 84, 125, 171, 230; James P. Sullivan, "Louisville and Her Southern Alliance, 1865–1890" (Ph.D. diss., University of Kentucky, 1965), passim.

8. Harrison and Klotter, *New History,* 205–206, 237–39; Coulter, *Civil War and Readjustment,* 152–56, 439; Allen W. Trelease, *White Terror* (1971), 124; W. A. Low, "The Freedmen Bureau in the Border States," in *Radicalism, Racism, and Party Alignment: The Border States during Reconstruction,* ed. Richard O. Curry (1969), 250–54; Ross A. Webb, *Kentucky in the Reconstruction Era* (1979); C. Vann Woodward, *Origins of the New South, 1877–1913* (1951), 6.

9. Tapp and Klotter, *Decades of Discord,* 22, 25–26, 46, 138, 170, 218, 235, 321; Ireland, "Elective Judiciary," 414.

10. Harrison and Klotter, *New History,* 241; *Lexington Observer and Reporter,* 4 January 1868; *Louisville Courier-Journal* (weekly), 10 May 1871.

11. Tapp and Klotter, *Decades of Discord,* 28, 26, 14, 22; *Frankfort Commonwealth* (semi-weekly), 9 August 1867; Lynn Douglas Morton, ed. *Weeden D. Gay's Diary, 1872–1888* (1994), 23; Ireland, "Elective Judiciary," 403–404; *New York Times,* 6 March 1882; Gaines M. Foster, *Ghosts of the Confederacy: Defeat, the Lost Cause, and the Emergence of the New South* (1985), 195–96.

12. "Memoirs of Henry V. Johnson of Scott County, Kentucky, 1852–1931," p. 65, Georgetown Public Library, Georgetown, Ky.; Klotter, *Breckinridges of Kentucky,* 306–307; William E. Knight, *The Wm. C. P. Breckinridge Defense* (1895), 30.

13. Harrison and Klotter, *New History,* 243–47, 257–69; Tapp and Klotter, *Decades of Discord,* passim.

14. Harrison and Klotter, *New History,* 242; Christopher R. Waldrep, "Rank-and-File Voters and the Coming of the Civil War: Caldwell County, Kentucky, as a Test Case," *Civil War History* 35 (1989): 59–72; Waldrep, "Who Were Kentucky's Whig Voters?" *Register of the Kentucky Historical Society* 79 (1981): 326–32; Thomas L. Connelly, "Neo-Confederatism or Power Vacuum: Post-War Kentucky Politics Reappraised," *Register of the Kentucky Historical Society* 64 (1966): 257–69; Leonard P. Curry, *Rail Routes South: Louisville's Fight for the Southern Market, 1865–1872* (1969), 4, 88; Tapp and Klotter, *Decades of Discord,* 29–36; *Flemingsburg Times-Democrat,* 24 June 1884; Webb, *Reconstruction Era,* 34–35.

15. Boyd and Boyd, *Mount Sterling,* 21–22, 57–58.

16. Richard Reid to Linda Jameson, 25 May 1869, quoted in *Judge Reid,* 48–49; *Paris True Kentuckian,* 7 May 1879.

17. *Richmond (Ky.) Register,* 28 March 1879; *Georgetown Weekly Times,* 2 April 1879; *Winchester Semi-Weekly Sun,* 18 April 1879; *Mount Sterling Democrat,* 4 February 1881; Ireland, "Buford-Elliott," 395–420. See also L. F. Johnson, *Tragedies and Trials,* 205–23.

18. *Winchester Semi-Weekly Sun,* 15 April 1879; *Frankfort Tri-Weekly Yeoman,* 1 April 1879; *Judge Reid,* 135–36.

19. *Winchester Semi-Weekly Sun,* 8 April 1879; *Judge Reid,* 136. On Hargis, see *Biographical Encyclopaedia,* 777–78; Levin, ed., *Lawyers and Lawmakers,* 93–94; John C. Doolan, "The Court of Appeals of Kentucky," *Green Bag* 12 (1900): 463.

20. *Winchester Semi-Weekly Sun,* 25, 29 April 1879; *Paris True Kentuckian,* 23, 30 April 1879; O'Rear, *Montgomery County Bar,* 56; *Richard Reid: A Memorial,* 23. The *Louisville*

Courier-Journal, 22 April 1884, later reported that Reid lost by only ½ vote in the "most excit-ing convention ever held in the mountains," but the 13-vote margin is supported elsewhere.

21. Robert M. Ireland, "The Green-Hargis Affair: Judicial Politics in Nineteenth-Century Kentucky," *Filson Club History Quarterly* 69 (1995): 366–89; *Arguments of Hon. Henry L. Stone of Mount Sterling, Ky., Delivered . . . in Behalf of the Defendant on the Trial of the Celebrated Libel Suit of Thomas M. Green vs. Thomas F. Hargis* (1881), 1–10, 114, 123; *Mount Sterling Democrat,* 11 June 1880.

22. A. E. Richards, "Superior Court of Kentucky," in *Lawyers and Lawmakers,* ed. Levin, 134–35; Tapp and Klotter, *Decades of Discord,* 183–84; *Judge Reid,* 137–39; *Mount Sterling Democrat,* 14, 21 April 1882; *Louisville Courier-Journal,* 15 June 1882; *Paris True Kentuck-ian,* 26 April, 7, 21 June 1882.

23. Richard Reid to Reid Rogers, 26 May 1883, quoted in *Judge Reid,* 160, 161.

24. Ibid., 9 October, 8 November 1883, 27 February 1884; Reid to Elizabeth Reid, 3, 9 October, 15 December 1883, 5 March 1884, quoted in *Judge Reid,* 161–67; *Maysville Bulle-tin,* 8 May 1884; *Biographical Encyclopaedia,* 28; E. P. Johnson, *History of Kentucky,* 3:1562–64.

CHAPTER 4

1. Thomas D. Clark, ed., *The Voice of the Frontier: John Bradford's Notes on Kentucky* (1993), 3, 12–20, 42–60; Harriette Simpson Arnow, *Seedtime on the Cumberland* (1960; 1983), 427, 346, 365; Perkins, *Border Life,* 135–38, 168; John Mack Faragher, *Daniel Boone* (1992), 70, 92–96, 121, 146–47, 218–22. Various, and differing, versions of McGary's words existed early. Humphrey Marshall's 1812 *History of Kentucky,* 164, gave it as cited in the text, sans the word "damned"; a similar version appears in Bradford's 1826 version (T. D. Clark, ed., *Voice of the Frontier,* 56). Faragher, above, cites an 1840s interview in the Draper manu-scripts, State Historical Society of Wisconsin, which offers, "Them that ain't cowards follow me." The version used here is from Daniel Boone's son, in Neal O. Hammon, ed., *My Father, Daniel Boone: The Draper Interviews with Nathan Boone* (1999), 76.

2. Faragher, *Daniel Boone,* 4–7; Michael A. Lofaro, "The Eighteenth Century 'Autobiog-raphies' of Daniel Boone," *Register of the Kentucky Historical Society* 76 (1978): 85–97; Rich-ard Slotkin, *Regeneration through Violence: The Mythology of the American Frontier, 1600–1860* (1973), 268–358; James W. Hammack Jr., *Kentucky and the Second American Revolution* (1976), 112, 83. See also James Russell Harris, "Kentuckians in the War of 1812: A Note on Numbers, Losses, and Sources," *Register of the Kentucky Historical Society* 82 (1984): 277–86.

3. J. Winston Coleman Jr., *Famous Kentucky Duels* (1953; 1969), 32–42; Robert V. Re-mini, *Henry Clay: Statesman for the Union* (1991), 293–95, 54–56; Bruce C. Baird, "The So-cial Aspects of Dueling in Virginia," in *Lethal Imagination: Violence and Brutality in American History,* ed. Michael A. BelleBiles (1999), 90; Melba Porter Hay, "Companion or Conspirator? Henry Clay and the Graves-Cilley Duel," in *A Mythic Land Apart: Reassessing Southerners and Their History,* ed. John David Smith and Thomas H. Appleton Jr. (1997), 57–79; *Portland (Maine) Transcript,* 5 June 1841, quoted in *Register of the Kentucky Historical Society* 97

(1999): 402. A story on the Graves duel appeared in the 30 December 1881 issue of the *Mount Sterling Democrat,* keeping that account before the public in Reid's hometown.

4. Elias Pym Fordham, *Personal Narratives of Travels . . .* (1906), 163; James Hall, *Sketches of History, Life, and Manners in the West,* 2 vols. (1835), 88, 70, 96; [Elizabeth R.] Steele, *A Summer Journey in the West* (1841), 251; *Autobiography of Nathaniel Southgate Shaler . . .* (1909), 41; Champ Clark, "Kentucky during the Civil War," in *Old Kentucky,* ed. J. F. Cook (1908), 218; Champ Clark, *My Quarter Century in American Politics,* 2 vols. (1920), 1:95–97, 78.

5. Ownby, *Subduing Satan,* 93, 21, 78, 53, 15; Lucas, *From Slavery to Segregation,* 43–50; Agnes G. McGann, *Nativism in Kentucky to 1860* (1944), 95–102; James Freeman Clarke, "George D. Prentice and Kentucky Thirty-Five Years Ago," *Old and New* 1 (1870): 741; Edward L. Ayers, *Vengeance and Justice: Crime and Punishment in the Nineteenth-Century American South* (1984), 270, 3; Dickson D. Bruce Jr., *Violence and Culture in the Antebellum South* (1979), 6.

6. Ireland, "Law and Disorder," 281; Ireland, "The Thompson-Davis Case and the Unwritten Law," *Filson Club History Quarterly* 62 (1988): 417–41; Ireland, "The Libertine Must Die: Sexual Dishonor and the Unwritten Law of the Nineteenth-Century United States," *Journal of Social History* 23 (1989): 37, 27–44; Hendrik Hartog, "Lawyering, Husband's Rights, and the 'Unwritten Law' in Nineteenth-Century America," *Journal of American History* 84 (1997): 78, 84.

7. *Louisville Commercial,* 24 April 1884; *Ashland Daily Independent,* 29 September 1954; Evelyn Jackson and William Talley, *Eastern Kentucky References* (1980), 369–72; *Louisville Courier-Journal,* 4 June 1882; *Kentucky Law Journal* 1 (1882): 617; Carter County Bicentennial Committee, *Carter County History, 1838–1976* (n.d.), 99–100; *Ashland Independent,* 1 March 1883, 24 April 1884; William E. Adams, *Our American Cousins* (1883), 253–54; *Mount Sterling Daily Sentinel-Democrat,* 30 April, 2 May 1884. See also J. M. Huff, *The Ashland Tragedy* (1969).

8. Charles Dudley Warner, "Comments on Kentucky," *Harper's New Monthly Magazine* 78 (1889): 270; Wright, *Racial Violence,* 26–60, 69–71; *Newport Kentucky State Journal,* 6 May 1884; *Louisville Commercial,* 17 April, 10 May 1884; *London (Ky.) Mountain Echo,* 16 May 1884; *Frankfort Weekly Kentucky Yeoman,* 13 May 1884.

9. Klotter, "Feuds in Appalachia," 290–317, 312; Altina L. Waller, "Feuding in Appalachia: Evolutions of a Cultural Stereotype," in *Appalachia in the Making: The Mountain South in the Nineteenth Century,* ed. Mary Beth Pudup, Dwight B. Billings, and Altina L. Waller (1995), 348, 347–76. See also Charles G. Mutzenberg, *Kentucky's Famous Feuds and Tragedies* (1897; rev. ed. 1917); Robert Maxwell Brown, *Strain of Violence: Historical Studies of American Violence and Vigilantism* (1975), 9–10; Ayers, *Vengeance and Justice,* 263–64; and John Ed Pearce, *Days of Darkness: The Feuds of Eastern Kentucky* (1994).

10. Klotter, "Feuds in Appalachia," 296–303; Altina L. Waller, *Feud: Hatfields, McCoys, and Social Change in Appalachia, 1860–1900* (1988); Otis K. Rice, *The Hatfields and the McCoys* (1978).

11. *Lexington Kentucky Statesman,* 17 August 1869; Boyd and Boyd, *Mount Sterling,* 54; Mathias, ed., *Thomas W. Parsons,* 145; G. C. Wright, *Racial Violence,* 310, 313; *Louisville Courier-Journal,* 16 February, 22 May, 19–20 November, 27 December 1878, 16 June 1882;

Mount Sterling Democrat, 10 February 1882; Richard E. Nisbett, "Violence and U.S. Regional Culture," *American Psychologist* 48 (1993): 444; Marc Howard Ross, "Internal and External Conflict and Violence: Cross-Cultural Evidence and a New Analysis," *Journal of Conflict Resolution* 29 (1985): 557, 561.

12. Bertram Wyatt-Brown, *Southern Honor: Ethics and Behavior in the Old South* (1982), xv, 369; Wyatt-Brown, *The House of Percy: Honor, Melancholy, and Imagination in a Southern Family* (1994), 9; Julian Pitt-Rivers, "Honor," in *International Encyclopedia of the Social Sciences,* ed. David L. Sills (1968), 6:503–506; T. V. Smith, "Honor," in *Encyclopedia of the Social Sciences,* ed. Edward R. A. Seligman, (1935), 7:456–58; Julian Pitt-Rivers, "Honour and Social Status," in *Honour and Shame: The Values of Mediterranean Society,* ed. J. G. Peristiany (1965), 21; Edward L. Ayers, "Honor," in *Encyclopedia of Southern Culture,* ed. Charles Reagan Wilson and William Ferris (1989), 1483–84; Kenneth S. Greenberg, *Honor and Slavery* (1996), xi–xiii, 9; Elliott J. Gorn, " 'Gourge and Bite, Pull Hair and Scratch': The Social Significance of Fighting in the Southern Backcountry," *American Historical Review* 90 (1985): 22, 39–40; Pablo Piccato, "Politics and the Technology of Honor: Dueling in Turn-of-the-Century Mexico," *Journal of Social History* 33 (1999): 331–35; Bertram Wyatt-Brown, *Honor and Violence in the Old South* (1986), viii; Wyatt-Brown, *The Shaping of Southern Culture: Honor, Grace, and War, 1760s–1880s* (2001), 35.

13. Coleman, *Famous Kentucky Duels,* 3–106; Robert D. Bamberg, ed., *The Confession of Jereboam O. Beauchamp* (1826; 1966), 9–134; Willard Rouse Jillson, "The Beauchamp-Sharp Tragedy in American Literature," *Register of the Kentucky State Historical Society* 36 (1938): 54; Robert M. Ireland, "Acquitted yet Scorned: The Ward Trial and the Traditions of Antebellum Kentucky Criminal Justice," *Register of the Kentucky Historical Society* 84 (1986): 107–45; L. F. Johnson, *Tragedies and Trials,* 44–57, 163–79; Bertram Wyatt-Brown, "Community, Class, and Snopesian Crime: Local Justice in the Old South," in *Class, Conflict, and Consensus: Antebellum Southern Community Studies,* ed. Orville Vernon Burton and Robert C. McMath Jr. (1982), 173–206.

14. Guy A. Cardwell, "The Duel in the Old South: Crux of a Concept," *South Atlantic Quarterly* 66 (1967): 53; Bruce, *Violence and Culture,* 79; W. Conrad Gass, "The Misfortune of a High Minded and Honorable Southern Gentleman: W. W. Avery and the Southern Code of Honor," *North Carolina Historical Review* 56 (1979): 278–97; *Frankfort Commonwealth,* 27 December 1853; Ayers, *Vengeance and Justice,* 20. Similar in manner, though using different weapons, was the famous 1856 caning of Charles Sumner by Representative Preston Brooks of South Carolina, in the Senate Chamber. See David H. Donald, *Charles Sumner and the Coming of the Civil War* (1960).

15. Wyatt-Brown, "Church, Honor, and Secession," 89; Wyatt-Brown, *Southern Honor,* 5; Wyatt-Brown, *Shaping of Southern Culture,* 214; Grady McWhiney, "Crackers and Cavaliers: Shared Courage," in *Plain Folk of the South Revisited,* ed. Samuel C. Hyde Jr. (1997), 201. See also Christopher J. Olsen, *Political Culture and Secession in Mississippi: Masculinity, Honor, and the Antiparty Tradition, 1830–1860* (2000).

16. Charles Reagan Wilson, *Baptized in Blood: The Religion of the Lost Cause, 1865–1920* (1980), 1, 5, 13; Alvin R. Sunseri, "Military and Economy," in *Encyclopedia of Southern Culture,* ed. Wilson and Ferris, 731; George C. Rable, *But There Was No Peace: The Role of Violence in the Politics of Reconstruction* (1984), 3–4, 187; Sheldon Hackney, "Southern

Violence," *Violence in America: Historical and Comparative Perspectives,* ed. Hugh Davis Graham and Ted Robert Gurr (1969), 515; W. J. Cash, *The Mind of the South* (1941), 130, 208.

17. John Wilson Townsend, *James Lane Allen* (1927), 95–96.

18. T. V. Smith, "Honor," 458; Pitt-Rivers, "Honor," 509–10; Ayers, *Vengeance and Justice,* 13, 23, 18; Wyatt-Brown, *Southern Honor,* 458; Edmund S. Morgan, "The Price of Honor," *New York Review of Books,* 31 May 2001, p. 36; Pearce, *Days of Darkness,* 8; Rob Weise to author, 31 January 2000; Richard E. Nisbett and Dov Cohen, *Culture of Honor: The Psychology of Violence in the South* (1996), xv–xvii; J. G. Peristiany, "Introduction," in *Honor and Shame: The Values of Mediterranean Society,* ed. J. G. Peristiany (1965), 9; Pitt-Rivers, "Honour and Social Status," 30; Christopher Waldrep, *Roots of Disorder: Race and Criminal Justice in the American South, 1817–1880* (1998), 2–3.

19. *Harper's* quoted in McWhiney, "Crackers and Cavaliers," 189; Ownby, *Subduing Satan,* 12–13. Definitions vary about what exactly is meant by the term "manhood." Generally, it is seen as a changing, culturally defined collection of attributes. One definition is that it "is the cultural process whereby concrete individuals are constituted as members of a preexisting social category—as men." See Bederman, *Manliness and Civilization,* 6–7. Michael Kimmel, in *Manhood in America,* 119, notes that the term "masculinity"—with more physical connotations—gradually replaced the word "manhood" by the end of the century.

20. Clyde Griffen, "Reconstructing Masculinity from the Evangelical Revival to the Waning of Progressivism: A Speculative Synthesis," in *Meanings for Manhood: Construction of Masculinity in Victorian America,* ed. Mark C. Carnes and Clyde Griffen (1990), 191, 183; Richard Hofstadter, *Social Darwinism in American Thought* (rev. ed., 1955), 201; Rotundo, *American Manhood,* 3–5, 224–25, 228; Bederman, *Manliness and Civilization,* 13, 84, 77; David D. Gilmore, *Manhood in the Making: Cultural Concepts of Masculinity* (1990), 222–23; David G. Pugh, *Sons of Liberty: The Masculine Mind in Nineteenth-Century America* (1983), xix, 114, 104.

21. Bederman, *Manliness and Civilization,* 25, 172; Gilmore, *Manhood in the Making,* 193, 222; Ayers, *Vengeance and Justice,* 19; Griffen, "Reconstructing Masculinity," 193.

22. *New York Times,* 16 October 1877, 9 December 1878; *Chicago Tribune,* 3 December 1878; Warner, "Comments on Kentucky," 269.

23. *New York Times,* 30 November 1878, 13 September 1879, 27 September 1880; *Lexington Kentucky Gazette,* 5 January 1878; *Midway Blue-Grass Clipper,* 5 April 1878; *Stanford Semi-Weekly Interior Journal,* 7 November 1882.

24. H. V. Redfield, *Homicide, North and South* (1880), 3–5, 12, 14, 36–62, 57, 188–89, 194, 207. Redfield's statistics appeared two years later in *The Nation* 35 (23 November 1882): 442, giving them additional national exposure.

25. Wyatt-Brown, "God and Honor," 295; Emory M. Thomas, *Robert E. Lee* (1995), 18, 145, 107, 413, 372, 413–14; Charles P. Roland, *Reflections on Lee: A Historian's Assessment* (1995), passim.

26. D. S. C. M. Potter to Richard Reid Rogers, 5 July 1884, in *Letters,* 94; Ayers, *Vengeance and Justice,* 28; Ownby, *Subduing Satan,* 12–14; Rotundo, *American Manhood,* 6; Wyatt-Brown, "God and Honor," 283. See also Theriot, *Mothers and Daughters,* 43, where she writes: "The ideal of the 'Christian Gentleman' who practiced self-denial and allowed his wife to dictate sexual interaction, was formulated by the 1850s."

CHAPTER 5

1. *Judge Reid,* 169–72; Lane interview.

2. Marriage bond, dated 22 August 1868, in *Montgomery County, Kentucky Marriage Bonds: White, 1864–1881,* transcribed by Thelma M. Dunn (1997), 24; Tenth Census of the United States, 1880: Montgomery County, Kentucky, microfilm, Kentucky Historical Society; Gladys Lee Aiken, transcriber, *1870 Census: Montgomery County, Kentucky* (n.d.), 109, 187: *Louisville Courier-Journal,* 21 April 1884; *Judge Reid,* 31; O'Rear, *Montgomery County Bar,* 66; Montgomery Co. Assessor's Book, 1883, Kentucky Department for Libraries and Archives; Lane interview, and author's observations; *Paris Kentuckian,* 23 April 1884. The house is still standing. The son of a farmer of modest means, Cornelison had grown up in nearby Madison County. See U.S. Census, 1860: Madison County, Kentucky, microfilm, University of Kentucky.

3. In addition to the sources cited in the Prologue, see also the affidavits of Sarah A. Jameson, 18 February 1885, and Mary E. Crouch, 9 June 1885, "Mrs. Reid's Statement," and "Speech of Col. Henry L. Stone," all in *Judge Reid,* 176–82, 560–62; *Paris Semi-Weekly Bourbon News,* 18 April 1884. Caswell Lane and John Marshall Prewitt each recall seeing the whip Cornelison used. Then in the possession of Dr. John Prewitt, it was lent to a person, and has since disappeared. Lane interview; John Marshall Prewitt, telephone interview by author, 26 August 2000.

4. *Judge Reid,* 183; *Louisville Courier-Journal,* 17, 21, 22, 25 April 1884; *Louisville Commercial,* 17, 21 April 1884; *Cincinnati Enquirer,* 21 April 1884.

5. *Howard* v. *Cornelison,* 5 Kentucky Law Reporter 902–21 (1884); *Judge Reid,* 545–46.

6. *Howard* v. *Cornelison,* 902–21; *Judge Reid,* 546–52; O'Rear, *Montgomery County Bar,* 67.

7. *Judge Reid,* 197–202, 207; *Christian Standard,* 31 May 1884, in *Richard Reid: A Memorial,* 93; *Mount Sterling Sentinel-Democrat,* 18 April 1884; *Louisville Commercial,* 20 April 1884. See Chapter 8 for further details of the political charge.

8. A. E. Richards to Richard Reid, 17 April 1884, in *Richard Reid: A Memorial,* 28; *Judge Reid,* 199–202; *Cornelison* v. *Commonwealth,* 84 Kentucky Reports 595 (1886); *Frankfort Weekly Kentucky Yeoman,* 22 April 1884. See also an excellent article on Reid by Robert M. Ireland in the *Filson Club History Quarterly* 71 (1997):123–45, 144 n.

9. *Judge Reid,* 204–205; L. F. Johnson, *Tragedies and Trials,* 248.

10. *Louisville Courier-Journal,* 17 April 1884. Cornelison, in fact, had confirmed already that Reid had offered to go to the two Superior Court judges and try to get them to revise their negative comments, if Cornelison wished him to do so. See *Louisville Courier-Journal,* 21 April 1884.

11. *Louisville Courier-Journal,* 22 April 1884; "Judge Reid's Speech," in *Judge Reid,* 223–25; *Paris Semi-Weekly Bourbon News,* 25 April 1884.

12. *Louisville Courier-Journal,* 22 April 1884; "Reid's Speech," 225–29. Reid gave similar versions of that speech across his district. See, for example, *Paris Semi-Weekly Bourbon News,* 29 April 1884. His call, "Who is on the side of the law?" echoes Exodus 32, verse 26, in the Bible, which asks, "Who is on the Lord's side?"

13. *Owensboro Semi-Weekly Messenger,* 25 April 1884; *Paris Semi-Weekly Bourbon*

News, 25 April 1884; *Georgetown Times,* 23 April 1884; *Louisville Commercial,* 19 April 1884; *Judge Reid,* 221, 331, 563.

14. *Owensboro Semi-Weekly Messenger,* 9 May 1884; *Christian Standard,* 31 May 1884, quoted in *Richard Reid: A Memorial,* 93, 39; *Judge Reid,* 535, 426, 342.

15. Richard Reid to Elizabeth Reid, 10 May 1884, A. E. Hobbs to Elizabeth Reid, 18 April 1884, W. E. Keller to Richard Reid, 19 April 1884, all in *Letters,* 9, 27, 30; *Louisville Courier-Journal,* 18 April 1884; *Paris Semi-Weekly Bourbon News,* 22 April 1884; *Georgetown Times,* 23 April 1884; *New York Times,* 19 April 1884; *San Francisco Daily Examiner,* 20 April 1884; *Judge Reid,* 409.

16. Lystra, *Searching the Heart,* 149; Rosenberg, "Sexuality, Class, and Role," 141; Ayers, *Vengeance and Justice,* 29; John H. Jameson to Elizabeth Reid, 5 May 1884, in *Letters,* 89; Kimmel, *Manhood in America,* 7–8; Gilmore, *Manhood in the Making,* vii.

17. Reid Rogers to Elizabeth Reid, 19 April 1884, in *Letters,* 72–73, and *Judge Reid,* 190–91. See also Pitt-Rivers, "Honour and Social Status," 28–29, who points out that under the ancient rules of honor, only family members "can pick up the glove" if a man is dishonored.

18. *Louisville Courier-Journal,* 22 April 1884; *Paris Kentuckian,* 23 April 1884; J. W. McGarvey in *The Pulpit,* quoted in *Richard Reid: A Memorial,* 80–81; *Judge Reid,* 409, 189; *New York Times,* 16 May 1884; *St. Louis Post-Dispatch,* 18 May 1884; *Chicago News,* cited in *Mount Sterling Daily Sentinel-Democrat,* 22 May 1884.

19. *Louisville Courier-Journal,* 16 May 1884; *Paris Kentuckian,* 22 May 1884; *Louisville Post,* 16 May 1884; Affidavit of Susan A. Jameson, 18 February 1885, and Elizabeth Reid to John Reid, 14 May 1884, both quoted in *Judge Reid,* 179, 364; Richard Reid to Elizabeth Reid, 10 May 1884, in *Letters,* 10.

CHAPTER 6

1. *Louisville Democrat,* quoted in *Paris Semi-Weekly Bourbon News,* 6 May 1884; *Louisville Commercial,* 19 April 1884; *Frankfort Weekly Kentucky Yeoman,* 22 April 1884; *Catlettsburg Central Methodist,* 26 April 1884; *Owensboro Semi-Weekly Messenger,* 22 April 1884; *Newport Kentucky State Journal,* 5 May 1884; *San Francisco Daily Examiner,* 20 April 1884; *Atlanta Constitution,* 19 April 1884.

2. *Paris Semi-Weekly Bourbon News,* 18, 22 April 1884; *Owen County Democrat,* quoted in *Richard Reid: A Memorial,* 48; *Stanford Semi-Weekly Interior Journal,* 22, 25 April 1884.

3. *Hickman Courier,* 25 April, 2 May 1884; *Covington Commonwealth,* quoted in *Owensboro Semi-Weekly Messenger,* 20 May 1884; *Louisville Times,* 15, 17 May 1884; James Lane Allen, "County Court Day in Kentucky," *Harper's* 79 (1889): 394. See also *Louisville Post,* quoted in *Mount Sterling Daily Sentinel-Democrat,* 23 April 1884.

4. *Hickman Courier,* 2 May 1884; *Philips v. Commonwealth,* 2 Duvall 328–32 (1866).

5. *Carico v. Commonwealth,* 7 Bush 124–30 (1870).

6. *Bohannon v. Commonwealth,* 8 Bush 481–90 (1871).

7. *Holloway v. Commonwealth,* 11 Bush 344–52 (1875).

8. *Judge Reid,* 347–49, 337–40; *Mount Sterling Daily Sentinel-Democrat,* 17, 18, April 1884; *Georgetown Times,* 30 April 1884; *Versailles Woodford Sun,* 25 April 1884; *Louisville*

Courier-Journal, 21, 23 April 1884; *Paris Semi-Weekly Bourbon News,* 25 April 1884. See also *Louisville Commercial,* 18 April 1884.

9. *Chicago Daily Tribune,* 20 April 1884; *St. Louis Post-Dispatch,* 17, 23 April 1884. For state comments on general justice issues see *Louisville Commercial,* 25 April 1884, and *Catlettsburg Central Methodist,* 26 April 1884.

10. *New York Times,* 18, 19 April 1884; *Brooklyn Union,* quoted in "M. A. M." to Richard Reid, May 1884, in *Letters,* 92–93; *New York Mercury,* quoted in *Newport State Journal,* 22 May 1884; *The Nation* 38 (15 May 1884): 416.

11. W. M. Beckner to Richard Reid, 18 April 1884, John S. Williams to Reid, 20 April 1884; E. H. Harding to Reid, 3 May 1884; M. M. Fisher to Reid, 7 May 1884, all in *Letters,* 12, 16, 42–43; Levin, ed., *Lawyers and Lawmakers,* 7, 664–65. See also *Judge Reid,* 238, 259, for the same.

12. Frank W. Allen to Richard Reid, 19 April 1884, in *Letters,* 30–31; John H. Jameson to Reid, 22 April 1884; H. A. Redfield to Reid, 25 April 1884, both in *Judge Reid,* 287–88, 292–93; Newton Burwell to Reid, 24 April 1884, in *Letters,* 81.

13. J. P. Hobson to Richard Reid, 19 April 1884, J. S. Sweeney to Reid, 19 April 1884, both in *Letters,* 14, 29; W. E. Keller to Reid, 19 April 1884, in *Judge Reid,* 249; Samuel McKee to Reid, 22 April 1884, in *Letters,* 19; *Biographical Encyclopaedia,* 145. The Sweeney letter also appeared in the *Paris Kentuckian,* 30 April 1884.

14. D. M. Harris to Richard Reid, 24 April 1884, in *Letters,* 36–37; W. R. Davis to Reid, 26 April 1884, in *Judge Reid,* 293–94.

15. Virgil M. Harris to Richard Reid, 5 May 1884, Linda Atkinson to Reid, 21 April 1884; George T. Edwards to Reid, 24 April 1884, all in *Letters,* 25, 53, 22, and *Judge Reid,* 269, 242. Linda Jameson Atkinson had named a son for Reid, as had her sister earlier. That son died in the same month as the attack. See *Letters,* 53 n.

16. W. G. Welch to Richard Reid, 19 April 1884, in *Letters,* 15.

17. *Owensboro Semi-Weekly Messenger,* 22 April 1884; *Louisville Courier-Journal,* 17, 18 April 1884; *Atlanta Constitution,* 19 April 1884; *Paris Semi-Weekly Bourbon News,* 22 April 1884; *Frankfort Weekly Kentucky Yeoman,* 29 April 1884; *Newport Kentucky State Journal,* 26 April 1884; *Paris Kentuckian,* 26 April 1884.

18. *Mount Sterling Sentinel-Democrat,* 18 April 1884; *Owensboro Semi-Weekly Messenger,* 22 April 1884; *Louisville Courier-Journal,* 20 April 1884.

19. Levin, ed., *Lawyers and Lawmakers,* 81–83; "The Matchless Argument of Dr. B. T. Kavanaugh," in *Richard Reid: A Memorial,* 101–106; *Paris Semi-Weekly Bourbon News,* 22 April 1884; *Louisville Courier-Journal,* 20 April 1884; *Mount Sterling Daily Sentinel-Democrat,* 21 April 1884; *Mount Sterling Democrat,* 14 May 1884; *Louisville Commercial,* 20 April 1884. See also *Judge Reid,* 216–20, and Lane interview.

20. Lane interview; O'Rear, *Montgomery County Bar,* 52; Ireland, "Elective Judiciary," 415; *Judge Reid,* 338–40.

21. *Judge Reid,* 340–47, 327; *Richard Reid: A Memorial,* 20; *Christian Standard,* 14 June 1884, clipping in Donaldson Papers; *Mount Sterling Daily Sentinel-Democrat,* 15 May 1884.

22. *Frankfort Weekly Kentucky Yeoman,* 29 April 1884; *Paris Kentuckian,* 26 April 1884; *Louisville Commercial,* 20 April 1884; *Paris Semi-Weekly Bourbon News,* 2 May 1884. Reid's itinerary can be reconstructed from letters and comments in *Judge Reid,* 317–24, and passim.

23. *Mount Sterling Daily Sentinel-Democrat,* 30 April 1884; *Louisville Courier-Journal,* 22 April 1884; *Richard Reid: A Memorial,* 23; O'Rear, *Montgomery County Bar,* 56.

24. *Paris Kentuckian,* 16 May, 23 April 1884; *Mount Sterling Daily Sentinel-Democrat,* 25 May 1884; *The Pulpit,* cited in *Richard Reid: A Memorial,* 79; *Frankfort Weekly Kentucky Yeoman,* 20 May 1884; *Maysville Bulletin,* 22 May 1884; *Judge Reid,* 314; *Christian Standard* and *Paris True Kentuckian,* both cited in *Richard Reid: A Memorial,* 89, 56; *Owensboro Semi-Weekly Messenger,* 22 April 1884; *Louisville Times,* 17 May 1884; *Paris Semi-Weekly Bourbon News,* 20 May 1884.

25. *Mount Sterling Gazette,* cited in *Richard Reid: A Memorial,* 10; *Louisville Post,* 16 May 1884; Richard Reid to Elizabeth Reid, 7, 8 May 1884, both in *Letters,* 8–9; Elizabeth Reid to Richard Reid, 1, 8, 9 May 1884, Richard Reid to Elizabeth Reid, 23 April 1884, all in *Judge Reid,* 325–29, 317; Richard Reid to Elizabeth Reid, 6 May 1884, in *Letters,* 8; *Mount Sterling Daily Sentinel-Democrat,* 16 May 1884.

26. *Richard Reid: A Memorial,* 20; *Newport Kentucky State Journal,* 24 April 1884; *Louisville Courier-Journal,* 22 April 1884; *Owensboro Semi-Weekly Messenger,* 20 May 1884; Richard Reid to Elizabeth Reid, 30 April, 4, 8, 10 May 1884, all in *Letters,* 7–10; *Judge Reid,* 325–26, 351–52, 365.

27. *Judge Reid,* 362–67, 371; *Louisville Courier-Journal,* 23 May 1884; *Christian Standard,* 31 May 1884, in *Richard Reid: A Memorial,* 94.

CHAPTER 7

1. *Paris Kentuckian,* 22 May 1884; *Mount Sterling Daily Sentinel-Democrat,* 16 May 1884; *Louisville Times,* 15 May 1884; *Paris Semi-Weekly Bourbon News,* 20 May 1884. See also "Map of Montgomery County Kentucky . . . 1879," Special Collections, Kentucky Historical Society.

2. *Paris Kentuckian,* 22 May 1884; *Mount Sterling Daily Sentinel-Democrat,* 16 May 1884; *Louisville Times,* 15 May 1884; *Cincinnati Enquirer,* 16 May 1884; and *Richard Reid: A Memorial,* 7–9. The Brock law office, heavily modified, still stands.

3. *Owensboro Semi-Weekly Messenger,* 20 May 1884; *Louisville Post,* 16 May 1884; *Mount Sterling Daily Sentinel-Democrat,* 17 May 1884; *Judge Reid,* 427; *Paris Semi-Weekly Bourbon News,* 16 May 1884; *Louisville Times,* 17 May 1884; *Louisville Post,* 17 May 1884.

4. *Judge Reid,* 368–69; *Louisville Post,* 15 May 1884; *Cincinnati Enquirer,* 16 May 1884.

5. *Paris Kentuckian,* 22 May 1884; *Mount Sterling Daily Sentinel-Democrat,* 16 May 1884; *Richard Reid: A Memorial,* 9.

6. *Mount Sterling Daily Sentinel-Democrat,* 14, 23 May 1884.

7. Anthony Giddens, introduction to *Suicide and the Meaning of Civilization,* by Thomas G. Masaryk, trans. William B. Weist and Robert G. Batson (1881; 1970), xxvii–xxx, xxxii n; Margaret Pabst Battin, *Ethical Issues in Suicide* (1982), 95, 177; Kay Redfield Jamison, *Night Falls Fast: Understanding Suicide* (1999), 13–116; Gerald C. Davison and John M. Neale, *Abnormal Psychology* (7th ed., 1998), 250; George Simpson, editor's introduction to *Suicide: A Study in Sociology,* by Emile Durkheim, trans. John A. Spaulding and George Simpson (1951), 23; Thomas E. Ellis and Cory F. Newman, *Choosing to Live: How to Defeat Suicide through*

Cognitive Therapy (1996), 9; Gustav Mikusch, "Suicide," in *Encyclopaedia of the Social Sciences,* ed. Edwin B. A. Seligman (1935), 14:456.

8. Giddens, introduction to *Suicide,* iv, xv, xiv, xxxv–xxxvii, xl, 140, 224; William Knighton, "Suicidal Mania," *Littell's Living Age* 148 (5 February 1881): 376–81; M. G. Mulhall, "Insanity, Suicide, and Civilization," *Contemporary Review* 43 (1883): 908. See also Howard I. Kushner, "Suicide, Gender, and the Fear of Modernity in Nineteenth-Century Medical and Social Thought," *Journal of Social History* 26 (1993): 466–67.

9. Battin, *Ethical Issues,* 28–39, 49–53; Jamison, *Night Falls Fast,* 14, 17; Mikusch, "Suicide," 456. The "Thou shall not kill" commandment is number five in the Catholic faith and sixth in the Protestant one.

10. Edwin S. Shneidman, "Suicide, Sleep, and Death," *Journal of Consulting Psychology* 28 (1964): 100; Battin, *Ethical Issues,* 63–69.

11. Davison and Neale, *Abnormal Psychology,* 252–53; Battin, *Ethical Issues,* 1; Ellis and Newman, *Choosing to Live,* 18; Jamison, *Night Falls Fast,* 206.

12. Edwin S. Shneidman, "Suicide: Psychological Aspects (1)," in *International Encyclopedia of the Social Sciences,* ed. David L. Sills (1968), 15:388; Norman L. Farberow and Edwin S. Shneidman, eds., *The Cry for Help* (1961), xi; Arthur L. Kobler and Ezra Stotland, *The End of Hope: A Social-Clinical Study of Suicide* (1964), 6–7; Battin, *Ethical Issues,* 8; Ellis and Newman, *Choosing to Live,* 16–18.

13. Alan L. Berman and David A. Jobes, *Adolescent Suicide: Assessment and Intervention* (1991), v; Davison and Neale, *Abnormal Psychology,* 254; Shneidman, "Suicide: Psychological Aspects," 15:389; Simpson, editor's introduction *Suicide,* by Durkheim, 24.

14. Shneidman, "Suicide: Psychological Aspects," 15: 389; Durkheim, *Suicide,* 9, 14–17, 345–58, and passim; Davison and Neale, *Abnormal Psychology,* 255; Kushner, "Suicide, Gender, and Fear of Modernity," 470–76; Battin, *Ethical Issues,* 10–11, 95. See also Jeffery W. Reimer, "Durkheim's 'Heroic Suicide' in Military Combat," *Armed Forces and Society* 25 (1998): 103–20.

15. Shneidman, "Suicide: Psychological Aspects," 15:389; Norman L. Farberow, "Suicide: Psychological Aspects (2)," in *International Encyclopedia of the Social Sciences,* ed. David L. Sills (1968), 15:391.

16. Battin, *Ethical Issues,* 6, 138; *Judge Reid,* 564, 536; *The Pulpit* and the *Christian Standard,* quoted in *Richard Reid: A Memorial,* 80, 90; Dr. Richard L. Lozano to the author, 19 March 1998 (hereinafter "Lozano letter").

17. Vgontzas and Kales, "Sleep and Its Disorders," 393; Ohayon, Guilleminault, and Priest, "Night Terrors," 268–76; Harvey Moldofsky et al., "Sleep-Related Violence," *Sleep* 18 (1995): 731–39; Hannu Lauerma, "Fear of Suicide during Sleepwalking," *Psychiatry* 59 (1996): 206–11; Roger J. Broughton et al., "Homicidal Somnambulism: A Case Report," *Sleep* 17 (1994): 253–64; Mark W. Mahowald et al., "Sleep Violence—Forensic Science Implications," *Journal of Forensic Sciences* 35 (1990): 413–32; *Fain* v. *Commonwealth* 78 Kentucky Reports 183–93 (1879); John Gilmore, "Murdering while Asleep," *Forensic Reports* 4 (1999): 455–59.

18. Davison and Neale, *Abnormal Psychology,* 251, 255–56; Battin, *Ethical Issues,* 5, 138; Richard B. Brandt, "The Morality and Rationality of Suicide," in *A Handbook for the Study of Suicide,* ed. Seymour Perlin (1975), 380; Ellis and Newman, *Choosing to Live,* 12; Shneidman, "Suicide, Sleep, and Death," 102. See also Wyatt-Brown, *House of Percy,* 35.

19. Kobler and Stotland, *End of Hope*, 1, 252; Davison and Neale, *Abnormal Psychology*, 252, 254; Ellis and Newman, *Choosing to Live*, 23; Lystra, *Searching the Heart*, 237; Kimmel, *Manhood in America*, 122; Rotundo, *American Manhood*, 110–15.

20. Dr. William Davis, quoted in *Judge Reid*, 6–7, 35; Lozano letter; J. Parsons Schaeffer, ed., *Morris' Human Anatomy* (1893; 11th ed., 1953), 1389–96. His minister said that "the crushing sorrow of his early childhood" made him "sensitive beyond all description" and gave him few friends, as a result. *Christian Standard*, 14 June 1884, clipping in Donaldson Collection. For medical thought on the subject near Reid's era, see Frederic S. Dennis, ed., *System of Surgery*, vol. 4: *Tumors-Hernia . . .* (1896), and for samples of trusses, see *Tafel Bros.' Illustrated Catalogue and Price List of Surgical and Electrical Instruments* (1855), 193.

21. Lozano letter; Mark Davenport, "Inguinal Hernia, Hydrocele, and the Undescended Testis," *British Medical Journal* 312 (1996): 564–67; Kushner, "Suicide, Gender, and Fear of Modernity," 469. See also Thomas A. Foster, "Deficient Husbands: Manhood, Sexual Incapacity, and Male Marital Sexuality in Seventeenth-Century New England," *William and Mary Quarterly*, 3rd series, 56 (1999): 733, 737, and Kevin J. Mumford, " 'Lost Manhood' Found: Male Sexual Impotence and Victorian Culture in the United States," *Journal of the History of Sexuality* 3 (1992): 33–57. A recent study (Davenport, above), noted that only 15 percent of those who had the condition of an undescended testis corrected by surgery after age thirteen became fertile.

22. *Judge Reid*, 7, 351–52, 362–63; Lystra, *Searching the Heart*, 225; Pitt-Rivers, "Honor," 6:506, 510.

23. Farberow, "Suicide," 15:390; Davison and Neale, *Abnormal Psychology*, 254. Most studies have found that the South, overall, shows low levels of suicide. See, for example, Austin L. Porterfield, "Indices of Suicide and Homicide by States and Cities," *American Sociological Review* 14 (1949): 481–90; Raymond D. Gastil, "Violence, Crime, and Punishment," in *Encyclopedia of Southern Culture*, ed. Charles Reagan Wilson and William Ferris (1989), 1473.

24. Pitt-Rivers, "Honor," 6:509.

25. Jack D. Douglas, "Suicide: Social Aspects," in *International Encyclopedia of the Social Sciences*, ed. David L. Sills (1968), 15:376.

26. Shakespeare, *Hamlet*, act 3, scene 1, lines 79–83; Reid, "Old Age of the Scholar," 393; Farberow, "Suicide," 15:393; Bruce, *Violence and Culture*, 14.

27. Shneidman, "Suicide, Sleep, and Death," 98; Pitt-Rivers, "Honor," 6:506; Farberow, "Suicide," 15:392–93; *Mount Sterling Daily Sentinel-Democrat*, 16 May 1884. See also Battin, *Ethical Issues*, 138–39, 7. Kenneth Greenberg in *Honor and Slavery*, 93–95, concludes of Edmund Ruffin's suicide soon after the end of the Civil War, as he declined to face a world in which the North dominated: "It demonstrated mastery and control rather than dependence and submission." He notes, however, that religious constraints turned most southerners away from that option.

28. C. C. Moore to Elizabeth Reid, n.d., in *Judge Reid*, 467; Wilson, *Baptized in Blood*, 5; Shakespeare, *King Richard the Second*, act 1, scene 1, line 183; T. V. Smith, "Honor," 7:457; Pitt-Rivers, "Honor," 6:504–505.

CHAPTER 8

1. Davison and Neale, *Abnormal Psychology*, 256; Ellis and Newman, *Choosing to Live*, 164–66; Battin, *Ethical Issues*, 114–15, 138–39.

2. *Frankfort Weekly Kentucky Yeoman,* 20 May 1884; *Mount Sterling Daily Sentinel-Democrat,* 18 May 1884; *Richard Reid: A Memorial,* 13–14; *Biographical Encyclopaedia,* 91; *Judge Reid,* 374–83.

3. *Biographical Cyclopedia of the Commonwealth of Kentucky* (1896), 147–48; *Judge Reid,* 383–87, 392; *Richard Reid: A Memorial,* 14–16; *Newport Kentucky State Journal,* 22 May 1884. Kentucky University is now Transylvania University.

4. *Louisville Courier-Journal,* 23 May 1884; Klotter, *Breckinridges of Kentucky,* 153; *Richard Reid: A Memorial,* 21–24; *Judge Reid,* 393–97.

5. *Baltimore Sun,* 16 May 1884; *New York Herald,* 16 May 1884; *Cleveland Plain Dealer,* 16 May 1884; *St. Louis Post-Dispatch,* 18 May 1884; *New York Times,* 16 May 1884; *San Francisco Daily Examiner,* 25 May 1884; *Chicago Daily Tribune,* 16 May 1884; Ireland, "Suicide of Judge Richard Reid," 137; *Nation* 38 (22 May 1884): 436. For other coverage of the suicide, see *Cincinnati Enquirer,* 16 May 1884; *Atlanta Constitution,* 16 May 1884; *New York Tribune,* 15 May 1884; *Washington Post,* 16 May 1884; *Washington Bee,* 24 May 1884.

6. *Louisville Courier-Journal,* quoted in *Richard Reid: A Memorial,* 46; *Catlettsburg Central Methodist,* 24 May 1884; *Paris Semi-Weekly Bourbon News,* 20 May 1884; *Lexington Transcript,* quoted in *Maysville Bulletin,* 22 May 1884; *Louisville Post,* 16 May 1884; *Richard Reid: A Memorial,* 39; *Judge Reid,* 468. On the crash, see also the *New York Tribune* and *New York Herald,* both of 15 May 1884.

7. *Louisville Post,* 16 May 1884; *Mayfield Monitor,* 23 May 1884; *Georgetown Times,* 21 May 1884; *Paris True Kentuckian,* quoted in *Judge Reid,* 401–402.

8. *Owensboro Semi-Weekly Messenger,* 20 May 1884; *Winchester Democrat, Courier-Journal, Vanceburg Courier,* all quoted in *Richard Reid: A Memorial,* 45, 49–61; *Louisville Times,* 16 May 1884; *Judge Reid,* 399–405. Supporting personal letters came to Mrs. Reid from across the nation. For a sampling, see *Judge Reid,* 438, 441, 451, 454–55, 457, 462–63.

9. *Hickman Courier,* 23 May 1884; *Newport Kentucky State Journal,* 17 May 1884; *Stanford Semi-Weekly Interior Journal,* 20 May 1884; *Breckinridge County News,* quoted in *Judge Reid,* 407; R. Graham to Elizabeth Reid, 18 October 1884, in *Letters,* 114.

10. *Louisville Commercial,* 22 April, 20 May 1884; *Louisville Courier-Journal,* 23 May 1884; Ireland, "Suicide of Judge Richard Reid," 139–40; "Speech of Col. Henry L. Stone," quoted in *Judge Reid,* 558; *New York Times,* 18 April 1884; *Richard Reid: A Memorial,* 54; *Judge Reid,* 364, 400, 332. See also *Frankfort Weekly Kentucky Yeoman,* 27 May 1884, and Dick Steward, whose *Duels and the Roots of Violence in Missouri* (2000) argues that duels were used as tools for political advancement.

11. "Sentinel-Democrat Clippings," 1884; *Flemingsburg Times-Democrat,* 23 May 1884; *Richard Reid: A Memorial,* 6, 30–31; *Judge Reid,* 335; *Stanford Semi-Weekly Interior Journal,* 27 May 1884; *Louisville Commercial,* 20 May 1884; *Frankfort Weekly Kentucky Yeoman,* 27 May, 3 June 1884.

12. *Paris Kentuckian,* 7, 11 June 1884; Ireland, "Suicide of Judge Richard Reid," 141–43; *London Mountain Echo,* 13 June 1884; *Frankfort Weekly Kentucky Yeoman,* 10, 17 June 1884; *Georgetown Times,* 11 June 1884; *Paris Semi-Weekly Bourbon News,* 13 June 1884. The numbers of ballots is variously given as 175, 176, and 177.

13. *Paris True Kentuckian,* 7 May 1879, 22 May 1884; *Judge Reid,* 387; *Richard Reid: A Memorial,* 26; *Mount Sterling Democrat,* 30 April 1880; O'Rear, *Montgomery County Bar,*

65; *London Mountain Echo,* 11, 25 July 1884; Doolan, "Court of Appeals," 465; *Maysville Bulletin,* 21 August, 17, 24 July 1884; *Frankfort Weekly Kentucky Yeoman,* 12 August 1884; *Judge Reid,* 336.

14. *Frankfort Weekly Kentucky Yeoman,* 12, 19, 26 August, 2 September 1884; Ireland, "Suicide of Judge Richard Reid," 142; "Kentucky," *Appleton's Annual Cyclopedia and Register of Important Events* (1884), 424; *London Mountain Echo,* 15 August 1884; Boyd and Boyd, *Mount Sterling,* 261; Doolan, "Court of Appeals," 463, 465; E. P. Johnson, *History of Kentucky,* 2:647; "May Stone," in Temple Bodley and Samuel M. Wilson, *History of Kentucky,* 4 vols. (1928), 3:24–28; Nancy Forderhase, "May Stone," in *Kentucky Encyclopedia,* ed. John E. Kleber (1992), 857. Reid's college classmate J. Q. A. Ward ran for and won the now-vacant seat on the Superior Court, defeating Cornelison ally and defense attorney Thomas Turner. See *Georgetown Times,* 28 May 1884, *Flemingsburg Times-Democrat,* 24 June 1884, and A. E. Richards, "Superior Court of Kentucky," in *Lawyers and Lawmakers,* ed. Levin, 136–37.

15. *Mount Sterling Daily Sentinel-Democrat,* 22 April 1884; *Louisville Times,* 15 May 1884; *Cornelison v. Commonwealth,* 7 Kentucky Law Reporter 346; *Judge Reid,* 500; Levin, ed., *Lawyers and Lawmakers,* 120, 124; L. F. Johnson, *Tragedies and Trials,* 253; O'Rear, *Montgomery County Bar,* 60. For Cornelison's response to the indictment, see John J. Cornelison to C. M. Clay, 17 March 1888, in Cassius M. Clay Papers, Special Collections, University of Kentucky.

16. *Cornelison v. Commonwealth,* 84 Kentucky Reports 591–96; *Judge Reid,* 502–504, 542–43. Some confusion exists on exactly when Cornelison changed his plea that last time. Newspaper reports, in *Judge Reid,* 502, suggested it came after the last defense argument. But the court decision, above, indicates it occurred as noted in the text.

17. *Judge Reid,* 541, 518–19, 508, 516, 534–35, 540–67.

18. Ibid., 504; *Cornelison v. Commonwealth,* 84 Kentucky Reports 591; L. F. Johnson, *Tragedies and Trials,* 256.

19. *Cornelison v. Commonwealth,* 7 Kentucky Law Reporter 344–56.

20. *Cornelison v. Commonwealth,* 84 Kentucky Reporter 583–623; Richard L. Troutman, ed., *The Heavens Are Weeping: The Diaries of George Richard Browder, 1852–1886* (1987), 408. The case also appeared in 2 Southwestern Reporter 235. Cornelison had another case before the court that term, involving a homestead mortgage. See *Cornelison v. Stephens,* 2 S. W. Reporter 122.

21. *Louisville Commercial,* 25, 29 July 1888; *Louisville Times,* 19–21 July 1888.

22. *Louisville Commercial,* 25, 29 July 1888. After seeing the whip years ago, John Marshall Prewitt still remembers it as "more like a club"—being one-half to three-quarters of an inch thick. Prewitt, communication to author, 8 August 2000.

23. *Louisville Courier-Journal,* 5, 6 August 1888; *Louisville Times,* 4 August 1888; "Executive Journal 1887–89, S. B. Buckner Governor," entry of 8 October 1888, Governors' Papers, Kentucky Department for Libraries and Archives; *Lexington Morning Herald,* 15 February 1899. Several sources incorrectly repeat that he served his full term. See, for example, L. F. Johnson, *Tragedies and Trials,* 256, and Boyd and Boyd, *Mount Sterling,* 64.

24. J. J. Cornelison to William Lindsay, 27 September 1890, Lindsay Papers; *Breckinridge County News,* quoted in *Richard Reid: A Memorial,* 67; *Lexington Daily Leader,* 14 February

1899; *Mount Sterling Advocate,* 21 February 1899; *Judge Reid,* 565; O'Rear, *Montgomery County Bar,* 67.

25. Farberow, "Suicide," 15:394; Davison and Neale, *Abnormal Psychology,* 252; Jamison, *Night Falls Fast,* 293–95; *The Pulpit,* quoted in *Richard Reid: A Memorial,* 81; *Louisville Post,* 17 May 1884.

26. Will of Richard Reid, dated 31 December 1883, Montgomery County Will Book G, Kentucky Department for Libraries and Archives; *Frankfort Weekly Kentucky Yeoman,* 3 June 1884; *New York Times,* 16 May 1884.

27. Elizabeth Reid to Cassius M. Clay, 1 June 1895, undated [June 1895], both in Clay Papers.

28. *Letters,* 44, 71, 116, 3, and passim; *Judge Reid,* x.

29. *Richard Reid: A Memorial,* passim; *Judge Reid,* x.

30. "Editor's Study," *Harper's New Monthly Magazine* 73 (1886): 965–66; *Judge Reid,* v–xiii; *Agents Wanted: Judge Richard Reid, a Biography* (n.d.).

31. *Judge Reid,* vii, passim. The statistics comparing the three books are the author's.

32. Ibid., 489, 576, passim.

33. Ibid., 465, 475, 478, 465–80, 371.

34. Davison and Neale, *Abnormal Psychology,* 252; Jamison, *Night Falls Fast,* 115.

35. Dudley Pope, *Guns* (1969), 191–92; Dr. Bruce D. Ragsdale to Dr. Richard L. Lozano, undated [1998]; Lozano letter; *Louisville Courier-Journal,* 16 May 1884; *Judge Reid,* 478.

36. Communication from John Marshall Prewitt to author, 8 August 2000; John Marshall Prewitt interview; Ann and Curt Steger interview; *Mount Sterling Advocate,* 8 July 1902, 26 February 1895; *Elizabeth Jameson Reid,* 13; O'Rear, *Montgomery County Bar,* 85; *New York Times,* 11 November 1949; Lane interview; Henry Prewitt, interview by author, Paris, Ky., 28 August 2000; "Notes from the Mount Sterling Advocate," May 1920 entry, Mount Sterling Public Library. Roger's wife was Eunice Tomlin. See Prewitt, *Prewitt Descendants,* 354.

37. Clipping, *Louisville Courier-Journal,* 29 April 1979, copy in author's possession; Chalkley, "*Magic Casements,*" 70–71; *New York Times,* 11 November 1949; John Marshall Prewitt interview; Henry Prewitt interview. Reid's brother, J. Davis Reid, lived until 29 June 1906, leaving an estate valued at a quarter of a million dollars, in that era's money. He owned 2,000 acres and had been a director of three banks. Of his ten children, the last died in 1944, the only one to live past age fifty-seven. See *Winchester Democrat,* 3 July 1906, and *Mount Sterling Democrat,* 4 July 1906.

EPILOGUE

1. See, for example, N. S. Shaler, *Kentucky: A Pioneer Commonwealth* (1884); W. H. Perrin, J. H. Battle, and G. C. Kniffin, *Kentucky: A History of the State* (1887); Z. F. Smith, *History of Kentucky* (1885; 1895); Robert M. McElroy, *Kentucky in the Nation's History* (1909); E. P. Johnson, *History of Kentucky;* Connelley and Coulter, *History of Kentucky;* Bodley and Wilson, *History of Kentucky;* Thomas D. Clark, *A History of Kentucky* (1937); Federal Writers' Project, *Kentucky* (1939); Steven A. Channing, *Kentucky: A Bicentennial History* (1977); James C. Klotter, ed., *Our Kentucky: A Study of the Bluegrass State* (2000); John E. Kleber, ed., *The Kentucky Encyclopedia* (1992); Harrison and Klotter, *New History.* Tapp and Klotter,

1899; *Mount Sterling Advocate,* 21 February 1899; *Judge Reid,* 565; O'Rear, *Montgomery County Bar,* 67.

25. Farberow, "Suicide," 15:394; Davison and Neale, *Abnormal Psychology,* 252; Jamison, *Night Falls Fast,* 293–95; *The Pulpit,* quoted in *Richard Reid: A Memorial,* 81; *Louisville Post,* 17 May 1884.

26. Will of Richard Reid, dated 31 December 1883, Montgomery County Will Book G, Kentucky Department for Libraries and Archives; *Frankfort Weekly Kentucky Yeoman,* 3 June 1884; *New York Times,* 16 May 1884.

27. Elizabeth Reid to Cassius M. Clay, 1 June 1895, undated [June 1895], both in Clay Papers.

28. *Letters,* 44, 71, 116, 3, and passim; *Judge Reid,* x.

29. *Richard Reid: A Memorial,* passim; *Judge Reid,* x.

30. "Editor's Study," *Harper's New Monthly Magazine* 73 (1886): 965–66; *Judge Reid,* v–xiii; *Agents Wanted: Judge Richard Reid, a Biography* (n.d.).

31. *Judge Reid,* vii, passim. The statistics comparing the three books are the author's.

32. Ibid., 489, 576, passim.

33. Ibid., 465, 475, 478, 465–80, 371.

34. Davison and Neale, *Abnormal Psychology,* 252; Jamison, *Night Falls Fast,* 115.

35. Dudley Pope, *Guns* (1969), 191–92; Dr. Bruce D. Ragsdale to Dr. Richard L. Lozano, undated [1998]; Lozano letter; *Louisville Courier-Journal,* 16 May 1884; *Judge Reid,* 478.

36. Communication from John Marshall Prewitt to author, 8 August 2000; John Marshall Prewitt interview; Ann and Curt Steger interview; *Mount Sterling Advocate,* 8 July 1902, 26 February 1895; *Elizabeth Jameson Reid,* 13; O'Rear, *Montgomery County Bar,* 85; *New York Times,* 11 November 1949; Lane interview; Henry Prewitt, interview by author, Paris, Ky., 28 August 2000; "Notes from the Mount Sterling Advocate," May 1920 entry, Mount Sterling Public Library. Roger's wife was Eunice Tomlin. See Prewitt, *Prewitt Descendants,* 354.

37. Clipping, *Louisville Courier-Journal,* 29 April 1979, copy in author's possession; Chalkley, *"Magic Casements,"* 70–71; *New York Times,* 11 November 1949; John Marshall Prewitt interview; Henry Prewitt interview. Reid's brother, J. Davis Reid, lived until 29 June 1906, leaving an estate valued at a quarter of a million dollars, in that era's money. He owned 2,000 acres and had been a director of three banks. Of his ten children, the last died in 1944, the only one to live past age fifty-seven. See *Winchester Democrat,* 3 July 1906, and *Mount Sterling Democrat,* 4 July 1906.

EPILOGUE

1. See, for example, N. S. Shaler, *Kentucky: A Pioneer Commonwealth* (1884); W. H. Perrin, J. H. Battle, and G. C. Kniffin, *Kentucky: A History of the State* (1887); Z. F. Smith, *History of Kentucky* (1885; 1895); Robert M. McElroy, *Kentucky in the Nation's History* (1909); E. P. Johnson, *History of Kentucky*; Connelley and Coulter, *History of Kentucky*; Bodley and Wilson, *History of Kentucky*; Thomas D. Clark, *A History of Kentucky* (1937); Federal Writers' Project, *Kentucky* (1939); Steven A. Channing, *Kentucky: A Bicentennial History* (1977); James C. Klotter, ed., *Our Kentucky: A Study of the Bluegrass State* (2000); John E. Kleber, ed., *The Kentucky Encyclopedia* (1992); Harrison and Klotter, *New History.* Tapp and Klotter,

Decades of Discord, mentions Reid but only in connection with the Superior Court. For southern history works sampled, see Francis B. Simkins and Charles P. Roland, *A History of the South* (1972); John Boles, *The South through Time: A History of an American Region* (1994); David C. Roller and Robert W. Twyman, *The Encyclopedia of Southern History* (1979); Wilson and Ferris, eds., *Encyclopedia of Southern Culture;* Woodward, *Origins of the New South;* Ayers, *Promise of the New South;* Cash, *Mind of the South.* Cash once taught at the college that Reid attended.

2. L. F. Johnson, *Tragedies and Trials,* 246–56; Jerry Lee Butcher, "A Narrative History of Selected Aspects of Violence in the New South, 1877–1920" (Ph.D. diss., University of Missouri, 1977), 75–76; Ireland, "Suicide of Judge Richard Reid," 123–45.

3. Gerda Lerner, *Why History Matters: Life and Thoughts* (1997), 52; John A. Dickinson to Richard Reid, 20 April 1884, George Darsie to Reid, 25 April 1884, W. R. Davis to Reid, 26 April 1884, D. M. Harris to Reid, 24 April 1884, Lee Wilson to Elizabeth Reid, 25 April 1884, all in *Letters,* 32, 38, 82, 36–37, 59; *Breckinridge County News,* quoted in *Richard Reid: A Memorial,* 68.

4. *Louisville Courier-Journal,* 8 September 1888; *Mount Sterling Advocate,* 17, 24 March, 7 April 1891, 6 November 1894; Boyd and Boyd, *Mount Sterling,* 87; G. C. Wright, *Racial Violence,* 316.

5. *Mount Sterling Advocate,* 4 December 1894, 3, 29 January, 5 February, 18 June, 13 August 1895; Boyd and Boyd, *Mount Sterling,* 87; G. C. Wright, *Racial Violence,* 326.

6. *Mount Sterling Advocate,* 15, 29 January 1895; *Twelfth Biennial Report of the Bureau of Agriculture . . . 1897* (1897), 119; A. B. Lipscomb, ed., *The Commercial History of the Southern States: Kentucky* (1903), 98; Edward F. Seiller, comp., *Kentucky: Natural Resources, Industrial Statistics, Industrial Directory, Description by Counties* ([1930]), 321–22; John Clements, *Kentucky Facts* (1990), 261; Carl B. Boyd Jr., "Montgomery County," in *Kentucky Encyclopedia,* ed. Kleber, 644; *Louisville Courier-Journal,* 8 June 1992.

7. *Frankfort Weekly Kentucky Yeoman,* 10, 17 June 1884; *Georgetown Times,* 11 June 1884; Kleber, ed., *Kentucky Encyclopedia,* 292, 947; *Maysville Bulletin,* 7, 14 August 1884; *Biographical Directory of the American Congress,* 1041, 1377, 1315. Culbertson lived until 1911 but did not serve in Congress after his term expired in 1885.

8. Tapp and Klotter, *Decades of Discord,* 402–404; L. F. Johnson, *Tragedies and Trials,* 282–91; William H. Townsend, *The Lion of White Hall* (1967), 30–33; *Cincinnati Enquirer,* 9 November 1889.

9. *Louisville Post,* 28 February, 3 March 1890; *Louisville Courier-Journal,* 1, 2, 5, 11–12 March 1890; *Frankfort Capital,* 1 March 1890; *New York Times,* 1 March 1890; James C. Klotter, "Sex, Scandal, and Suffrage in the Gilded Age," *Historian* 42 (1980): 225–26.

10. *Mount Sterling Advocate,* 7 May 1895.

11. James C. Klotter, *William Goebel: The Politics of Wrath* (1977), 33–37, 100–25; Urey Woodson, *The First New Dealer: William Goebel* (1939), 241–46; *Louisville Courier-Journal,* 12 April 1895, 31 January, 1–3 February 1900; *Official Report of the Proceedings and Debates in the Convention . . . to Adopt, Amend, or Change the Constitution of the State of Kentucky,* 4 vols. (1890), 4:4690.

12. William E. Ellis, " 'The Harvest Moon Was Shinin' on the Streets of Shelbyville': Southern Honor and the Death of General Henry H. Denhardt, 1937," *Register of the Ken-*

2. *Frankfort Weekly Kentucky Yeoman*, 20 May 1884; *Mount Sterling Daily Sentinel-Democrat*, 18 May 1884; *Richard Reid: A Memorial*, 13–14; *Biographical Encyclopaedia*, 91; *Judge Reid*, 374–83.

3. *Biographical Cyclopedia of the Commonwealth of Kentucky* (1896), 147–48; *Judge Reid*, 383–87, 392; *Richard Reid: A Memorial*, 14–16; *Newport Kentucky State Journal*, 22 May 1884. Kentucky University is now Transylvania University.

4. *Louisville Courier-Journal*, 23 May 1884; Klotter, *Breckinridges of Kentucky*, 153; *Richard Reid: A Memorial*, 21–24; *Judge Reid*, 393–97.

5. *Baltimore Sun*, 16 May 1884; *New York Herald*, 16 May 1884; *Cleveland Plain Dealer*, 16 May 1884; *St. Louis Post-Dispatch*, 18 May 1884; *New York Times*, 16 May 1884; *San Francisco Daily Examiner*, 25 May 1884; *Chicago Daily Tribune*, 16 May 1884; Ireland, "Suicide of Judge Richard Reid," 137; *Nation* 38 (22 May 1884): 436. For other coverage of the suicide, see *Cincinnati Enquirer*, 16 May 1884; *Atlanta Constitution*, 16 May 1884; *New York Tribune*, 15 May 1884; *Washington Post*, 16 May 1884; *Washington Bee*, 24 May 1884.

6. *Louisville Courier-Journal*, quoted in *Richard Reid: A Memorial*, 46; *Catlettsburg Central Methodist*, 24 May 1884; *Paris Semi-Weekly Bourbon News*, 20 May 1884; *Lexington Transcript*, quoted in *Maysville Bulletin*, 22 May 1884; *Louisville Post*, 16 May 1884; *Richard Reid: A Memorial*, 39; *Judge Reid*, 468. On the crash, see also the *New York Tribune* and *New York Herald*, both of 15 May 1884.

7. *Louisville Post*, 16 May 1884; *Mayfield Monitor*, 23 May 1884; *Georgetown Times*, 21 May 1884; *Paris True Kentuckian*, quoted in *Judge Reid*, 401–402.

8. *Owensboro Semi-Weekly Messenger*, 20 May 1884; *Winchester Democrat, Courier-Journal, Vanceburg Courier*, all quoted in *Richard Reid: A Memorial*, 45, 49–61; *Louisville Times*, 16 May 1884; *Judge Reid*, 399–405. Supporting personal letters came to Mrs. Reid from across the nation. For a sampling, see *Judge Reid*, 438, 441, 451, 454–55, 457, 462–63.

9. *Hickman Courier*, 23 May 1884; *Newport Kentucky State Journal*, 17 May 1884; *Stanford Semi-Weekly Interior Journal*, 20 May 1884; *Breckinridge County News*, quoted in *Judge Reid*, 407; R. Graham to Elizabeth Reid, 18 October 1884, in *Letters*, 114.

10. *Louisville Commercial*, 22 April, 20 May 1884; *Louisville Courier-Journal*, 23 May 1884; Ireland, "Suicide of Judge Richard Reid," 139–40; "Speech of Col. Henry L. Stone," quoted in *Judge Reid*, 558; *New York Times*, 18 April 1884; *Richard Reid: A Memorial*, 54; *Judge Reid*, 364, 400, 332. See also *Frankfort Weekly Kentucky Yeoman*, 27 May 1884, and Dick Steward, whose *Duels and the Roots of Violence in Missouri* (2000) argues that duels were used as tools for political advancement.

11. "Sentinel-Democrat Clippings," 1884; *Flemingsburg Times-Democrat*, 23 May 1884; *Richard Reid: A Memorial*, 6, 30–31; *Judge Reid*, 335; *Stanford Semi-Weekly Interior Journal*, 27 May 1884; *Louisville Commercial*, 20 May 1884; *Frankfort Weekly Kentucky Yeoman*, 27 May, 3 June 1884.

12. *Paris Kentuckian*, 7, 11 June 1884; Ireland, "Suicide of Judge Richard Reid," 141–43; *London Mountain Echo*, 13 June 1884; *Frankfort Weekly Kentucky Yeoman*, 10, 17 June 1884; *Georgetown Times*, 11 June 1884; *Paris Semi-Weekly Bourbon News*, 13 June 1884. The numbers of ballots is variously given as 175, 176, and 177.

13. *Paris True Kentuckian*, 7 May 1879, 22 May 1884; *Judge Reid*, 387; *Richard Reid: A Memorial*, 26; *Mount Sterling Democrat*, 30 April 1880; O'Rear, *Montgomery County Bar*,

65; *London Mountain Echo,* 11, 25 July 1884; Doolan, "Court of Appeals," 465; *Maysville Bulletin,* 21 August, 17, 24 July 1884; *Frankfort Weekly Kentucky Yeoman,* 12 August 1884; *Judge Reid,* 336.

14. *Frankfort Weekly Kentucky Yeoman,* 12, 19, 26 August, 2 September 1884; Ireland, "Suicide of Judge Richard Reid," 142; "Kentucky," *Appleton's Annual Cyclopedia and Register of Important Events* (1884), 424; *London Mountain Echo,* 15 August 1884; Boyd and Boyd, *Mount Sterling,* 261; Doolan, "Court of Appeals," 463, 465; E. P. Johnson, *History of Kentucky,* 2:647; "May Stone," in Temple Bodley and Samuel M. Wilson, *History of Kentucky,* 4 vols. (1928), 3:24–28; Nancy Forderhase, "May Stone," in *Kentucky Encyclopedia,* ed. John E. Kleber (1992), 857. Reid's college classmate J. Q. A. Ward ran for and won the now-vacant seat on the Superior Court, defeating Cornelison ally and defense attorney Thomas Turner. See *Georgetown Times,* 28 May 1884, *Flemingsburg Times-Democrat,* 24 June 1884, and A. E. Richards, "Superior Court of Kentucky," in *Lawyers and Lawmakers,* ed. Levin, 136–37.

15. *Mount Sterling Daily Sentinel-Democrat,* 22 April 1884; *Louisville Times,* 15 May 1884; *Cornelison v. Commonwealth,* 7 Kentucky Law Reporter 346; *Judge Reid,* 500; Levin, ed., *Lawyers and Lawmakers,* 120, 124; L. F. Johnson, *Tragedies and Trials,* 253; O'Rear, *Montgomery County Bar,* 60. For Cornelison's response to the indictment, see John J. Cornelison to C. M. Clay, 17 March 1888, in Cassius M. Clay Papers, Special Collections, University of Kentucky.

16. *Cornelison v. Commonwealth,* 84 Kentucky Reports 591–96; *Judge Reid,* 502–504, 542–43. Some confusion exists on exactly when Cornelison changed his plea that last time. Newspaper reports, in *Judge Reid,* 502, suggested it came after the last defense argument. But the court decision, above, indicates it occurred as noted in the text.

17. *Judge Reid,* 541, 518–19, 508, 516, 534–35, 540–67.

18. Ibid., 504; *Cornelison v. Commonwealth,* 84 Kentucky Reports 591; L. F. Johnson, *Tragedies and Trials,* 256.

19. *Cornelison v. Commonwealth,* 7 Kentucky Law Reporter 344–56.

20. *Cornelison v. Commonwealth,* 84 Kentucky Reporter 583–623; Richard L. Troutman, ed., *The Heavens Are Weeping: The Diaries of George Richard Browder, 1852–1886* (1987), 408. The case also appeared in 2 Southwestern Reporter 235. Cornelison had another case before the court that term, involving a homestead mortgage. See *Cornelison v. Stephens,* 2 S. W. Reporter 122.

21. *Louisville Commercial,* 25, 29 July 1888; *Louisville Times,* 19–21 July 1888.

22. *Louisville Commercial,* 25, 29 July 1888. After seeing the whip years ago, John Marshall Prewitt still remembers it as "more like a club"—being one-half to three-quarters of an inch thick. Prewitt, communication to author, 8 August 2000.

23. *Louisville Courier-Journal,* 5, 6 August 1888; *Louisville Times,* 4 August 1888; "Executive Journal 1887–89, S. B. Buckner Governor," entry of 8 October 1888, Governors' Papers, Kentucky Department for Libraries and Archives; *Lexington Morning Herald,* 15 February 1899. Several sources incorrectly repeat that he served his full term. See, for example, L. F. Johnson, *Tragedies and Trials,* 256, and Boyd and Boyd, *Mount Sterling,* 64.

24. J. J. Cornelison to William Lindsay, 27 September 1890, Lindsay Papers; *Breckinridge County News,* quoted in *Richard Reid: A Memorial,* 67; *Lexington Daily Leader,* 14 February

tucky Historical Society 84 (1986): 361–96; *Louisville Courier-Journal Magazine,* 8 December 1985; James C. Klotter, *Kentucky: Portrait in Paradox, 1900–1950* (1996), 70–71.

13. G. C. Wright, *Racial Violence,* 118–19, 163, 71.

14. Numerous primary sources document the mountain troubles. As an example, see *New York Times,* 17 September, 15, 24–28 October, 13 November 1889, 15 June, 28 August, 2 September 1890, 5, 23 May, 20 June, 15 August, 23 September 1903, 3 April, 16 May 1904. More specifically, see Thomas C. Ballou, "A Cumberland Vendetta" (manuscript book, Kentucky Historical Society); Mutzenberg, *Kentucky's Feuds,* 187–253; Pearce, *Days of Darkness,* 170; Dwight B. Billings and Kathleen M. Blee, *The Road to Poverty: The Making of Wealth and Hardship in Appalachia* (2000); E. L. Noble, *Bloody Breathitt's Feuds,* 4 vols. (1936–47), 3:6, 35–37, 41, 46, 55–58, 97–100, 116–18; Klotter, *Portrait in Paradox,* 55–57; Waller, "Feuding in Appalachia," 347–76; Klotter, "Feuds in Appalachia," 290–317.

15. On the Tollgate War, see J. Winston Coleman Jr., *Stage-Coach Days in the Bluegrass* (1935; 1995), 238–46; Tapp and Klotter, *Decades of Discord,* 404–408; Kentucky House of Representatives, *Journal of the Regular Session of the House of Representatives of the Commonwealth of Kentucky* (1898), 24–27.

16. A rich literature exists on the Black Patch War. See, for instance, John L. Mathews, "The Farmers' Union and the Tobacco Pool," *Atlantic Monthly* 102 (1908): 482–91; James O. Nall, *The Tobacco Night Riders of Kentucky and Tennessee* (1939); Rick S. Gregory, "Desperate Farmers: The Dark Tobacco District Planters' Protective Association of Kentucky and Tennessee, 1904–1914" (Ph.D. diss., Vanderbilt University, 1989); Tracy Campbell, *The Politics of Despair* (1993); Christopher R. Waldrep, *Night Riders* (1993); Suzanne Marshall, *Violence in the Black Patch of Kentucky and Tennessee* (1994).

17. Klotter, *Portrait in Paradox,* 243–44; *Golden Pond Moonshine* (pamphlet), 1. On Harlan, see John W. Hevener, *Which Side Are You On? The Harlan County Coal Miners, 1931–39* (1978); Paul F. Taylor, *Bloody Harlan* (1990); Tony Bubka, "The Harlan County Coal Strike of 1931," *Labor History* 11 (1970); National Committee for the Defense of Political Prisoners, *Harlan Miners Speak* (1932); U.S. Senate, *Violation of Free Speech and Rights of Labor Hearing,* 75th Cong., 1st Sess. (1937); Alessandro Portelli, "History-Telling and Time: An Example from Kentucky," *Oral History Review* 20 (1992): 61.

18. *Hazel Green Herald,* 12 August 1887; *Louisville Courier-Journal,* 2 January 1890.

19. *New York Times,* 27 June 1887; "The Kentucky Tragedy," *The Nation* 49 (14 November 1889): 382–83; "The Progress of the World," *American Monthly Review of Reviews* 21 (1900): 274; James G. Speed, "The Kentuckian," *Century Magazine* 59 (1900): 946–47.

20. *Chicago Tribune,* 23 July 1885; *Report on Crime . . . in the United States at the Eleventh Census: 1890* (1895), 173; Harrison and Klotter, *New History,* 434; *Bulletin of the State Board of Health of Kentucky* 6 (June 1934): 30; Robert W. Bingham to Barry Bingham, 8 March [1935] (copy), Papers of Robert Worth Bingham, Manuscript Division, Library of Congress; *Louisville Courier-Journal,* 19 January 1906; Joseph L. McConnell, "Growth of Manufacturing in Kentucky, 1904 to 1929" (master's thesis, University of Kentucky, 1932), 18–22, 11–12, passim; Klotter, *Portrait in Paradox,* 131–32.

21. Harrison and Klotter, *New History,* table 25.2, 434; Raymond D. Gastil, *Cultural Regions of the United States* (1975), 107; *Lexington Herald-Leader,* 5 August 1991, 12 March 1995.

22. William G. Thomas III, "'Under Indictment': Thomas Lafayette Rosser and the New South," *Virginia Magazine of History and Biography* 100 (1992): 207; Rable, *But There Was No Peace,* 3–4, 187. As defined, the South includes the eleven Confederate states, plus Kentucky. (The Gallup Poll includes all those, plus Oklahoma, in its definition.)

23. B. J. Ramage, "Homicide in the Southern States," *Sewanee Review* 4 (1896): 212–14, 219, 222–23; Ayers, *Vengeance and Justice,* 266–67; Butcher, "Narrative History of Selected Aspects of Violence," 52; Austin L. Porterfield, "A Decade of Serious Crime in the United States: Some Trends and Hypotheses," *American Sociological Review* 13 (1948): 49.

24. Hackney, "Southern Violence," 479–84, 491–93; Raymond D. Gastil, "Homicide and a Regional Culture of Violence," *American Sociological Review* 36 (1971): 414–15, 419–20, 425; Gastil, *Cultural Regions,* 97–116; John Shelton Reed, "To Live and Die in Dixie: A Contribution to the Study of Southern Violence," *Political Science Quarterly* 76 (1971): 429–45; Reed, *The Enduring South* (1975), 45–55; C. Loftin and R. H. Hill, "Regional Subculture and Homicide: An Examination of the Gastil-Hackney Thesis," *American Sociological Review* 39 (1974): 714–24; Lin Huff-Corzine, Jay Corzine, and David C. Moore, "Southern Exposure: Deciphering the South's Influence on Homicide Rates," *Social Forces* 64 (1986): 906–24; William C. Bailey, "Some Further Evidence on Homicide and a Regional Culture of Violence," *Omega: Journal of Death and Dying* 7 (1976): 145–70.

25. Wyatt-Brown, *Southern Honor*; Wyatt-Brown, *Honor and Violence*; Ayers, *Vengeance and Justice,* 270; Nisbett, "Violence and Culture," 441–49, 442; Dov Cohen et al., "Insult, Aggression, and the Southern Culture of Honor," *Journal of Personality and Social Psychology* 70 (1996): 945–60, 946. I remain stubbornly unconvinced by the so-called Celtic Thesis, but for a good presentation of that argument, see Grady McWhiney, *Cracker Culture: Celtic Ways in the Old South* (1988), and Forrest McDonald and Grady McWhiney, "The Antebellum Southern Herdsman: A Reinterpretation," *Journal of Southern History* 41 (1975): 47–66.

26. Nisbett and Cohen, *Culture of Honor,* xv–xviii, 4–5, 26–38, 43–48, 81–82, 92–94; Gastil, "Violence, Crime, and Punishment," 1475.

27. *Turner* v. *Commonwealth* 89 Kentucky 78 (1887); *Commonwealth* v. *Rudert* 109 Kentucky 653–60 (1901).

28. *Springfield* v. *State* 11 Southern Reporter 250–53 (1892); *State* v. *Bartlett* 71 S.W. Reporter 148–53 (1902).

29. Joseph H. Beale Jr., "Retreat from a Murderous Assault," *Harvard Law Review* 16 (1903): 567, 576–82.

30. *Gibson* v. *Commonwealth* 34 S.W. Reporter, 2d 936 (1931); Daniel T. Goyette, "Development in Cases Involving Self-Defense," in *Kentucky Bar Association Update '99* (1999), 404–405; Robert G. Lawson and William H. Fortune, *Kentucky Criminal Law* (1998), 146, 146 n. See also William S. Cooper and Robert G. Lawson, "Self Defense in Kentucky: A Need for Clarification or Revision," *Kentucky Law Journal* 76 (1987–88): 167–99.

31. John C. Klotter, *Criminal Law,* 6th ed. (2001), iii, 98–105; Lawson and Fortune, *Kentucky Criminal Law,* 362–64; Reed, *Enduring South,* 97.

32. David McCullough, *Mornings on Horseback* (1981), 283–88, 317–50; Kimmel, *Manhood in America,* 182; Bederman, *Manliness and Civilization,* 175–86, 15; Theodore Roosevelt, *The Winning of the West,* 6 vols. (1889–96); John A. Lucas and Ronald A. Smith, *Saga*

of American Sport (1978), 240; Robert J. Higgs, *God in the Stadium: Sports and Religion in America* (1995), 126; Robert F. Martin, "Billy Sunday and Christian Manliness," *Historian* 58 (1996): 812–13, 817–19.

33. Kristin L. Hoganson, *Fighting for American Manhood: How Gender Politics Provoked the Spanish-American and Philippine-American Wars* (1998), 12–14, 202–203; Griffen, "Reconstructing Masculinity," 191, 199; *Louisville Courier-Journal*, 2 June 1898; *Courier-Journal*, 29 November 1899, quoted in Daniel S. Margolies, "God's Promise Redeemed: Marse Henry Watterson and the Compromises of American Empire" (Ph.D. diss., University of Wisconsin, 1999), 392; Bederman, *Manliness and Civilization*, 193, 214.

34. Walter Millis, *The Martial Spirit* (1931; 1965), 340; Lewis L. Gould, *The Spanish-American War and President McKinley* (1982), 123–26; William E. Leuchtenburg, *The Perils of Prosperity, 1914–32* (1958), 36–37, 47, 142–46, 158; Henry F. May, *The End of American Innocence* (1959), 393–98; David M. Kennedy, *Freedom from Fear: The American People in Depression and War, 1929–1945* (1999), 160–74, 190–96; Selig Adler, *The Isolationist Impulse: Its Twentieth-Century Reaction* (1957), 250–90.

35. On the Gilded Age, see, for example, Vincent P. DeSantis, *The Shaping of Modern America* (2nd ed., 1989), 1–120; John A. Garraty, *The New Commonwealth, 1877–1890* (1968); Morton Keller, *Affairs of State: Public Life in Nineteenth Century America* (1977); Robert H. Wiebe, *The Search for Order, 1877–1920* (1967), 1–163; Mark W. Summers, *The Gilded Age* (1997); and Nell Irvin Painter, *Standing at Armageddon: The United States, 1877–1919* (1987).

36. Rotundo, *American Manhood*, 285–86; Susan Faludi, "The Betrayal of the American Man," *Newsweek*, 13 September 1999, p. 48.

37. Pitt-Rivers, "Honor," 6:510; Wyatt-Brown, *Shaping of Southern Culture*, 299; Ruth Horowitz and Gary Schwartz, "Honor, Normative Ambiguity, and Gang Violence," *American Sociological Review* 39 (1974): 238–40; Nisbett and Cohen, *Culture of Honor*, 90–91; Faludi, "Betrayal"; Ayers, *Vengeance and Justice*, 275.

38. Reed, *Enduring South*, 45; Nisbett and Cohen, *Culture of Honor*, 38; *Tampa Tribune*, 22 July 1996; David Burner, *Making Peace with the Sixties* (1996), 113; Waller R. Newell, "The Crisis of Manliness," *Weekly Standard* 3 (3 August 1998): 19; David Chaney, "The Spectacle of Honour: The Changing Dramatization of Status," *Theory, Culture, and Society* 12 (1995): 159; Faludi, "Betrayal."

Bibliography

MANUSCRIPTS

Bourbon County, Ky., Clerk's Office, Paris, Ky.
    Deed Book 70.
    Order Book T.
    Will Book S.
Georgetown College, Georgetown, Ky.
  College Archives
    Catalogue of the Students of Georgetown College with a List of Academic Honors Confirmed by the College.
    James Tevis Diary.
    Records of the Faculty, vol. 1.
    Records of Georgetown College, 1859–1887.
    Records of the Trustees of Georgetown College from 1837 to 1865.
Kentucky Department for Libraries and Archives, Frankfort, Ky.
    Executive Journal, 1887–89, S. B. Buckner, Governor's Papers.
    Montgomery County, Ky., Assessor's Book, 1883.
    Montgomery County, Ky., Will Book G.
Kentucky Historical Society, Frankfort, Ky.
  Special Collections.
    Map of Montgomery County, Kentucky . . . 1879.
    Mrs. Richard Reid Collection.
Library of Congress, Washington, D.C.
  Manuscript Division
    Papers of Robert Worth Bingham.

Montgomery County, Ky., Clerk's Office, Mount Sterling, Ky.
    Deed Books 20–21, 36–37, 40–41.
Mount Sterling Public Library, Mount Sterling, Ky.
    "Clippings from the 'Looking Backward' Column of *Mount Sterling Sentinel-Democrat*"
    "Notes from the Mount Sterling Advocate"
Private Collections
    Donaldson, Everett, Mount Sterling, Ky.
        Everett Donaldson Papers
    Klotter, James C., Lexington, Ky.
        Lozano, Richard L., to James C. Klotter
        Prewitt, John Marshall, to James C. Klotter
        Ragsdale, Bruce D., to Richard Lozano
        Weise, Robert, to James C. Klotter
    Roseberry, Kenney, Paris, Ky.
        Kenney Roseberry Family Files
United States Census (manuscript)
        1850: Montgomery County, Ky.
        1860: Madison County, Ky.
        1880: Montgomery County, Ky.
University of Kentucky, Lexington, Ky.
    Special Collections
        Cassius M. Clay Papers.
        Lindsay Papers.
        John White Stevenson Collection.
University of North Carolina, Chapel Hill, N.C.
    Southern Historical Collection.
        James M. Saffell Scrapbooks.

NEWSPAPERS

Kentucky

Ashland Independent, 1883–84, 1954.
Catlettsburg Central Methodist, 1884.
Flemingsburg Times-Democrat, 1884.
Frankfort Capital, 1890.
Frankfort Commonwealth, 1867.
*Frankfort Yeoman,*1879–80, 1884.

Georgetown Times, 1879, 1884.
Hartford Herald, 1884.
Hazel Green Herald, 1887.
Hickman Courier, 1884.
Lexington Daily Leader, 1899.
Lexington Herald-Leader, 1991, 1995.
Lexington Kentucky Gazette, 1866, 1878.
Lexington Kentucky Statesman, 1869.
Lexington Morning Herald, 1899.
Lexington Observer and Reporter, 1868.
Lexington Press, 1874.
London Mountain Echo, 1884.
Louisville Commercial, 1884, 1888.
Louisville Courier-Journal, 1871, 1878, 1882–85, 1888, 1890, 1895–1900, 1906,
    1960, 1979, 1985.
Louisville Post, 1884, 1890.
Louisville Times, 1884, 1888.
Mayfield Monitor, 1884.
Maysville Bulletin, 1884.
Midway Blue-Grass Clipper, 1878.
Mount Sterling Advocate, 1891, 1894–95, 1899, 1902.
Mount Sterling Democrat, 1880–82, 1884, 1906.
Mount Sterling Kentucky Sentinel, 1865.
Mount Sterling Sentinel-Democrat, 1884.
Newport Kentucky State Journal, 1884.
Owensboro Messenger, 1884.
Paris Bourbon News, 1884.
Paris Kentuckian, 1884.
Paris True Kentuckian, 1879, 1882.
Richmond Register, 1879.
Stanford Interior Journal, 1882, 1884.
Versailles Woodford Sun, 1884.
Winchester Democrat, 1906.
Winchester Sun, 1879.

Other

Atlanta Constitution, 1884.
Baltimore Sun, 1884.
Chicago Tribune, 1884–85.

Cincinnati Enquirer, 1884, 1889.
Cincinnati Gazette, 1867.
Cleveland Plain Dealer, 1884.
Fulton (Mo.) Telegraph, 1863, 1873.
Nashville Banner, 1884.
New York Herald, 1884.
New York Times, 1878–80, 1882, 1884, 1887, 1889–90, 1903–04, 1949.
New-York Tribune, 1884.
Portland (Maine) Transcript, 1841.
St. Louis Post-Dispatch, 1884.
San Francisco Examiner, 1884.
Tampa Tribune, 1996.
Washington (D.C.) Bee, 1884.
Washington Post, 1884.

Court Cases

Bohannon v. *Commonwealth* 8 Bush 481 (1871).
Carico v. *Commonwealth* 7 Bush 124 (1870).
Commonwealth v. *Rudert* 109 Kentucky 653 (1901).
Cornelison v. *Commonwealth* 84 Kentucky Reports 595 (1886).
Cornelison v. *Stephens* 2 S.W. Reporter 122 (1884).
Fain v. *Commonwealth* 78 Kentucky Reports 183 (1879).
Gibson v. *Commonwealth* 34 S.W. Reporter, 2d 936 (1931).
Holloway v. *Commonwealth* 11 Bush 344 (1875).
Howard v. *Cornelison* 5 Kentucky Law Reporter 902 (1884).
Philips v. *Commonwealth* 2 Duvall 328 (1866).
Springfield v. *State* 11 Southern Reporter 250 (1892).
State v. *Bartlett* 71 S.W. Reporter 148 (1902).
Turner v. *Commonwealth* 89 Kentucky 78 (1889).

Interviews

Lane, Caswell, interview by author, Mount Sterling, 1 October 1999.
Murphy, Terry, interview by author, Mount Sterling, 11 June 2001.
Prewitt, Henry, interview by author, Paris, 28 August 2000.
Prewitt, John Marshall, telephone interview by author, 26 August 2000.
Steger, Ann and Curt, interview by author, Mount Sterling, 15 June 2001.

Books

Adams, William E. *Our American Cousins*. London: Walter Scott, 1883.

Adler, Selig. *The Isolationist Impulse: Its Twentieth-Century Reaction*. New York: Free Press, 1957.

Agents Wanted: Judge Richard Reid, a Biography.N.p., n.d.

Aiken, Gladys Lee, transcriber. *1870 Census: Montgomery County, Kentucky*. N.p., n.d.

Allen, James Lane. *The Blue Grass Region of Kentucky*. New York: Macmillan, 1892.

Apple, Lindsey, Frederick A. Johnston, and Ann B. Bevins, eds. *Scott County, Kentucky: A History*. Georgetown, Ky.: Scott County Historical Society, 1993.

Appleton's Annual Cyclopedia and Register of Important Events. New York: D. Appleton, 1866, 1884.

Arguments of Hon. Henry L. Stone of Mount Sterling, Ky., Delivered . . . in Behalf of the Defendant, on the Trial of the Celebrated Libel Suit of Thomas M. Green vs. Thomas F. Hargis. Frankfort, Ky.: Roundabout Office, 1881.

Arnow, Harriette Simpson. *Seedtime on the Cumberland*. Lexington: University Press of Kentucky, 1983.

Aron, Stephen. *How the West Was Lost: The Transformation of Kentucky from Daniel Boone to Henry Clay*. Baltimore: Johns Hopkins University Press, 1996.

Ayers, Edward L. *The Promise of the New South: Life after Reconstruction*. New York: Oxford University Press, 1992.

———. *Vengeance and Justice: Crime and Punishment in the Nineteenth-Century American South*. New York: Oxford University Press, 1984.

Baird, Nancy Disher. *Luke Pryor Blackburn: Physician, Governor, Reformer*. Lexington: University Press of Kentucky, 1979.

Bamberg, Robert D., ed. *The Confession of Jereboam O. Beauchamp*. Philadelphia: University of Pennsylvania Press, 1966.

Bardaglio, Peter W. *Reconstructing the Household: Families, Sex, and the Law in the Nineteenth-Century South*. Chapel Hill: University of North Carolina, 1995.

Battin, Margaret Pabst. *Ethical Issues in Suicide*. Englewood Cliffs, N.J.: Prentice-Hall, 1982.

Bederman, Gail. *Manliness and Civilization: A Cultural History of Gender and Race in the United States, 1880–1917*. Chicago: University of Chicago, 1995.

Berman, Alan L., and David A. Jobes. *Adolescent Suicide: Assessment and Intervention*. Washington, D.C.: American Psychological Association, 1991.

Billings, Dwight B., and Kathleen M. Blee. *The Road to Poverty: The Making of Wealth and Hardship in Appalachia*. Cambridge: Cambridge University Press, 2000.

Billington, Monroe L. *The American South*. New York: Charles Scribner's Sons, 1971.

Biographical Cyclopedia of the Commonwealth of Kentucky. Chicago: John M. Gresham, 1896.

Biographical Directory of the American Congress, 1774–1949. Washington, D.C.: Government Printing Office, 1950.

Biographical Encyclopaedia of Kentucky. Cincinnati: J. M. Armstrong, 1878.

Bodley, Temple, and Samuel M. Wilson. *History of Kentucky.* 4 vols. Chicago: S. J. Clarke, 1928.

Boles, John. *The South through Time: A History of an American Region.* Upper Saddle River, N.J.: Prentice-Hall, 1994.

Bourbon County, Kentucky, Tombstone Inscriptions. N.p., n.d..

Boyd, Carl B., Jr., and Hazel M. Boyd. *A History of Mount Sterling, Kentucky, 1792–1918.* N.p, 1984.

Boyd, Hazel M. *Some Marriages in Montgomery County, Kentucky, before 1864.* N.p., 1961.

Brown, Robert Maxwell. *Strain of Violence: Historical Studies of American Violence and Vigilantism.* New York: Oxford University Press, 1975.

Brownell, Blaine A., and David R. Goldfield, eds. *The City in Southern History.* Port Washington, N.Y.: Kennikat Press, 1977.

Bruce, Dickson D., Jr. *Violence and Culture in the Antebellum South.* Austin: University of Texas Press, 1979.

Burner, David. *Making Peace with the Sixties.* Princeton, N.J.: Princeton University Press, 1996.

Burton, Orville Burton and Robert C. McMath, eds. *Class, Conflict, and Consensus: Antebellum Southern Community Studies.* Westport, Conn.: Greenwood Press, 1982.

Campbell, Tracy. *The Politics of Despair.* Lexington: University Press of Kentucky, 1993.

Carnes, Mark C. *Secret Ritual and Manhood in Victorian America.* New Haven, Conn.: Yale University Press, 1989.

Carnes, Mark C., and Clyde Griffen, eds. *Meanings for Manhood: Construction of Masculinity in Victorian America.* Chicago: University of Chicago Press, 1990.

Carter County Bicentennial Committee. *Carter County History, 1838–1976.* N.p., n.d.

Cash, W. J. *The Mind of the South.* New York: Vintage Books, 1941.

Catalogue of Georgetown College, Kentucky, 1859–1860. Frankfort, Ky.: A. G. Hodges, 1860.

Catalogue of the Officers and Students of Georgetown College, Kentucky, 1855–1856. Louisville: Hull and Brothers, 1856.

Catalogue of the Officers and Students of Georgetown College, Kentucky, 1856–1857. Cincinnati: Geo. S. Blanchard, 1857.

Catalogue of the Officers and Students of Georgetown College, Kentucky, 1857–1858. Cincinnati: Geo. S. Blanchard, 1858.

Catalogue of the Officers and Students of Georgetown College, Kentucky, 1858–1859. Frankfort, Ky.: A. G. Hodges, 1859.

Catalogue of the Students of Georgetown College. N.p., n.d.

Chalkley, Eleanor Breckinridge. *"Magic Casements."* Frankfort: Kentucky Historical Society, 1982.

Channing, Steven A. *Kentucky: A Bicentennial History.* New York: W. W. Norton, 1977.

Clark, Champ. *My Quarter Century in American Politics.* 2 vols. New York: Harper and Brothers, 1920.

Clark, Thomas D. *A History of Kentucky.* Lexington: John Bradford Press, 1937.

————, ed. *The Voice of the Frontier: John Bradford's Notes on Kentucky.* Lexington: University Press of Kentucky, 1993.

Clements, John. *Kentucky Facts.* Dallas: Clements Research, 1990.

Clift, G. Glenn. *Governors of Kentucky, 1792–1942.* Cynthiana, Ky.: Hobson Press, 1942.

Coleman, J. Winston, Jr. *Famous Kentucky Duels.* Lexington: Henry Clay Press, 1969.

————. *Stage-Coach Days in the Bluegrass.* Lexington: University Press of Kentucky, 1995.

Collins, Lewis, and Richard H. Collins. *History of Kentucky.* 2 vols. Covington, Ky.: Collins, 1874.

Compendium of the Ninth Census. Washington, D.C.: Government Printing Office, 1870.

Connelley, William E., and E. Merton Coulter. *History of Kentucky.* 5 vols. Chicago: American Historical Society, 1922.

Cook, J. F. *Old Kentucky.* New York: Neale, 1908.

Coulter, E. Merton. *The Civil War and Readjustment in Kentucky.* Chapel Hill: University of North Carolina Press, 1926.

Curry, Leonard P. *Rail Routes South: Louisville's Fight for the Southern Market, 1865–1872.* Lexington: University of Kentucky Press, 1969.

Curry, Richard O., ed. *Radicalism, Racism, and Party Alignment: The Border States during Reconstruction.* Baltimore: Johns Hopkins University Press, 1969.

Davis, William C., and Meredith L. Swentor, eds. *Bluegrass Confederate: The Headquarters Diary of Edward O. Guerrant.* Baton Rouge: Louisiana State University Press, 1999.

Davison, Gerald C., and John M. Neale. *Abnormal Psychology.* 7th ed. New York: John Wiley and Sons, 1998.

Degler, Carl N. *At Odds: Women and the Family in America from the Revolution to the Present.* New York: Oxford University Press, 1980.

D'Emilio, John, and Estelle B. Freedman. *Intimate Matters: A History of Sexuality in America.* New York: Harper and Row, 1988.

Dennis, Frederic S., ed. *System of Surgery*. Vol. 4, Philadelphia: Lea Brothers, 1896.

DeSantis, Vincent P. *The Shaping of Modern America*. 2nd ed. Wheeling, Ill.: Forum Press, 1989.

Donald, David H. *Charles Sumner and the Coming of the Civil War*. New York: Knopf, 1960.

Drabble, Margaret, ed. *The Oxford Companion to English Literature*. 5th ed. New York: Oxford University Press, 1991.

Dunn, Thelma, transcriber. *Montgomery County, Kentucky, County Clerk Tax Assessment Records, 1806–1807–1808–1809–1810 and the 1810 Census Record*. N.p., 1996.

———. *Montgomery County, Kentucky, Marriage Bonds: White, 1864–1881*. Atoka, Tenn.: Thelma Dunn, 1997.

Durkheim, Emile. *Suicide: A Study in Sociology*. Translated by John Spaulding and George Simpson. Glencoe, Ill.: Free Press, 1951.

Elizabeth Jameson Reid: A Tribute. N.p., 1904.

Eller, Ronald D. *Miners, Millhands, and Mountaineers: Industrialization of the Appalachian South, 1880–1930*. Knoxville: University of Tennessee Press, 1982.

Ellis, Thomas E., and Cory F. Newman. *Choosing to Live: How to Defeat Suicide through Cognitive Therapy*. Oakland: New Harmony Publications, 1996.

Everman, H. E. *Bourbon County since 1865*. N.p., 1999.

Faragher, John Mack. *Daniel Boone*. New York: Henry Holt, 1992.

Farberow, Norman L., and Edwin S. Shneidman, eds. *The Cry for Help*. New York: McGraw-Hill, 1961.

Federal Writers Project. *Kentucky*. New York: Harcourt, Brace, 1939.

Fields, Carl R. *A Sesquicentennial History of Georgetown College*. Georgetown, Ky.: Georgetown College Press, 1979.

Fordham, Elias Pym. *Personal Narratives of Travels. . . .* Cleveland: Arthur H. Clark, 1906.

Foster, Gaines M. *Ghosts of the Confederacy: Defeat, the Lost Cause, and the Emergence of the New South*. New York: Oxford University Press, 1985.

Fox, John Jr. *The Little Shepherd of Kingdom Come*. New York: Avon Books, 1973.

Frank, Stephen M. *Life with Father: Parenthood and Masculinity in the Nineteenth-Century North*. Baltimore: Johns Hopkins University Press, 1998.

Friend, Craig T., ed. *The Buzzel about Kentuck: Settling the Promised Land*. Lexington: University Press of Kentucky, 1999.

Fuller, Paul E. *Laura Clay and the Woman's Rights Movement*. Lexington: University Press of Kentucky, 1975.

Garraty, John A. *The New Commonwealth, 1877–1890*. New York: Harper and Row, 1968.

Gastil, Raymond D. *Cultural Regions of the United States*. Seattle: University of Washington Press, 1975.

Gilmore, David D. *Manhood in the Making: Cultural Concepts of Masculinity.* New Haven, Conn.: Yale University Press, 1990.

Goldfield, David R. *Cotton Fields and Skyscrapers: Southern City and Region, 1607–1980.* Baton Rouge: Louisiana State University Press, 1982.

Gould, Lewis L. *The Spanish-American War and President McKinley.* Lawrence: University Press of Kansas, 1982.

Graham, Hugh Davis, and Ted Robert Gurr, eds. *Violence in America: Historical and Comparative Perspectives.* New York: Signet Books, 1969.

Green, Thomas Marshall. *Historic Families of Kentucky.* Cincinnati: Robert Clarke, 1889.

Greenberg, Kenneth S. *Honor and Slavery.* Princeton, N.J.: Princeton University Press, 1996.

Hall, James. *Sketches of History, Life, and Manners in the West.* 2 vols. Philadelphia: Harrison Hall, 1835.

Hammack, James W., Jr. *Kentucky and the Second American Revolution.* Lexington: University Press of Kentucky, 1976.

Hammon, Neal O., ed. *My Father, Daniel Boone: The Draper Interviews with Nathan Boone.* Lexington: University Press of Kentucky, 1999.

Harrison, Lowell H. *The Civil War in Kentucky.* Lexington: University Press of Kentucky, 1975.

———. *Lincoln and Kentucky.* Lexington: University Press of Kentucky, 2000.

Harrison, Lowell H., and James C. Klotter. *A New History of Kentucky.* Lexington: University Press of Kentucky, 1997.

Harrison, Richard L., Jr. *From Camp Meeting to Church: A History of the Christian Church (Disciples of Christ) in Kentucky.* Lexington: Christian Board of Publications, 1992.

Hevener, John W. *Which Side Are You On? The Harlan County Coal Miners, 1931–1939.* Urbana: University of Illinois Press, 1978.

Higgs, Robert J. *God in the Stadium: Sports and Religion in America.* Lexington: University Press of Kentucky, 1995.

Hofstadter, Richard. *Social Darwinism in American Thought.* Rev. ed. Boston: Beacon Press, 1955.

Hoganson, Kristin L. *Fighting for American Manhood: How Gender Politics Provoked the Spanish-American and Philippine-American Wars.* New Haven, Conn.: Yale University Press, 1998.

Howard, Victor B. *Black Liberation in Kentucky: Emancipation and Freedom, 1862–1884.* Lexington: University Press of Kentucky, 1983.

Hubble, Anna Joy Munday, comp. *Bourbon County, Kentucky, 1850 Census.* N.p., 1986.

Huebner, Timothy S. *The Southern Judicial Tradition: State Judges and Sectional Distinctiveness, 1790–1890.* Athens: University of Georgia Press, 1999.

Huff, J. M. *The Ashland Tragedy*. Ashland, Ky.: Boyd County Historical Society, 1969.

Hyde, Samuel C., Jr., ed. *Plain Folk of the South Revisited*. Baton Rouge: Louisiana State University Press, 1997.

Ireland, Robert M. *Little Kingdoms: The Counties of Kentucky, 1850–1891*. Lexington: University Press of Kentucky, 1977.

Jackson, Evelyn, and WilliamTalley. *Eastern Kentucky References*. Utica, Ky.: McDowell Publishers, 1980.

Jamison, Kay Redfield. *Night Falls Fast: Understanding Suicide*. New York: Vintage Books, 1999.

Johnson, E. Polk. *A History of Kentucky and Kentuckians*. 3 vols. Chicago: Lewis, 1912.

Johnson, L. F. *Famous Kentucky Tragedies and Trials*. Rev. ed. Lexington: Henry Clay Press, 1972.

Johnston, J. Stoddard, ed. *Memorial History of Louisville*. 2 vols. Chicago: American Biographical Publishing Co., 1896.

Jordan, Winthrop D. *White over Black: American Attitudes toward the Negro, 1550–1812*. Baltimore: Penguin Books, 1968.

Keller, Morton. *Affairs of State: Public Life in Nineteenth-Century America*. Cambridge, Mass.: Belknap Press, 1977.

Kennedy, David M. *Freedom from Fear: The American People in Depression and War, 1929–1945*. New York: Oxford University Press, 1999.

Kentucky House of Representatives. *Journal of the Regular Session of the House of Representatives of the Commonwealth of Kentucky*. Louisville: Geo. G. Fetter, 1898.

Kentucky State Directory, Travelers and Shippers Guide for 1870–1871. Louisville: John P. Morton, 1870.

Kimmel, Michael. *Manhood in America: A Cultural History*. New York: Free Press, 1996.

Kleber, John E., ed. *The Kentucky Encyclopedia*. Lexington: University Press of Kentucky, 1992.

Klotter, James C. *The Breckinridges of Kentucky*. Lexington: University Press of Kentucky, 1986.

———. *Kentucky: Portrait in Paradox, 1900–1950*. Frankfort: Kentucky Historical Society, 1996.

———. *William Goebel: The Politics of Wrath*. Lexington: University Press of Kentucky, 1977.

———, ed. *Our Kentucky: A Study of the Bluegrass State*. Rev. ed. Lexington: University Press of Kentucky, 2000.

Klotter, John C. *Criminal Law*. 6th ed. Cincinnati: Anderson, 2001.

Kobler, Arthur L., and Ezra Stotland. *The End of Hope: A Social-Clinical Study of Suicide*. London: Free Press of Glencoe, 1964.

Knight, William E. *The Wm. C. P. Breckinridge Defence*. Colfax, Iowa: Weekly Clipper, 1895.

Langsam, Walter E., and William Gus Johnson. *Historic Architecture of Bourbon County, Kentucky*. Paris, Ky.: Historic Paris-Bourbon County, 1985.

Larsen, Lawrence. *The Rise of the Urban South*. Lexington: University Press of Kentucky, 1985.

————. *The Urban South: A History*. Lexington: University Press of Kentucky, 1990.

Lawson, Robert G., and William H. Fortune. *Kentucky Criminal Law*. Charlottesville, Va.: Lexis Law Publishing, 1998.

Lawson, Rowena, transcriber. *Montgomery County, Kentucky, 1850 Census*. Bowie, Md.: Heritage Books, 1986

Lerner, Gerda. *Why History Matters: Life and Thought*. New York: Oxford University Press, 1997.

Letters. N.p., n.d.

Leuchtenburg, William E. *The Perils of Prosperity, 1914–1932*. Chicago: University of Chicago Press, 1958.

Levin, H., ed. *Lawyers and Lawmakers of Kentucky*. Chicago: Lewis, 1897.

Lewis, Alvin F. *History of Higher Education in Kentucky*. Washington, D.C.: Government Printing Office, 1899.

Ligon, Moses. *A History of Public Education in Kentucky*. Lexington: Bureau of School Service, 1942.

Lipscomb, A. B., ed. *The Commercial History of the Southern States: Kentucky*. Louisville: John P. Morton, 1903.

Lucas, John A., and Ronald A. Smith. *Saga of American Sport*. Philadelphia: Lea and Febiger, 1978.

Lucas, Marion B., and George C. Wright. *A History of Blacks in Kentucky*. 2 vols. Frankfort: Kentucky Historical Society, 1992.

Lystra, Karen. *Searching the Heart: Women, Men, and Romantic Love in Nineteenth-Century America*. New York: Oxford University Press, 1989.

McAllister, J. Gray, and Grace O. Guerrant. *Edward O. Guerrant*. Richmond, Va.: Richmond Press, 1950.

McCullough, David. *Mornings on Horseback*. New York: Simon and Schuster, 1981.

McElroy, Robert M. *Kentucky in the Nation's History*. New York: Moffat, Yard, 1909.

McGann, Agnes G. *Nativism in Kentucky to 1860*. Washington, D.C.: Catholic University of America Press, 1944.

McVey, Frank L. *The Gates Open Slowly: A History of Education in Kentucky*. Lexington: University of Kentucky Press, 1949.

McWhiney, Grady. *Cracker Culture: Celtic Ways in the Old South*. University, Ala.: University of Alabama Press, 1988.

Majority and Minority Reports and Testimony Taken by the Rowan County Investigating Committee. Frankfort, Ky.: J. D. Woods, 1888.

Mangan, J. A., and James Walvin, eds. *Manliness and Morality: Middle-Class Masculinity in Britain and America, 1800–1940.* New York: St. Martin's Press, 1987.

Marshall, Humphrey. *History of Kentucky.* Frankfort, Ky.: Henry Gore, 1812.

Marshall, Suzanne. *Violence in the Black Patch of Kentucky and Tennessee.* Columbia: University of Missouri Press, 1994.

Masaryk, Thomas G. *Suicide and the Meaning of Civilization.* Translated by William B. Weist and Robert J. Batson. Chicago: University of Chicago Press, 1970.

Mathias, Frank F., ed. *Incidents and Experiences in the Life of Thomas W. Parsons.* Lexington: University Press of Kentucky, 1975.

May, Henry F. *The End of American Innocence.* New York: Alfred A. Knopf, 1959.

Meyer, Leland W. *Georgetown College.* Louisville: Western Recorder, 1929.

———. *The Life and Times of Colonel Richard M. Johnson of Kentucky.* New York: Columbia University Press, 1932.

Miller, Randall M., Harry S. Stout, and Charles Reagan Wilson, eds., *Religion and the American Civil War.* New York: Oxford University Press, 1998.

Millis, Walter. *The Martial Spirit.* New York: Viking Press, 1965.

Montgomery County, Kentucky, Bicentennial, 1774–1974. N.p., n.d.

Moore, Arthur K. *The Frontier Mind: A Cultural Analysis of the Kentucky Frontiersman.* Lexington: University of Kentucky Press, 1957.

Morton, Lynn Douglas, ed. *Weeden D. Gay's Diary, 1872–1888.* Stanton, Ky.: Lynn Douglas Morton, 1994.

Mutzenburg, Charles G. *Kentucky's Famous Feuds and Tragedies.* New York: R. F. Fenno, 1917.

Nagle, Eric C. *Vital Records from Newspapers of Paris, Kentucky, 1813–1870.* Dayton: n.p., 1994.

Nall, James O. *The Tobacco Night Riders of Kentucky and Tennessee.* Louisville: Standard Press, 1939.

National Committee for the Defense of Political Prisoners. *Harlan Miners Speak.* New York: Harcourt, Brace, 1932.

Ninth Census. Washington, D.C.: Government Printing Office, 1870.

Nisbett, Richard E., and Dov Cohen. *Culture of Honor: The Psychology of Violence in the South.* Boulder, Colo.: Westview Press, 1996.

Noble, E. L. *Bloody Breathitt's Feuds.* 4 vols. Jackson, Ky.: Jackson Times, 1936–47.

Official Report of the Proceedings and Debates in the Convention . . . to Adopt, Amend, or Change the Constitution of the State of Kentucky. 4 vols. Frankfort, Ky.: E. Polk Johnson, 1890.

Olsen, Christopher J. *Political Culture and Secession in Mississippi: Masculinity, Honor, and the Antiparty Tradition, 1830–1860.* New York: Oxford University Press, 2000.

O'Rear, Edward C. *History of the Montgomery County (Ky.) Bar.* N.p., 1945.

Ownby, Ted. *Subduing Satan: Religion, Recreation, and Manhood in the Rural South, 1865–1920.* Chapel Hill: University of North Carolina Press, 1990.

Painter, Nell Irvin. *Standing at Armageddon: The United States, 1877–1919.* New York: W. W. Norton, 1987.

Pearce, John Ed. *Days of Darkness: The Feuds of Eastern Kentucky.* Lexington: University Press of Kentucky, 1994.

Peristiany, J. G., ed. *Honour and Shame: The Values of Mediterranean Society.* London: Weidenfeld and Nicolson, 1965.

Perkins, Elizabeth A. *Border Life: Experience and Memory in the Revolutionary Ohio Valley.* Chapel Hill: University of North Carolina Press, 1998.

Perlin, Seymore, ed. *A Handbook for the Study of Suicide.* New York: Oxford University Press, 1975.

Perrin, W. H., J. H. Battle, and G. C. Kniffen. *Kentucky: A History of the State.* Louisville: F. A. Battey, 1887.

Pope, Dudley. *Guns.* New York: Delacorte Press, 1969.

Prewitt, Richard A. *Michael Prewitt, Sr., and His Descendants, 1720–1977.* Grimes, Iowa: Prewitt, 1977.

Price, W. T. *Without Scrip or Purse; or, The "Mountain Evangelist," George O. Barnes.* Louisville: W. T. Price, 1883.

Pudup, Mary Beth, Dwight B. Billings, and Altina L. Waller, eds. *Appalachia in the Making: The Mountain South in the Nineteenth Century.* Chapel Hill: University of North Carolina Press, 1995.

Pugh, David G. *Sons of Liberty: The Masculine Mind in Nineteenth-Century America.* Westport, Conn.: Greenwood Press, 1983.

Rable, George C. *But There Was No Peace: The Role of Violence in the Politics of Reconstruction.* Athens: University of Georgia Press, 1984.

Ramage, James A. *Rebel Raider: The Life of General John Hunt Morgan.* Lexington: University Press of Kentucky, 1986.

Redfield, H. V. *Homicide, North and South.* Philadelphia: J. B. Lippincott, 1880.

Reed, John Shelton. *The Enduring South.* Chapel Hill: University of North Carolina Press, 1975.

Reid, Elizabeth Jameson. *Judge Richard Reid: A Biography.* Cincinnati: Standard Publishing Co., 1886.

Reid, Richard. *Historical Sketches of Montgomery County.* Lexington: James M. Byrnes, 1926.

Remini, Robert. *Henry Clay: Spokesman for the Union.* New York: W. W. Norton, 1991.

Rennick, Robert M. *Kentucky Place Names.* Lexington: University Press of Kentucky, 1984.

Report on Crime . . . in the United States at the Eleventh Census: 1890. Washington, D.C.: Government Printing Office, 1895.

Rice, Otis K. *The Hatfields and the McCoys*. Lexington: University Press of Kentucky, 1978.

Richard Reid: A Memorial. Louisville: Bradley and Gilbert, 1884.

Richards, J. A. *History of Bath County*. Yuma, Ariz.: Southwest Printers, 1961.

Roland, Charles P. *Reflections on Lee: A Historian's Assessment*. Mechanicsburg, Pa.: Stackpole Books, 1995.

Roller, David C., and Robert W. Twyman. *Encyclopedia of Southern History*. Baton Rouge: Louisiana State University Press, 1979.

Roosevelt, Theodore. *The Winning of the West*. 6 vols. New York: G. P. Putnam's Sons, 1889–1896.

Rotundo, E. Anthony. *American Manhood: Transformations in Masculinity from the Revolution to the Modern Era*. New York: Basic Books, 1993.

Rudolph, Frederick. *The American College and University: A History*. New York: Alfred A. Knopf, 1962.

Schaeffer, J. Parsons, ed. *Morris' Human Anatomy*. 11th ed. New York: McGraw-Hill, 1953.

Seiller, Edward F., comp. *Kentucky: Natural Resources, Industrial Statistics, Industrial Directory, Description by Counties*. Frankfort, Ky.: Bureau of Agriculture, [1930].

Seventeenth Annual Commencement of Georgetown College. N.p., n.d.

Shaler, Nathaniel Southgate. *Autobiography of Nathaniel Southgate Shaler*. Boston: Houghton Mifflin, 1909.

———. *Kentucky: A Pioneer Commonwealth*. Boston: Houghton, Mifflin, 1884.

Simkins, Francis B., and Charles P. Roland. *A History of the South*. 4th ed. New York: Alfred A. Knopf, 1972.

Slotkin, Richard. *Gunfighter Nation*. New York: Atheneum, 1992.

———. *Regeneration through Violence: The Mythology of the American Frontier, 1600–1860*. Middletown, Conn.: Wesleyan University Press, 1973.

Smith, Edward C. *The Borderland in the Civil War*. New York: Macmillan, 1927.

Smith, John David, and Thomas H. Appleton Jr., eds. *A Mythic Land Apart: Reassessing Southerners and Their History*. Westport, Conn.: Greenwood Press, 1997.

Smith, Z. F. *History of Kentucky*. Louisville: Prentice Press, 1895.

Snyder, Robert. *A History of Georgetown College*. Georgetown, Ky.: Georgetown College, 1979.

Steele, [Elizabeth R.]. *A Summer Journey in the West*. 2 vols. New York: John S. Taylor, 1841.

Steward, Dick. *Duels and the Roots of Violence in Missouri*. Columbia: University of Missouri Press, 2000.

Stone, Henry Lane. *"Morgan's Men": A Narrative of Personal Experiences*. Louisville: Westerfield-Bonte, 1919.

Summers, Mark W. *The Gilded Age*. Upper Saddle River, N.J.: Prentice-Hall, 1997.

Tafel Bros.' Illustrated Catalogue and Price List of Surgical and Electrical Instruments. Louisville: n.p., 1855.

Tapp, Hambleton, and James C. Klotter. *Kentucky: Decades of Discord, 1865–1900.* Frankfort: Kentucky Historical Society, 1977.

Taylor, Paul F. *Bloody Harlan.* Lanham, Md.: University Press of America, 1990.

Theriot, Nancy M. *Mothers and Daughters in Nineteenth-Century America.* Lexington: University Press of Kentucky, 1996.

Thomas, Emory M. *Robert E. Lee.* New York: Norton, 1995.

Townsend, John Wilson. *James Lane Allen.* Louisville: Courier-Journal Job Printing Co., 1927.

Townsend, William H. *The Lion of White Hall.* Dunwoody, Ga.: Norman S. Berg, 1967.

Trelease, Allen W. *White Terror.* New York: Harper and Row, 1971.

Troutman, Richard L., ed. *The Heavens Are Weeping: The Diaries of George Richard Browder, 1852–1886.* Grand Rapids, Mich.: Zondervan, 1987.

Twelfth Biennial Report of the Bureau of Agriculture, Labor, and Statistics of the State of Kentucky. Louisville: Geo. G. Fetter, 1897.

U.S. Senate. *Violations of Free Speech and Rights of Labor Hearing.* 75th Congress, 1st Session. Washington, D.C.: Government Printing Office, 1937.

Waldrep, Christopher R. *Night Riders.* Durham, N.C.: Duke University Press, 1993.

———. *Roots of Disorder: Race and Criminal Justice in the American South.* Urbana: University of Illinois Press, 1998.

Wall, Joseph F. *Henry Watterson: Reconstructed Rebel.* New York: Oxford University Press, 1956.

Waller, Altina L. *Feud: Hatfields, McCoys, and Social Change in Appalachia, 1860–1900.* Chapel Hill: University of North Carolina Press, 1988.

Webb, Ross A. *Kentucky in the Reconstruction Era.* Lexington: University Press of Kentucky, 1979.

Werner, Emmy E., and Ruth S. Smith. *Vulnerable but Invincible: A Longitudinal Study of Resilient Children and Youth.* New York: McGraw-Hill, 1982.

Wiebe, Robert H. *The Search for Order, 1877–1920.* New York: Hill and Wang, 1967.

Wilson, Charles Reagan. *Baptized in Blood: The Religion of the Lost Cause, 1865–1920.* Athens: University of Georgia Press, 1980.

Wilson, Charles Reagan, and William Ferris, eds. *Encyclopedia of Southern Culture.* Chapel Hill: University of North Carolina Press, 1989.

Winks, Robin. *The Historian as Detective: Essays on Evidence.* New York: Harper and Row, 1968.

Witherspoon, Pattie French. *Through Two Administrations: Character Sketches of Kentucky.* Chicago: T. B. Arnold, 1897.

Woodson, Urey. *The First New Dealer: William Goebel.* Louisville: Standard Press, 1939.

Woodward, C. Vann. *Origins of the New South, 1877–1913*. Baton Rouge: Louisiana State University Press, 1951.

Wright, George C. *Racial Violence in Kentucky, 1865–1940*. Baton Rouge: Louisiana State University Press, 1990.

Wright, John D., Jr. *Transylvania: Tutor to the West*. Lexington: Transylvania University, 1975.

Wyatt-Brown, Bertram. *Honor and Violence in the Old South*. Oxford: Oxford University Press, 1986.

———. *The House of Percy: Honor, Melancholy, and Imagination in a Southern Family*. New York: Oxford University Press, 1994.

———. *The Shaping of Southern Culture: Honor, Grace, and War*. Chapel Hill: University of North Carolina Press, 2001.

———. *Southern Honor: Ethics and Behavior in the Old South*. Oxford: Oxford University Press, 1982.

ARTICLES

Allen, James Lane. "County Court Day in Kentucky." *Harper's* 78 (1889): 383–97.

Bailey, William C. "Some Further Evidence on Homicide and a Regional Culture of Violence." *Omega: Journal of Death and Dying* 7 (1976): 145–70.

Baird, Bruce C. "The Social Origins of Dueling in Virginia." In *Lethal Imagination: Violence and Brutality in American History,* ed. Michael A. Bellesiles. New York: New York University Press, 1999.

Beale, Joseph H., Jr. "Retreat from a Murderous Assault." *Harvard Law Review* 16 (1903): 567–82.

Brandt, Richard B. "The Morality and Rationality of Suicide." In *A Handbook for the Study of Suicide,* ed. Seymour Perlin. Oxford: Oxford University Press, 1975.

Broughton, Roger J., et al. "Homicidal Somnambulism: A Case Report." *Sleep* 17 (1994): 253–64.

Bubka, Tony. "The Harlan County Coal Strike of 1931." *Labor History* 11 (1970): 41–57.

Bulletin of the State Board of Health of Kentucky 6 (June 1934): 30.

Cardwell, Guy A. "The Duel in the Old South: Crux of a Concept." *South Atlantic Quarterly* 66 (1967): 50–69.

Chaney, David. "The Spectacle of Honour: The Changing Dramatization of Status." *Theory, Culture, and Society* 12 (1995): 147–67.

Clark, Champ. "Kentucky during the Civil War." In *Old Kentucky,* ed. J. F. Cook. New York: Neale, 1908.

Clarke, James Freeman. "George D. Prentice and Kentucky Thirty-Five Years Ago." *Old and New* 1 (1870): 739–44.

Cohen, Dov, Richard E. Nisbett, Brian F. Bowdle, and Norbert Schwarz. "Insult, Aggression, and the Southern Culture of Honor." *Journal of Personality and Social Psychology* 70 (1996): 945–60.

Cominos, Peter T. "Late-Victorian Sexual Responsibility and the Social System." *International Review of Social History* 8 (1963): 18–48, 216–50.

Connelly, Thomas L. "Neo-Confederatism or Power Vacuum: Post-War Kentucky Politics Reappraised." *Register of the Kentucky Historical Society* 64 (1966): 257–69.

Cooper, William S., and Robert G. Lawson. "Self Defense in Kentucky: A Need for Clarification or Revision." *Kentucky Law Journal* 76 (1987–88): 167–99.

Curtis, Susan. "The Son of Man and God the Father: The Social Gospel and Victorian Masculinity." In *Meanings for Manhood*, ed. Mark C. Carnes and Clyde Griffen. Chicago: University of Chicago Press, 1990.

Davenport, Mark. "Inguinal Hernia, Hydrocele, and the Undescended Testis." *British Medical Journal* 312 (1996): 564–67.

Doolan, John C. "The Court of Appeals of Kentucky." *Green Bag* 12 (1900): 408–19, 458–66.

Douglas, Jack D. "Suicide: Social Aspects." In *International Encyclopedia of the Social Sciences*, ed. David L. Sills. Vol. 15. 1968.

Drake, Ella W. "Choctaw Academy: Richard M. Johnson and the Business of Indian Education." *Register of the Kentucky Historical Society* 91 (1993): 260–97.

"Editor's Study." *Harper's New Monthly Magazine*. 73 (1886): 965–66.

Ellis, William E. " 'The Harvest Moon Was Shinin' on the Streets of Shelbyville': Southern Honor and the Death of General Henry H. Denhardt, 1937." *Register of the Kentucky Historical Society* 84 (1986): 361–96.

Faludi, Susan. "The Betrayal of the American Man." *Newsweek,* 13 September 1999.

Farberow, Norman L. "Suicide: Psychological Aspects (2)." In *International Encyclopedia of the Social Sciences*, ed. David L. Sills. Vol. 15. 1968.

Foster, Thomas A. "Deficient Husbands: Manhood, Sexual Incapacity, and Male Marital Sexuality in Seventeenth-Century New England." *William and Mary Quarterly* (3rd series) 56 (1999): 723–44.

Gass, W. Conrad. " 'The Misfortune of a High Minded and Honorable Gentleman': W.W. Avery and the Southern Code of Honor." *North Carolina Historical Review* 56 (1979): 278–97.

Gastil, Raymond D. "Homicide and a Regional Culture of Violence." *American Sociological Review* 36 (1971): 412–26.

———. "Violence, Crime, and Punishment." In *The Encyclopedia of Southern Culture,* ed. Charles Reagan Wilson and William Ferris. Chapel Hill: University of North Carolina Press, 1989.

Gilliam, Will D., Jr. "Family Friends and Foes." *Louisville Courier-Journal Magazine,* 20 November 1960.

Gilmore, John. "Murdering while Asleep." *Forensic Reports* 4 (1999): 455–59.

Gorn, Elliott J. "'Gourge and Bite, Pull Hair and Scratch': The Social Significance of Fighting in the Southern Backcountry." *American Historical Review* 90 (1985): 18–43.

Goyette, Daniel T. "Developments in Cases Involving Self-Defense." In *Kentucky Bar Association Update '99.* 1999.

Griffen, Clyde. "Reconstructing Masculinity from the Evangelical Revival to the Waning of Progressivism." In *Meanings for Manhood,* ed. Mark C. Carnes and Clyde Griffen. Chicago: University of Chicago Press, 1990.

Hackney, Sheldon. "Southern Violence." In *Violence in America,* ed. Hugh Davis Graham and Ted Robert Gurr. New York: Signet Books, 1969.

Hardy, Sallie E. M. "Some Kentucky Lawyers of the Past and Present." *Green Bag* 9 (1897): 260–350.

Harris, James Russell. "Kentuckians in the War of 1812: A Note on Numbers, Losses, and Sources." *Register of the Kentucky Historical Society* 82 (1984): 277–86.

Hartog, Hendrik. "Lawyering, Husband's Rights, and the 'Unwritten Law' in Nineteenth-Century America." *Journal of American History* 84 (1997): 67–96.

Hay, Melba Porter. "Companion or Conspirator? Henry Clay and the Graves-Cilley Duel." In *A Mystic Land Apart,* ed. John David Smith and Thomas H. Appleton Jr. Westport, Conn.: Greenwood Press, 1997.

Hill, Samuel S. "Outline Sketch of Georgetown College." *Filson Club History Quarterly* 26 (1952): 166–71.

Horowitz, Ruth, and Gary Schwartz. "Honor, Normative Ambiguity, and Gang Violence." *American Sociological Review* 39 (1974): 238–51.

Huff-Corzine, Lin, Jay Corzine, and David C. Moore. "Southern Exposures: Deciphering the South's Influence on Homicide Rates." *Social Forces* 64 (1986): 906–24.

Ireland, Robert M. "Acquitted yet Scorned: The Ward Trial and the Traditions of Antebellum Kentucky Criminal Justice." *Register of the Kentucky Historical Society* 84 (1986): 107–45.

———. "The Buford-Elliott Tragedy and the Traditions of Kentucky Criminal Justice." *Filson Club History Quarterly* 66 (1992): 395–419.

———. "The Green-Hargis Affair: Judicial Politics in Nineteenth-Century Kentucky." *Filson Club History Quarterly* 69 (1995): 366–89.

———. "Law and Disorder in Nineteenth-Century Kentucky." *Vanderbilt Law Review* 32 (1979): 281–99.

———. "The Libertine Must Die: Sexual Dishonor and the Unwritten Law in the Nineteenth-Century United States." *Journal of Social History* 23 (1989): 27–44.

———. "The Nineteenth-Century Criminal Jury: Kentucky in the Context of the American Experience." *Kentucky Review* 4 (1983): 52–70.

———. "The Politics of the Elective Judiciary during the Period of Kentucky's Third Constitution." *Register of the Kentucky Historical Society* 93 (1995): 387–421.

———. "The Suicide of Judge Richard Reid: Politics and Honor Run Amok." *Filson Club History Quarterly* 71 (1997): 123–45.

———. "The Thompson-Davis Case and the Unwritten Law." *Filson Club History Quarterly* 62 (1988): 417–41.

———. "Violence." In *Our Kentucky*, ed. James C. Klotter. Rev. ed. Lexington: University Press of Kentucky, 2000.

Jillson, Willard Rouse. "The Beauchamp-Sharp Tragedy in American Literature." *Register of the Kentucky Historical Society* 36 (1938): 54–60.

"The Kentucky Tragedy." *The Nation* 49 (14 November 1889): 382–83.

Klotter, James C. "Feuds in Appalachia: An Overview." *Filson Club History Quarterly* 56 (1982): 290–317.

———. "Sex, Scandal, and Suffrage in the Gilded Age." *Historian* 42 (1980): 225–43.

Knighton, William. "Suicidal Mania." *Littell's Living Age* 148 (5 February 1881): 376–81.

Kushner, Howard I. "Suicide, Gender, and the Fear of Modernity in Nineteenth-Century Medical and Social Thought." *Journal of Social History* 26 (1993): 461–90.

Lauerma, Hannu. "Fear of Suicide during Sleepwalking." *Psychiatry* 59 (1996): 206–11.

Lebanon [pseud.]. "Suggested Thoughts." *Ciceronian Magazine* 1 (1856): 269–71.

Lofaro, Michael A. "The Eighteenth Century 'Autobiographies' of Daniel Boone." *Register of the Kentucky Historical Society* 76 (1978): 85–97.

Loftin, C., and R. H. Hill. "Regional Subculture and Homicide: An Examination of the Gastil-Hackney Thesis." *American Sociological Review* 39 (1974): 714–24.

Low, W. A. "The Freedmen's Bureau in the Border States." In *Radicalism, Racism, and Party Realignment*, ed. Richard O. Curry. Baltimore: Johns Hopkins University Press, 1969.

Lucas, Marion B. "Kentucky Blacks: The Transition from Slavery to Freedom." *Register of the Kentucky Historical Society* 91 (1993): 403–19.

McDonald, Forrest, and Grady McWhiney. "The Antebellum Southern Herdsman: A Reinterpretation." *Journal of Southern History* 41 (1975): 47–66.

McWhiney, Grady. "Crackers and Cavaliers: Shared Courage." In *Plain Folk of the South Revisited*, ed. Samuel C. Hyde. Baton Rouge: Louisiana State University Press, 1997.

Mahowald, Mark W., Scott R. Bundlie, Thomas D. Hurwitz, and Carlos H. Schenck. "Sleep Violence—Forensic Science Implications." *Journal of Forensic Sciences* 35 (1990): 413–32.

Martin, Robert F. "Billy Sunday and Christian Manliness." *Historian* 58 (1996): 811–23.

Mathews, John L. "The Farmers' Union and the Tobacco Pool." *Atlantic Monthly* 102 (1908): 482–91.

Mathias, Frank M. "Kentucky's Struggle for Common Schools, 1820–1850." *Register of the Kentucky Historical Society* 82 (1984): 214–34.

Mikusch, Gustav. "Suicide." In *Encyclopaedia of the Social Sciences,* ed. Edwin R. A. Seligman. Vol 14. 1935.

Moldofsky, Harvey, Russell Gilbert, Franklin A. Lue, and Alistair W. MacLean. "Sleep-Related Violence." *Sleep* 18 (1995): 731–39.

Morgan, Edmund S. "The Price of Honor." *New York Review of Books,* 31 May 2001.

"Mr. Richard Reid." *Kentucky Law Journal* 2 (1882): 3.

Mulhall, M. G. "Insanity, Suicide, and Civilization." *Contemporary Review* 43 (1883): 42–44.

Mumford, Kevin J. " 'Lost Manhood' Found: Male Sexual Impotence and Victorian Culture in the United States." *Journal of the History of Sexuality* 3 (1992): 33–57.

Newell, Waller R. "The Crisis of Manliness." *Weekly Standard* 3 (3 August 1998): 18–21.

Nisbett, Richard E. "Violence and U.S. Regional Culture." *American Psychologist* 48 (1993): 441–49.

Ohayon, Maurice M., Christian Guilleminault, and R. G. Priest. "Night Terrors, Sleepwalking, and Confusional Arousals in the General Population." *Journal of Clinical Psychiatry* 60 (1999): 268–78.

Piccato, Pablo. "Politics and the Technology of Honor: Dueling in Turn-of-the-Century Mexico." *Journal of Social History* 33 (1999): 331–54.

Pitt-Rivers, Julian. "Honor." In *International Encyclopedia of the Social Sciences,* ed. David E. Sills. Vol. 6. 1968.

———. "Honour and Social Status." In *Honour and Shame: The Values of Mediterranean Society,* ed. J. G. Peristiany. London: Weidenfeld and Nicholson, 1965.

Portelli, Allessandro. "History-Telling and Time: An Example from Kentucky." *Oral History Review* 20 (1996): 51–66.

Porterfield, Austin L. "A Decade of Serious Crime in the United States: Some Trends and Hypotheses." *American Sociological Review* 13 (1948): 44–54.

———. "Indices of Suicide and Homicide by States and Cities." *American Sociological Review* 14 (1949): 481–90.

"The Progress of the World." *American Monthly Review of Reviews* 21 (1900): 274–76.

Rabinowitz, Howard N. "Continuity and Change: Southern Urban Development, 1860–1900." In *The City in Southern History,* ed. Blaine A. Brownell and David R. Goldfield. Port Washington, N.Y.: Kennikat Press, 1977.

Ramage, B. J. "Homicide in the Southern States." *Sewanee Review* 4 (1896): 212–32.

Reed, John Shelton. "To Live and Die in Dixie: A Contribution to the Study of Southern Violence." *Political Science Quarterly* 76 (1971): 429–45.

[Reid, Richard]. "The Martyr to Science." *Georgetown College Magazine* 1 (1857): 197–99.

[————]. "Music." *Ciceronian Magazine* 1 (1856): 67–71.

Reid, Richard. "The Old Age of the Scholar." *Ciceronian Magazine* 1 (1857); 388–93.

————. "Unity of Purpose in Life." *Ciceronian Magazine* 1 (1856): 216–19.

Reimer, Jeffrey W. "Durkheim's 'Heroic Suicide' in Military Combat." *Armed Forces and Society* 25 (1998): 103–20.

Rosenberg, Charles E. "Sexuality, Class, and Role in Nineteenth-Century America." *American Quarterly* 25 (1973): 131–53.

Ross, Marc Howard. "Internal and External Conflict and Violence: Cross-Cultural Evidence and a New Analysis." *Journal of Conflict Resolution* 29 (1985): 547–79.

Shneidman, Edwin S. "Suicide: Psychological Aspects (1)." In *International Encyclopedia of the Social Sciences,* ed. David L. Sills. Vol. 15. 1968.

————. "Suicide, Sleep, and Death." *Journal of Consulting Psychology* 28 (1964): 95–106.

Smith, John David. "Kentucky's Civil War Recruits: A Medical Profile." *Medical History* 24 (1980): 185–96.

Smith, Peter C., and Karl B. Raitz. "Negro Hamlets and Agricultural Estates in Kentucky's Inner Bluegrass." *Geographical Review* 64 (1974): 217–34.

Smith, T. V. "Honor." In *Encyclopedia of the Social Sciences,* ed. Edward R. A. Seligman. Vol. 7. 1935.

Speed, James G. "The Kentuckian." *Century Magazine* 59 (1900): 946–52.

Sprague, Stuart S. "The Death of Tecumseh and the Rise of Rumpsey Dumpsey: The Making of a Vice President." *Filson Club History Quarterly* 59 (1985): 455–61.

Tachau, Mary K. Bonsteel. "Comment." *Vanderbilt Law Review* 32 (1979): 301–304.

Thomas, William G., III. "Under Indictment: Thomas Lafayette Rosser and the New South." *Virginia Magazine of History and Biography* 100 (1992): 207–31.

Vgontzas, A. N., and A. Kales. "Sleep and Its Disorders." *Annual Review of Medicine* 50 (1999): 387–400.

Waldrep, Christopher R. "Rank-and-File Voters and the Coming of the Civil War: Caldwell County, Kentucky, as a Test Case." *Civil War History* 35 (1989): 59–72.

————. "Who Were Kentucky's Whig Voters?" *Register of the Kentucky Historical Society* 79 (1981): 326–32.

Waller, Altina L. "Feuding in Appalachia: Evolutions of a Cultural Sterotype." In *Appalachia in the Making,* ed. Mary Beth Pudup, Dwight B. Billings, and Altina L. Waller. Chapel Hill: University of North Carolina Press, 1995.

Warner, Charles Dudley. "Comments on Kentucky." *Harper's New Monthly Magazine* 78 (1889): 255–71.

Woodworth, Steven E. " 'The Indeterminate Qualities': Jefferson Davis, Leonidas Polk, and the End of Kentucky's Neutrality, September 1861." *Civil War History* 38 (1992): 289–97.

Wyatt-Brown, Bertram. "Church, Honor, and Secession." In *Religion in the American Civil War,* ed. Randall M. Miller, Harry S. Stout, and Charles Reagan Wilson. New York: Oxford University Press, 1998.

———. "Community, Class, and Snopesian Crime: Local Justice in the Old South." In *Class, Conflict, and Consensus,* ed. Orville Vernon Burton and Robert C. McMath. Westport, Conn.: Greenwood Press, 1982.

———. "God and Honor in the Old South." *Southern Review* 25 (1989): 283–96.

Unpublished Works

Alband, Jo Della. "A History of the Education of Women in Kentucky." Master's thesis, University of Kentucky, 1954.

Ballou, Thomas C. "A Cumberland Vendetta." Kentucky Historical Society, n.d.

Boyd, John A. "Neutrality and Peace: Kentucky and the Secession Crisis of 1861." Ph.D. diss., University of Kentucky, 1999.

Butcher, Jerry Lee. "A Narrative History of Selected Aspects of Violence in the New South, 1877–1920." Ph.D. diss., University of Missouri, 1977.

Gregory, Rick S. "Desperate Farmers: The Dark Tobacco District Planters' Protective Association of Kentucky and Tennessee, 1904–1914." Ph.D. diss., Vanderbilt University, 1989.

Johnson, Henry V. "Memoirs of Henry V. Johnson of Scott County, Kentucky, 1852–1931." Georgetown (Ky.) Public Library, n.d.

Jones, Jonathan M. "The Making of a Vice President: The National Political Career of Richard M. Johnson of Kentucky." Ph.D. diss., University of Memphis, 1998.

McConnell, Joseph L. "Growth of Manufacturing in Kentucky, 1904 to 1929." Master's thesis, University of Kentucky, 1932.

Margolies, Daniel S. "God's Promise Redeemed: Marse Henry Watterson and the Compromises of American Empire." Ph.D. diss., University of Wisconsin, 1999.

"Notes from the Mt. Sterling Advocate." Mount Sterling Public Library, n.d.

Russell, Timothy. "Neutrality and Ideological Conflict in Kentucky during the First Year of the American Civil War." Ph.D. diss., University of New Mexico, 1989.

Sullivan, James P. "Louisville and Her Southern Alliance, 1865–1890." Ph.D. diss., University of Kentucky, 1965.

Index

CPSIA information can be obtained
at www.ICGtesting.com
Printed in the USA
LVHW011802031218
599103LV00020B/431